PSYCHOLOGY OF EMOTIONS, MOTIVATIONS AND ACTIONS

# SUICIDE FROM A GLOBAL PERSPECTIVE: PSYCHOSOCIAL APPROACHES

# PSYCHOLOGY OF EMOTIONS, MOTIVATIONS AND ACTIONS

Additional books in this series can be found on Nova's website under the Series tab.

Additional E-books in this series can be found on Nova's website under the E-book tab.

PSYCHOLOGY OF EMOTIONS, MOTIVATIONS AND ACTIONS

# SUICIDE FROM A GLOBAL PERSPECTIVE: PSYCHOSOCIAL APPROACHES

AMRESH SHRIVASTAVA,
MEGAN KIMBRELL AND DAVID LESTER
EDITORS

Nova Science Publishers, Inc.
*New York*

Copyright © 2012 by Nova Science Publishers, Inc.

**All rights reserved.** No part of this book may be reproduced, stored in a retrieval system or transmitted in any form or by any means: electronic, electrostatic, magnetic, tape, mechanical photocopying, recording or otherwise without the written permission of the Publisher.

For permission to use material from this book please contact us:
Telephone 631-231-7269; Fax 631-231-8175
Web Site: http://www.novapublishers.com

## NOTICE TO THE READER

The Publisher has taken reasonable care in the preparation of this book, but makes no expressed or implied warranty of any kind and assumes no responsibility for any errors or omissions. No liability is assumed for incidental or consequential damages in connection with or arising out of information contained in this book. The Publisher shall not be liable for any special, consequential, or exemplary damages resulting, in whole or in part, from the readers' use of, or reliance upon, this material. Any parts of this book based on government reports are so indicated and copyright is claimed for those parts to the extent applicable to compilations of such works.

Independent verification should be sought for any data, advice or recommendations contained in this book. In addition, no responsibility is assumed by the publisher for any injury and/or damage to persons or property arising from any methods, products, instructions, ideas or otherwise contained in this publication.

This publication is designed to provide accurate and authoritative information with regard to the subject matter covered herein. It is sold with the clear understanding that the Publisher is not engaged in rendering legal or any other professional services. If legal or any other expert assistance is required, the services of a competent person should be sought. FROM A DECLARATION OF PARTICIPANTS JOINTLY ADOPTED BY A COMMITTEE OF THE AMERICAN BAR ASSOCIATION AND A COMMITTEE OF PUBLISHERS.

Additional color graphics may be available in the e-book version of this book.

LIBRARY OF CONGRESS CATALOGING-IN-PUBLICATION DATA

Suicide from a global perspective : psychosocial approaches / editors, Amresh Shrivastava, Megan Kimbrell, David Lester.
 p. cm.
 Includes bibliographical references and index.
 ISBN 978-1-61470-965-7 (hardcover)
 1. Suicide. 2. Suicide--Psychological aspects. 3. Suicide--Sociological aspects. I. Shrivastava, Amresh. II. Kimbrell, Megan. III. Lester, David.
 HV6545.S8293 2011
 362.28--dc23
                              2011028727

*Published by Nova Science Publishers, Inc. † New York*

# Contents

| | | |
|---|---|---|
| **Preface** | | ix |
| **Contributing Authors** | | xi |
| **Foreword** | | xv |
| **Part 1: Psychological Approaches** | | 1 |
| Chapter 1 | Cognition and Suicide<br>*Michelle M. Cornette, Charles W. Mathias, Dawn M. Marsh, Terri A. deRoon-Cassini and Donald M. Dougherty* | 3 |
| Chapter 2 | Loss, Hopelessness and Suicide<br>*Paolo Scocco and Elena Toffol* | 11 |
| Chapter 3 | Self-Destructive Motivation: An Evolutionary Perspective<br>*R. Michael Brown and Stephanie L. Brown* | 19 |
| Chapter 4 | Suicide and Life Events<br>*Andrew M. Busch, Michelle M. Cornette, Charles W. Mathias, Dawn M. Marsh and Donald M. Dougherty* | 27 |
| Chapter 5 | Stress, Lifestyle and Suicidal Behavior<br>*Lourens Schlebusch* | 33 |
| Chapter 6 | What Can We Learn from Suicide Notes? A Study in India<br>*Antoon A. Leenaars, T.D. Dogra, Shalina Girdhar and Lindsey Leenaars* | 41 |
| Chapter 7 | Childhood Trauma in Suicidal Behavior<br>*Marco Sarchiapone, Vladimir Carli and Alec Roy* | 47 |
| Chapter 8 | Suicide Protectors<br>*Leo Sher* | 57 |
| **Part 2: Environmental Approaches to Suicide** | | 67 |
| Chapter 9 | Sociological Perspectives on Suicide<br>*Masahito Fushimi* | 69 |

| | | |
|---|---|---|
| **Chapter 10** | Advances in Sociological Approaches to Understanding Suicide<br>*Augustine J. Kposowa* | 75 |
| **Chapter 11** | Suicide and Unemployment<br>*Steven Stack* | 81 |
| **Chapter 12** | Suicide and Economic Status<br>*Augustine J. Kposowa* | 87 |
| **Chapter 13** | Suicide in Rural and Urban Communities<br>*Ping Qin* | 93 |
| **Chapter 14** | Suicide, Environment and Ecology<br>*Mark S. Kaplan and Stacey A. Sobell* | 101 |
| **Chapter 15** | Immigration and Risk for Suicide<br>*Megan E. Johnston* | 109 |
| **Chapter 16** | The Impact of the Media on Suicide<br>*Steven Stack* | 115 |
| **Chapter 17** | A Strain Theory of Suicide<br>*Jie Zhang* | 119 |
| **Chapter 18** | Suicide and Disasters<br>*Dusica Lecic-Tosevski, Milica Pejovic Milovancevic and Smiljka Popovic Deusic* | 127 |
| **Part 3: Suicide Across Cultures** | | 135 |
| **Chapter 19** | Cultural Psychodynamics and Suicidal Behavior<br>*Vijoy K. Varma* | 137 |
| **Chapter 20** | Hidden Suicide in the Developing World<br>*Colin Pritchard* | 145 |
| **Chapter 21** | Suicide in Sri Lanka<br>*Waltraud Bolz* | 153 |
| **Chapter 22** | Suicide in the Former Soviet Union (USSR)<br>*Airi Värnik* | 159 |
| **Chapter 23** | Suicide in the People's Republic of China<br>*Colin Pritchard* | 165 |
| **Chapter 24** | Suicide in Japan<br>*Mutsuhiro Nakao* | 169 |
| **Chapter 25** | Suicide in Israel<br>*Eliezer Witztum and Daniel Stein* | 175 |
| **Chapter 26** | Suicide in India<br>*G. Gururaj* | 181 |
| **Chapter 27** | Suicide in Sub-Saharan Africa<br>*Sussie Eshun and Paul Bartoli* | 195 |

| **Chapter 28** | Sub-Syndromal Suicide: An Arab Perspective<br>*Ahmed Okasha, Aida Seif El Dawla and Tarek Okasha* | **199** |
| **Chapter 29** | Outcome and Implications of Research in<br>Suicidology from Developing Countries<br>*Anju Kuruvilla and K. S. Jacob* | **205** |
| **Index** | | **215** |

# PREFACE

These volumes survey the field of suicidology with two goals. As well as inviting well-known scholars from the field of suicidology to present their latest thoughts on the topics that they study, we have invited other scholars to apply the insights from their disciplines and their fields of study to the problem of understanding and preventing suicide.

Second, we have made an effort to invite scholars from the non-Western regions of the world to contribute their perspectives about suicidal behavior, thereby enriching our understanding of suicide. As a result, this volume has chapters from scholars whose work is not typically found in other edited books on suicidal behavior. For example, chapters cover the role of the environment and ecology in suicide, suicide in those with intellectual disabilities, and hidden suicide in the developing world, to name a few.

With these two goals, we have endeavored both to present contemporary thought about suicide and to break new boundaries in the ongoing efforts to understand this perplexing behavior.

Suicide is a multi-factorial problem, arising in a complex way from biological, psychological, sociological, cultural, environmental and geographical factors. An attempt has been made to bring in all of these factors into these volumes. This is the first of the series and covers psychological, sociological and anthropological approaches to the study of suicidal behavior.

# Contributing Authors

## Editors

Amresh Shrivastava, MD
University of Western Ontario, Canada
dr.amresh@gmail.com

Megan Kimbrell, MA
The University of Akron
megan@justmegan.com

David Lester, PhD
The Richard Stockton College of New Jersey
lesterd@stockton.edu

## Corresponding Authors

Waltraud Bolz, Dipl. Psych.
Kronberg, Germany
waltraud.bolz@gmx.de

R. Michael Brown, PhD
Pacific Lutheran University
rmikebrown@wavecable.com

Michelle M. Cornette, PhD
Zablocki VA Medical Center, Milwaukee, WI
Michelle.Cornette@va.gov

Sussie Eshun, PhD
East Stroudsburg University of Pennsylvania
seshun@po-box.esu.edu

Masahito Fushimi, MD
Akita Prectural Mental Health & Welfare Center,
Japan
fushimi@pref.akita.lg.jp

G. Gururaj, MD
National Institute of Mental Health & Neuro
Sciences, Bengaluru, India
guru@nimhans.kar.nic.in

K. S. Jacob, MD
Christian Medical College, Vellore, India
ksjacob@cmvellore.ac.in

Megan E. Johnston
University of Toronto, Canada
megan.johnston@utoronto.ca

Augustine Kposowa, PhD
University of California, Riverside, California
ajkposowa@sbcglobal.net

Antoon A. Leenaars, PhD
Private Practice, Windsor, Ontario, Canada
draalee@sympatico.ca

Mutsuhiro Nakao, MD
Teikyo University School of Medicine, Japan
psm110@med.teikyo-u.ac.jp

Ahmed Okasha, MD
Ain Shams University, Cairo, Egypt
aokasha35@gmail.com

Colin Pritchard, PhD
Bournemouth University, UK
CPritchard@bournemouth.ac.uk

Ping Qin, MD
University of Aarhus, Denmark
pq@ncrr.dk

Marco Sarchiapone, MD
University of Molise, Italy
marco.sarchiapone@me.com

Norman Sartorius, MD
Association for the Improvement of Mental Health
Programs, Geneva, Switzerland
sartorius@normansartorius.com

Lourens Schlebusch, MD
University of KwaZulu-Natal, South Africa
schlebusch@ukzn.ac.za

Paolo Scocco, MD
Mental Health Department, Padova, Italy
scocco.paolo@virgilio.it

Leo Sher, MD
Mount Sinai School of Medicine, New York
drleosher@gmail.com

Stacey Ananda Sobell, MPH
Ecotrust, Portland, Oregon
ssobell@ecotrust.org

Steven Stack, PhD
Wayne State University
steven_stack@hotmail.com

Daniel Stein, MD
Tel Aviv University, Israel
danil49@netvision.net.il

Dusica Lecic Tosevski, MD
Belgrade University School of Medicine, Serbia
dusica.lecictosevski@gmail.com

Airi Värnik, MD
Tallinn University, Estonia
airiv@online.ee

Vijoy Varma, FRCPsych
vijoyv@frontier.com

Jie Zhang, PhD
Buffalo State College
Zhangj@buffalostate.edu

# FOREWORD

Suicide is the cause of death for nearly one million people a year. Death by suicide is often reported as being due to other causes to avoid stigmatization and other negative consequences of suicide for the family. It can, therefore, be assumed that the number of people who commit suicide is much higher than this number. Attempts at suicide, estimated to be ten times more frequent than completed suicide, often cause permanent impairment and disability. Suicide can stigmatize families across generations. The loss of life caused by suicide presents a significant loss for the communities in which it occurs – socially, economically and by blocking progress towards the creation of a civic society.

The aging of populations and the high prevalence of chronic diseases, both of which are risk factors for suicide and both of which characterize an increasing number of countries, as well as the increasing prevalence of several mental disorders (for example, depressive disorders) and the continuing growth of several other risk factors for suicide, make it possible to predict an increase in suicide rates worldwide unless resolute action is undertaken to prevent suicidal behavior. A major problem in that respect is that, in many countries, suicide is not seen as a major public health problem despite its frequency and the severity of its consequences. In part this is so because of a vicious circle. Methods of suicide prevention have not been sufficiently widely and vigorously applied, so that public health authorities, until now, have only a very limited number of compelling examples of successful suicide prevention programs. Therefore, these do not provide the resources for such programs, which in turn limits the possibility of producing successful programs that would convince them to continue their investment in this area of public health. In part, however, the absence of resolute action against suicide is due to the insufficient awareness of the magnitude and severity of the problem (and of the possibilities of effective intervention to reduce the problem) by the general population, by health and social service decision makers and by health professionals.

A textbook bringing together current knowledge about suicide, its causes and its prevention is a precious tool for public health efforts and for clinicians' daily work. The availability of an assembly of carefully and critically presented facts in the form of chapters responding to specific problems can help in the education of health professionals and provide them with data that they can use in developing proposals for action. It can draw attention to methods of work that have been tried elsewhere and found useful. It can provide a better understanding of the genesis of problem and its progression. When such a textbook is produced by an international group of experts from some thirty countries – developing and developed, North and South, East and West, characterized by different religions, traditions and cultures – it becomes even more useful because it presents knowledge seen through the eyes of professionals with rich experience gathered in dealing with the same problem under different circumstances prevailing in different parts of the world. These experts represent several disciplines that are involved in research and in practical work with people who may be at risk of suicide, and this multidisciplinary approach is another asset of this voluminous work.

It is, therefore, a pleasure to congratulate the authors of this work and to express the hope that the book will be read and used by many. The application of the knowledge that is assembled – in conducting further research, in education of different categories of personnel, and in providing care – will be the most significant reward for those who produced this book and, given the quality of their work and the efforts that they have made to make it such, they richly deserve it.

*Professor N. Sartorius*

# Part 1: Psychological Approaches

*Chapter 1*

# COGNITION AND SUICIDE

*Michelle M. Cornette, Charles W. Mathias, Dawn M. Marsh, Terri A. deRoon-Cassini and Donald M. Dougherty*

Central to addressing what motivates an individual to consider and act upon suicidal impulses is furthering our understanding of the processes and content of the cognitions which precede suicidal ideation and behaviors. Aspects of social and neurocognition are among the most salient risk factors for suicide, and include our perceptions of ourselves and our future, our beliefs about how we believe we measure up to the standards set by ourselves and others, and how adept we are at solving interpersonal dilemmas. This chapter provides an overview of key cognitive risk factors, process-oriented models, and related approaches to treating suicidal symptoms from a cognitive perspective.

## HOPELESSNESS

Expectations about one's future can affect one's likelihood of attempting suicide. Hopelessness, defined as the perception that one's negative life circumstances are unlikely to improve, or that there is no way to solve an important problem or escape psychological pain, can at times lead individuals to seek escape through suicide. Weishaar (2000) described hopelessness as the social cognitive risk factor "most consistently related to suicidal ideation, intent, and completion" in both adult and child clinical populations. Research has suggested that hopelessness may be a stronger predictor of completed suicide than depression (Steer, et al., 1993), even when other important third variables, including a prior history of attempts, are controlled for statistically. Hopelessness has been shown to be more predictive of suicidal *intent* than depression among both suicide ideators and attempters (Wen-Hung, et al., 2004). In particular, prospective longitudinal studies have demonstrated that hopelessness predicts eventual suicide over periods of ten years or more in adult psychiatric inpatients and outpatients (Beck, et al., 1985, 1990).

## COGNITIVE VULNERABILITY TO SUICIDE

Beyond hopelessness, research suggests that certain styles of cognition may predispose individuals to engage in suicidal behaviors. Cognitive risk, measured via both negative cognitive styles (Abramson, et al., 1989) and dysfunctional assumptions (Wilson, et al., 2005), have been found to predict suicidality (Abramson, et al., 1998). Factors such as hopelessness and ruminative thinking have been found to mediate the relationship between cognitive risk and the presence/duration of suicidal thinking (Smith, et al., 2006).

## PERFECTIONISM/ELEVATED SELF-STANDARDS

Cognitions related to unmet, often elevated, self-standards have been implicated in suicide and suicidal behaviors. In a study comparing a sample of adolescent suicidal versus non-suicidal inpatients (Orbach, et al., 1998), suicidal adolescents reported more negative self-representations, a less complex organization of self-attributes and a higher discrepancy between their ideal and *ought-to-be* selves. In an investigation of the link between self-discrepancies and suicidal ideation (Cornette, et al., 2007), self-perceptions which were discrepant from both ideal and ought-to-be standards were associated with suicidal ideation. Discrepancies between actual and ideal standards which a person believed were unlikely to resolve in the future were also more strongly associated with suicidal ideation, highlighting the importance of belief patterns which reflect hopelessness about the likelihood of attaining one's desired self-attributes.

Perfectionism, in which the individual determinedly pursues self-imposed, personally demanding standards, despite adverse consequences, represents an extreme cognitive emphasis on ameliorating a perceived disparity between reality and standards. Perfectionism has been found to be predictive of suicidal ideation and attempts in both adolescent and adult samples (Hewitt, et al., 1994). Some research has suggested that socially prescribed perfectionism may be the most salient form of perfectionism for suicidality (Dean, et al., 1996), as it seems to confer vulnerability to suicidal behaviors by depriving people of the benefits of social connection and exposing them to the costs of social disconnection. Socially-prescribed perfectionism has been associated with more serious suicide intent among suicide attempters (Boergers, et al., 1998). In addition, some research has suggested that socially-prescribed perfectionism is discriminately associated with important mediators of suicidality, while self-oriented perfectionism is not (Dean, et al., 1996).

## PROBLEM-SOLVING DEFICITS

Problem solving ability, especially for interpersonal dilemmas, is a cognitive process found to be deficient in suicidal patients (Sidley, et al., 1997). In one study (Williams, et al., 2005), those formerly depressed individuals with a history of suicidal ideation produced significantly less effective solutions to interpersonal problems following a mood challenge, an effect that was moderated by insufficient specificity in autobiographical memory. In another study, problem-solving deficiencies were shown to mediate the relationship between a family history of suicide attempts and multiple suicide attempt status (Jeglic, et al., 2005).

## AUTOBIOGRAPHICAL MEMORY

Research suggests that deficiencies in the ability to generate specific, detailed autobiographical memories may be associated with suicide risk (Pollock & Williams, 2001). A number of prospective studies suggest that one of the maladaptive effects of overgeneralized memory is delaying recovery from affective disturbance, ultimately lengthening the time-frame for suicide risk (Brittlebank, et al., 1993).

Hopelessness about the future can also be affected by overgeneralized autobiographical memory. In particular, suicidal patients with less specific memories are less able to generate specific future scenarios compared with non-suicidal individuals (Williams, et al., 1996). Such failure may impact the formation and implementation of future plans, possibly perpetuating hopelessness.

Finally, overgeneralized autobiographical memory has been identified as a major contributor to social problem-solving deficits (another known risk factor for suicidal behavior) among suicidal individuals, who may experience difficulties retrieving information from past experiences to solve current interpersonal problems (Kaviani, et al., 2005).

## PERCEIVED BURDENSOMENESS AND THWARTED BELONGINGNESS

Perceptions of oneself as burdensome to and/or disenfranchised from others may be important risk factors for suicide. Perceptions of interpersonal burdensomeness and social isolation have stood apart as risk factors for suicide (de Catanzaro, 1995). Perceived burdensomeness has stood out as a unique and specific predictor of suicide (Brown, et al., 1999), as well as a predictor of the medical lethality of suicide attempts (Joiner, et al., 2002). Research has shown that suicide notes from individuals completing suicide contain more references to perceived burdensomeness than the notes of individuals attempting suicide (Joiner, et al., 2002). Brown and colleagues (2002) further reported that, whereas non-suicidal self-injury was often driven by a desire to express anger or punish oneself, suicide attempts were often motivated by a desire to make others better off. Support for the role of objective and perceived thwarted belongingness in suicidal thinking can be found in numerous studies of clinical and community samples (Sokero, et al., 2003).

## DISSOCIATION AND PERCEPTUAL TOLERANCE

Dissociation (a disruption in the integrated functions of consciousness, memory or perception) and perceptual tolerance (the need for higher levels of a stimulus to achieve the same effect) may also be associated with susceptibility to suicidal behavior. Orbach (2006) examined cognitions surrounding harm to the self, introducing the concept of the *suicidal body*. He argued that, for individuals who undergo unbearable psychological circumstances (such as abuse), the "threshold for pain and other senses are heightened to assuage the effect of the unpleasant conditions." Following prolonged use of dissociation as a defense mechanism, Orbach argued that thresholds can become stuck at elevated levels regardless of whether current experiences are positive or negative. Subsequently, numbness, detachment, insensitivity to pain and estrangement toward the body occur, potentially allowing one to overcome psychological obstacles (e.g., fear of pain or fear of death) to engaging in suicidal behaviors. He further argued that individuals who develop perceptual tolerance may also experience lessened sensitivity to physical and perhaps other pleasures and, therefore, may feel they have little to lose through bodily detachment or suicide.

## COGNITIVE MODELS OF SUICIDE RISK

A number of models of suicide risk which incorporate various components of cognition outlined above have been introduced over the past decade. The following is a select overview of some of the more compelling conceptual models which incorporate a focus on acute suicide risk, direct links to treatment, or the psychological processes which discriminate suicide ideators from those who go on to engage in serious suicide attempts.

In Baumeister's escape theory (1990), suicidal behavior is conceptualized as an attempt to escape from aversive self-awareness when other strategies have failed. The causal chain culminating in suicidal behavior begins with events which fall significantly below standards. If internal attributions are made for failures, Baumeister argues that negative self-awareness follows, which subsequently leads to negative affect (e.g., depression, anxiety and anger). Both are the proximal motivating causes of escape through cognitive deconstruction, which involves shrinking the world to the immediate temporal and spatial present. The deconstructed state facilitates avoidance of higher level, meaningful thought necessary for comparisons between self and standards which can foster and maintain aversive self-awareness and negative affect. According to Baumeister, the consequences of cognitive deconstruction include disinhibition, irrational thought, lack of emotionality and passivity. Since the deconstructed state is a rejection of meaningful thought, inhibitions and other barriers to suicidal behaviors are reduced. For those whose troubling thoughts and feelings are neither adequately shut down by cognitive deconstruction or addressed successfully through reinterpretation, suicide may be seen as the one remaining outlet for escape from suffering.

Based on Beck's original cognitive theory of depression, Brown and Wenzel (2007) outlined a cognitive model of suicidal behavior which distinguishes between cognitive processes associated with psychiatric disturbance and those associated with suicidal crises. They argue that state hopelessness and selective attention both contribute to attentional fixation which, when influenced by suicidal cognitive schemas (e.g., I'm worthless or life has no meaning) and subsequent negative automatic thoughts (e.g., I can't take it anymore or things will never change), lead to suicidal ideation. When ideation exceeds an individual's tolerance, suicidal behavior becomes likely.

The fluid vulnerability theory (Rudd, 2006) is a vulnerability-stress model of suicide which accounts for the fluctuations in suicidal ideation often observed over time. Rudd builds upon the work of Beck and colleagues, arguing that internal or external precipitants can trigger "orienting schemas," based upon an individual's psychiatric and developmental history, which assign preliminary meaning to stressors. These orienting schemas may then trigger the "suicidal mode," "a suicidal episode or state that is characterized by specific or core cognitive schemas, acute dysphoria and related physiological arousal (i.e., Axis I symptoms), and associated death-related behaviors." According to the theory, core cognitive schemas which are likely to trigger the suicidal "mode" cluster around four themes: (1) unlovability, (2) helplessness, (3) distress tolerance and (4) perceived burdensomeness. Rudd and colleagues argue that the threshold for the activation of the suicidal mode decreases among individuals with a history of previous suicide attempts.

Joiner's (2005) interpersonal-psychological model outlines core interpersonal cognitions (perceived burdensomeness and thwarted belongingness) which he argues are most critical for developing suicidal ideation. Joiner argues that even among individuals who experience suicidal ideation, barriers to engaging in serious suicidal behaviors exist, and that acquired ability, comprised of (1) reduced fear about self-injury, (2) heightened tolerance to pain, and (3) acquisition of a knowledge base regarding means for self-harm, is central to risk for serious self-injury.

## TREATMENT IMPLICATIONS

Historically, treatments for depression have been employed in the treatment of suicidal symptoms. This was based upon the premise that effective treatment of depression would result in effective amelioration of suicide symptoms. Ultimately though there has been a lack of randomized controlled trials indicating that depression treatment prevents suicide attempts (Brown & Wenzel, 2007). What has been developed is a cognitive-behavioral-based psychotherapy which is specific in its treatment of the symptoms of suicide and of the specific proximal vulnerability factors that precede suicidal behaviors (e.g., hopelessness, poor problem solving, poor impulse control, noncompliance with the health system, social isolation, etc.) (Brown, et al., 2006). Cognitive coping strategies include modifying suicide relevant beliefs (through guided discovery or future time-imaging), building problem-solving skills, identifying reasons for living, creating coping cards and reducing impulsivity.

Some evidence also exists for the efficacy of treatments specifically targeting interpersonal problem-solving skills (Joiner, et al., 2001). In addition, dialectical behavior therapy, which incorporates cognitive strategies to include problem-solving, cognitive restructuring, and contingency clarification, has demonstrated efficacy in reducing suicidal symptoms among individuals with borderline personality disorder (Linehan, et al, 2006).

Rudd and his colleagues (2001) developed a treatment for suicidal behavior based upon the principles of cognitive therapy and self-determination theory (SDT; Ryan & Deci, 2000), arguing that suicidal clients' motivation can be increased through supporting their sense of autonomy as well as their perceived sense of competence in therapy. SDT techniques can also directly facilitate the satisfaction of unmet psychological needs for autonomy (through choice and rationale provision), relatedness (through the therapeutic alliance), and competence (through skill building). The unmet psychological needs outlined in Joiner's (2005) theory of suicidal behavior are consistent with SDT principles, mapping onto neglected autonomy and competence needs (perceptions of thwarted belongingness) and neglected relatedness needs (perceived burdensomeness).

## CONCLUSION

Much information has been amassed on cognitive risk factors for suicide. Recent theories provide a conceptual framework for understanding how cognitive risk factors interact with one another as well as with other important risk factors for suicide. Cognitive risk factors and theory have also been influential in informing treatments for suicidal behaviors.

## REFERENCES

Abramson, L. Y., Alloy, L. B., Hogan, M. E., et al. (1998). Suicidality and cognitive vulnerability to depression among college students: a prospective study. *Journal of Adolescence*, 21, 473-487.

Abramson, L. Y., Metalsky, G. I., & Alloy, L. B. (1989). Hopelessness depression: a theory-based subtype of depression. *Psychological Review*, 96, 358-372.

Baumeister, R. F. (1990). Suicide as escape from self. *Psychological Review*, 97, 90-113.

Beck., A. T., Steer, R. A., Kovacs, M., et al. (1985). Hopelessness and eventual suicide: a 10-year prospective study of patients hospitalized with suicidal ideation. *American Journal of Psychiatry*, 142, 559-563.

Beck, A. T., Brown, G., Berchick, R. J., et al. (1990). Relationship between hopelessness and ultimate suicide: a replication with psychiatric outpatients. *American Journal of Psychiatry*, 147, 190-195.

Boergers, J., Spirito, A., & Donaldson, D. (1998). Reasons for adolescent suicide attempts: associations with psychological functioning. *Journal of the American Academy of Child & Adolescent Psychiatry*, 37, 1287-1293.

Brittlebank, A. D., Scott, J., Williams, J. M. G., et al. (1993). Autobiographical memory in depression: state or trait marker? *British Journal of Psychiatry*, 162, 118-121.

Brown, G. K., & Wenzel, A. (2007). Cognitive therapy for suicide prevention. Presentation for the Veterans Affairs conference on evidence-based interventions for suicidal persons. Denver, CO.

Brown, G. K., Comtois, K. A., & Linehan, M. M. (2002). Reasons for suicide attempts and non-suicidal self-injury in women with borderline personality disorder. *Journal of Abnormal Psychology*, 111, 198-202.

Brown, R. M., Dahlen, E., Mills, C., et al. (1999). Evaluation of an evolutionary model of self- preservation and self-destruction. *Suicide & Life-Threatening Behavior*, 29, 58-71.

Brown, G. K., Jeglic, E., Henriques, G. R., et al. (2006). Cognitive therapy, cognition and suicidal behavior. In T. E. Ellis (Ed) *Cognition and suicide: theory, research and therapy*, pp. 53-74. Washington DC: American Psychological Association.

Cornette, M. M., Strauman, T. J., Abramson, L. Y., et al. (2009). Self-discrepancy and suicidal ideation. *Cognition & Emotion*, 23, 504-527.

Dean, P. J., Range, L. M., & Goggin, W. C. (1996). The escape theory of suicide in college students: testing a model that includes perfectionism. *Suicide& Life-Threatening Behavior*, 26, 181-186.

de Catanzaro, D. (1995). Reproductive status, family interactions, and suicidal ideation: surveys of the general public and high-risk groups. *Ethology & Sociobiology,* 16, 385-394.

Hewitt, P. L., Flett, G. L., & Weber, C. (1994). Perfectionism, hopelessness, and suicide ideation. *Cognitive Therapy & Research,* 18, 439-460.

Jeglic, E. L., Sharp, I. R., Chapman, J. E., et al. (2005). History of family suicide behaviors and negative problem solving in multiple suicide attempters. *Archives of Suicide Research,* 9, 135-146.

Joiner, T. (2005). *Why people die by suicide.* Cambridge, MA: Harvard University Press.

Joiner, T. E., Pettit, J. W., Walker, et al. (2002). Perceived burdensomeness and suicidality: two studies on the suicide notes of those attempting and completing suicide. *Journal of Social & Clinical Psychology,* 21, 531-545.

Joiner, T.E., Voelz, Z.R., & Rudd, M.D. (2001). For suicidal young adults with comorbid depressive and anxiety disorders, problem-solving treatment may be better than treatment as usual. *Professional Psychology: Research & Practice,* 32, 278-282.

Kaviani, H., Rahimi-Darabad, P., & Naghavi, H.R. (2005). Autobiographical memory retrieval and problem solving deficits of Iranian depressed patients attempting suicide. *Journal of Psychopathology & Behavioral Assessment,* 27, 39-44.

Linehan, M. M., Comtois, K. A., Murray, A. M, et al. (2006). Two-year randomized controlled trial and follow-up of dialectical behavior therapy vs. therapy by experts for suicidal behaviors and borderline personality disorder. *Archives of General Psychiatry,* 63, 757-766.

Orbach, I. (2006). The body-mind of a suicidal person. In T. E. Ellis (Ed) *Cognition and suicide: theory, research and therapy,* pp.193-214.Washington DC: American Psychological Association.

Orbach, I., Mikulincer, M., Stein, D., et al. (1998). Self-representation of suicidal adolescents. *Journal of Abnormal Psychology,* 107, 435-439.

Pollock, L. R. & Williams, J. M. G. (2001). Effective problem solving in suicide attempters depends on specific autobiographical recall. *Suicide & Life-Threatening Behavior,* 31, 386-396.

Rudd, M. D. (2006). Fluid vulnerability theory: a cognitive approach to understanding the process of acute and chronic suicide risk. In T. E. Ellis (Ed) *Cognition and suicide: theory, research and therapy,* pp.355-368.Washington DC: American Psychological Association.

Rudd, M. D., Joiner, T., & Rajab, M. (2001) Treating suicidal behavior: an effective, time-limited approach. New York: Guilford.

Ryan, R. M., & Deci, E. L. (2000). Self-determination theory and the facilitation of intrinsic motivation, social development, and well-being. *American Psychologist,* 55, 68-78.

Sidley, G. L., Whitaker, K., Calam, R., et al. (1997). The relationship between problem-solving and autobiographical memory in parasuicide patients. *Behavioural & Cognitive Psychotherapy,* 25, 195-202.

Smith, J. M., Alloy, L. B., & Abramson, L. Y. (2006). Cognitive vulnerability to depression, rumination, hopelessness, and suicidal ideation: multiple pathways to self-injurious thinking. *Suicide & Life-Threatening Behavior,* 36, 443-454.

Sokero, T. P., Melartin, T. K., Rytsala, H. J., et al. (2003). Suicidal ideation and attempts among psychiatric patients with major depressive disorder. *Journal of Clinical Psychiatry*, 64, 1094-1100.

Steer, R. A., Kumar, G., & Beck, A. T. (1993). Hopelessness in adolescent psychiatric inpatients. *Psychological Reports,* 72, 559-564.

Weishaar, M. E. (2000). Cognitive risk factors in suicide. In R. W. Maris, S. S., Canetto, J. L. McIntosh, & M. M. Silverman (Eds.) *Review of suicidology*, pp.112-139. New York: Guilford.

Wen-Hung, K. Gallo, J. J., & Eaton, W. W. (2004). Hopelessness, depression, substance disorder, and suicidality: a 13-year community-based study. *Social Psychiatry & Psychiatric Epidemiology*, 39, 497-501.

Williams, J. M. G., Ellis, N. C., Tyers, C., et al. (1996). The specificity of autobiographical memory and imageability of the future. *Memory & Cognition*, 24, 116-125.

Williams, J. M. G., Branhofer, T. Crane, C., et al. (2005). Problem solving deteriorates following mood challenge in formerly depressed patients with a history of suicidal ideation. *Journal of Abnormal Psychology*, 114, 421-431.

Wilson, C. J., Deane, F. P., & Ciarrochi, J. (2005). Can hopelessness and adolescents' beliefs and attitudes about seeking help account for help negation? *Journal of Clinical Psychology*, 61, 1525-1539.

*Chapter 2*

# LOSS, HOPELESSNESS AND SUICIDE

### *Paolo Scocco and Elena Toffol*

Real or psychological loss and a feeling of hopelessness are very common experiences, often associated with the onset of psychiatric disorders such as schizophrenia, mood or panic disorders, but also with mental suffering, or "psychache," which is not specific to any one disorder. These events are also triggers of behavioral disorders such as alcohol and drug abuse, binge eating or suicidal behaviors. Research has shown that suicidal behaviors (i.e., completed suicide, attempted suicide, self-injurious behaviors and suicidal ideation) are often associated with stressful and traumatic life events (Kolves, et al., 2006), inevitably related to a feeling of loss and hopelessness. On psychological autopsy, people who die by suicide often have a history of recent loss and/or hopelessness (Cassells, et al., 2005). Loss and hopelessness may also follow a suicidal gesture (Krysinka, 2003). Conversely, suicidal gestures can leave bereaved relatives and friends with a mixture of loss, hopelessness, grief and shame (Harwood, et al., 2002).

## WHAT IS A LOSS?

Loss is a common word with a broad spectrum of meanings, linked to experiences that vary according to one's theoretical approach. For example, a loss may relate to "somebody," such as the bereavement of a close friend or family member, to a "real object," or a social or interpersonal role, or it may be related to self, identity or culture.

According to the original psychodynamic (Freudian) theory, depression and suicide are the natural result of failure to work through the bereavement process with subsequent identification with the lost object. Abraham and Freud hypothesized a turned-inward anger model for depression, where the loved object becomes internalized in an attempt to prevent the traumatic loss. Consequently the patient becomes the target of his/her own death impulses. Bowlby's object-loss model consists of a two-step process, in which an early break in affectional bonds causes a behavioral predisposition to depression, and then subsequent adult losses lead to revival of memories of traumatic childhood losses, thereby precipitating depressive episodes. The cognitive model presumes a cognitive triad, in which patients consider themselves helpless, interpret most events unfavorably vis-à-vis the self, and believe the future to be hopeless (Kaplan, et al., 1999). Interpersonal theory is based on the premise that people with chronic or recurrent interpersonal problems may be more susceptible to loss of self-esteem or to develop hopelessness, anxiety and psychopathology. In particular, it suggests that social and interpersonal deficits and losses may act both as antecedents to and consequences of psychopathology, since mental illness impairs the ability to perform social roles (Weissmann, et al., 2000).

These briefly described theories show quite clearly that there is a correlation between the loss experience and suicidal phenomena. In order to simplify closer investigation of this correlation, we make a distinction between:

1) loss as bereavement
2) loss as role transition
3) culture loss or disruption of self-identity

## BEREAVEMENT AND SUICIDAL PHENOMENA

Bereavement is considered to be one of the most stressful life events. Experiencing the death of a relative or friend is always difficult to cope with and is often associated with such severe grief that some people perceive the need for professional help. It can also lead to a specific syndrome in adults (so-called "traumatic grief"), which is distinct from complicated and uncomplicated grief, and associated with higher suicidal ideation (Prigerson, et al., 1996).

It has been shown that the presence of suicidal thoughts, loneliness, hopelessness, depressive anxiety and complicated grief in bereaved people increases the suicidal risk for the survivors themselves (Szanto, et al., 1997), whatever their age, gender, marital status or social group. It has also been demonstrated that early parental loss, especially when it results in a long-term disruption of family life, increases the probability of suicidal ideation and suicidal behavior in young people (Adam, et al., 1982). Finally, suicide risk is higher after a perinatal loss (Hutti, 2005).

The role of bereavement in increasing suicidal risk is particularly pertinent to suicide survivors (Groot, et al., 2006). Bereavement after a violent death (i.e., by accident, homicide or suicide) often leads to complicated grief. In particular, it is hard to comprehend a sudden violent loss, to make sense of it and to find meaning in the loss itself (Currier, et al., 2006). It is thus understandable that, more commonly than in other causes of death, relatives bereaved by suicide feel guilt, rejection, shame or stigma (Harwood, et al., 2002), that is, they experience the so-called "suicide survivor syndrome" (Krysinka, 2003).

## ROLE TRANSITION AND SUICIDAL PHENOMENA

On the basis of Weissman and colleagues' (2000) definition, "role transition" includes any important change in life status associated with both positive and negative aspects (e.g., the beginning or the end of a relationship or career, a move, a promotion, retirement, graduation or a diagnosis of medical illness). In such circumstances an individual has to deal with the loss of a role which he/she can overcome only by finding and developing a new role. Whatever one's age, role transition may cause symptoms as individuals try to adapt to a new set of circumstances.

Accordingly, suicide rates are somewhat higher in people experiencing a role transition or a specific age-related life event, a physical illness, or interpersonal/familial problems (Rubenowitz, et al., 2001; Duberstein, et al., 2004). Age-related variations have also been reported in the pattern of recent life events. Events such as separation, serious family disputes, job problems, unemployment and residence changes are more common among younger suicides, whereas in middle-age stressful role transition events commonly include somatic illness, job change or loss, retirement, losing a spouse or becoming caretaker of a parent (Heikkinen, et al., 1995).

Adolescent suicide deserves particular attention since completed suicide rates are low during childhood, but rise sharply at puberty. Attempted suicide rates are also higher, and suicidal thoughts are even higher in adolescence (Lipschitz, et al., 2001). The high rate (20% to 30%) of suicidal thoughts in adolescents suggests that ideation is not always pathological, but may be related to a specific stage of adolescence when teens first address or deal with the theme of their own mortality (Evans, et al., 2005). In addition, in many countries, children leave their home and family during adolescence and start their own life as independent adults. This role transition can be a highly stressful event for young adolescents and is often associated with other stress precipitating factors such as the loss of a romantic relationship (Gould, et al., 1996). Finally, it has been demonstrated that attempted suicide is far more common among adopted adolescents than among teens living with their biological families (Slap, et al., 2001). Adoption itself could be an event that leads to an identity disruption just when teenagers are beginning to develop their own identity.

## DISRUPTION OF SELF-IDENTITY AND CULTURE LOSS AND SUICIDE

Almost all the above issues can bring about disruption of self-identity. Indeed, the loss of a close friend or family member or a role transition may be associated with the fear of losing one's sense of self-identity. The same applies to people who experience a culture loss. Indeed, suicide is more common in ethnic minorities and in immigrants. In particular it seems that suicide rates are higher in second-generation immigrants, probably due to age-specific vulnerability and sensitivity to the adverse conditions of life as an immigrant. Environmental factors may contribute, together with individual factors, in determining the suicide risk in immigrants, as may socio-economic stress, racism, loss of ties with religious affiliations, difficulty in forming a new social identity and loss of support from the family or community of origin (McKenzie, et al., 2003). Immigrants tend to concentrate in some city areas and to maintain their own traditions until the group experiences a push towards assimilation from children and grandchildren. Obstructing this tendency towards ethnic concentration by "forced" dilution of the various ethnic groups in any one country can have severe healthcare and social repercussions (e.g., an increase in the occurrence of psychiatric pathologies, suicide and antisocial behavior) (Scocco, et al., 2006).

Increasing levels of suicide have been found among Inupiat youths, an ethnic group living in Northwest Alaska (Wexler, 2006), and among youths in Greenland (Leineweber, et al., 2001). Both are probably related to rapid socio-cultural change, or "acculturation stress," and consequent progressive culture loss.

Then there is the case of borderline personality structure, characterized by disruption in self-identity. Indeed, the typical features of a borderline structure are lack of self-identity, chronic feelings of emptiness and the lack of a sense of self-cohesion. These patients usually lack a sense of integration between the self and objects related to the self, and between good and bad aspects of the self and reality. Here archaic defense mechanisms, such as splitting and projective identification, generally come into play (Kernberg, 1984). People with this type of personality structure cannot easily describe themselves when asked, and often act out their sense of emptiness or loss, for example by a suicidal gesture.

Another example of loss of self-identity leading to suicide can be found in homosexual populations, where suicidality is higher than among heterosexuals (Ploderl, et al., 2005), particularly just after coming-out (Cato, et al., 2003). The trigger factor for a suicide attempt in homosexuals is often intrapersonal distress, related to a not yet established "positive gay identity" (i.e., ego dystonic homosexuality), and to possible experiences of homosexuality-related rejection. The need to come to terms with an emerging homosexual identity can frighten youth and subsequently lead to suicidal behaviors (Schneider, et al., 1989).

## HOPELESSNESS AND SUICIDAL PHENOMENA

Hopelessness is closely related to bereavement, role transition, culture loss and self-identity disruption since it is the common emotional reaction to all these. In any event, hopelessness may be the consequence of many other material circumstances related to everyday life, including one's occupational levels or poor physical health. All these events may cause negative expectations about the future (i.e., hopelessness), dissatisfaction with life and demoralization (Butterworth, et al., 2006). There are several links between hopelessness and suicidal ideation, attempted and completed suicide (Beck, et al., 1993). The Beck Hopelessness Scale (Beck, et al., 1990) is a sensitive indicator of suicidal potential recognized worldwide. Hopelessness has also been deemed to act as a mediator with other risk factors (dysfunctional attitudes, childhood maltreatment and life stress) to increase suicidality (Rudd, 1990) and to contribute to perseverance of suicidal thoughts (Smith, et al., 2006).

Work by Dieserud, et al. (2001) shows the close connection between the main topics of this review (loss, hopelessness and suicide). The authors highlight two paths in the pattern of suicide attempt. The first begins with low self-esteem (=self-disruption), separation or divorce (=role transition), advances to depression, and ends with a suicide attempt mediated by hopelessness. The second path begins with low self-esteem and a low sense of self-efficacy and advances to attempted suicide through poor interpersonal and problem solving skills (Dieserud, et al., 2001).

## THERAPEUTIC IMPLICATIONS AND CONCLUSIONS

The main therapeutic implication of this review is, once again, the importance of closely supervising patients experiencing hopelessness, loss, self-hate, anguish, and other feelings that increase suicidal risk. It is good clinical practice to regard these patients as suicidal (Maltsberger, 2001) and to help them seek and find appropriate help.

It would be useful to take particular care of bereaved people, for example by arranging specific programs of psychiatric help and consultation, with psychotherapeutic (e.g., interpersonal and cognitive-behavioral psychotherapies) and/or psychopharmacological approaches. People bereaved by the suicide of a relative or friend deserve particular attention since they too are at risk.

On the basis of our experience with suicide survivors, we suggest the need to undertake a specific strategy for people at risk due to loss or hopelessness. Since 2005, our Mental Health Department has adopted an interpersonal psychotherapeutic approach (IPT) for clients surviving the death by suicide of a friend or relative. We chose this approach since these people usually have to deal not only with loss, but also with role dispute or interpersonal deficits, ideal foci for IPT. Using this approach, we have found a general amelioration in depressive symptomatology, both in complicated grief and in suicidal ideation (Scocco, et al., 2005, 2006). This approach also acts by lowering the stigma that usually follows a suicide. Further research, however, is warranted to confirm these results.

## REFERENCES

Adam, K. S., Lohrenz, J. G., Harper, D., et al. (1982). Early parental loss and suicidal ideation in university students. *Canadian Journal of Psychiatry*, 27, 275-281.

Beck, A. T., Brown, G., Berchick, R. J., et al. (1990). Relationship between hopelessness and ultimate suicide: a replication with psychiatric outpatients. *American Journal of Psychiatry*, 147,190-195.

Beck, A. T., Steer, R. A., Brown, G. (1993). Dysfunctional attitudes and suicidal ideation in psychiatric outpatients. *Suicide & Life-Threatening Behavior*, 23, 11-20.

Butterworth, P., Fairweather, A. K., Anstey, K. J., et al. (2006). Hopelessness, demoralization and suicidal behaviour: the backdrop to welfare reform in Australia. *Australia & New Zealand Journal of Psychiatry*, 40, 648-656.

Cassells, C., Paterson, B., Dowding, D., et al. (2005). Long- and short-term risk factors in the prediction of inpatient suicide: a review of the literature. *Crisis*, 26, 53-63.

Cato, J. E., & Canetto, S. S. (2003). Young adults' reactions to gay and lesbian peers who became suicidal following "coming out" to their parents. *Suicide & Life-Threatening Behavior*, 33, 201-210.

Currier, J. M., Holland, J. M., & Neimeyer, R. A. (2006). Sense-making, grief, and the experience of violent loss: toward a meditational model. *Death Studies*, 30, 403-428.

Dieserud, G., Roysamb, E., Ekeberg, O., et al. (2001). Toward an integrative model of suicide attempt: a cognitive psychological approach. *Suicide & Life-Threatening Behavior*, 31, 153-168.

Duberstein, P. R., Conwell, Y., Conner, K. R., et al. (2004). Suicide at 50 years of age and older: perceived physical illness, family discord and financial strain. *Psychological Medicine*, 34, 137-146.

Evans, E., Hawton, K., Rodham, K., et al. (2005). The prevalence of suicidal phenomena in adolescents: a systematic review of population-based studies. *Suicide & Life-Threatening Behavior*, 35, 239-250.

Gould, M., Fisher, P., Parides, M., et al. (1996). Psychosocial risk factors of child and adolescent completed suicide. *Archives of General Psychiatry*, 53, 1155-1164.

Groot, M. H., Keijser, J., Neeleman, J. (2006). Grief shortly after suicide and natural death: a comparative study among spouses and first-degree relatives. *Suicide & Life-Threatening Behaviour*, 36, 418-431.

Harwood, D., Hawton, K., Hope, T., et al. (2002). The grief experiences and needs of bereaved relatives and friends of older people dying through suicide: a descriptive and case-control study. *Journal of Affective Disorders*, 72, 185-194.

Heikkinen, M. E., Isometsa, E. T., Aro, H. M., et al. (1995). Age-related variation in recent life-events preceding suicide. *Journal of Nervous & Mental Disease*, 183, 325-31.

Hutti, M. H. (2005). Social and professional support needs of families after perinatal loss. *Journal of Obstetric, Gynecological & Neonatal Nursing*, 34, 630-638.

Kaplan, H. I., & Sadock, B. J. (1999). Kaplan and Sadock's synopsis of psychiatry-behavioral sciences/clinical psychiatry. 8th Ed. Philadelphia, PA: Lippincott Williams & Wilkins.

Kernberg, O. (1984). *Severe personality disorders.* New Haven, CT: Yale University Press.

Klerman, G. L., Weissman, M. M., Rounsaville, B. J., et al. (1984). *Interpersonal psychotherapy for depression.* New York: Basic Books.

Kolves, K., Varnik, A., Schneider, B., et al. (2006). Recent life events and suicide: a case-control study in Tallinn and Frankfurt. *Social Science & Medicine*, 62, 2887-2896.

Krysinka, K. E. (2003). Loss by suicide: a risk factor for suicidal behaviour. *Journal of Psychosocial Nursing Mental Health Services*, 41, 34-41.

Leineweber, M., Bjerregaard, P., Bareveldt, C., et al. (2001). Suicide in a society in transition. *International Journal of Circumpolar Health.* 60, 280-287.

Lipschitz, A. (2001). Suicidal adolescents in managed care. In J.M. Ellison (Ed.) *Treatment of suicidal patients in managed care,* pp.59-83. Washington, DC: American Psychiatric Press.

Maltsberger, J. T. (2001). Treating suicidal patients in the managed care environment. In J. M. Ellison (Ed.) *Treatment of suicidal patients in managed care,* pp.1-13. Washington, DC: American Psychiatric Press.

McKenzie, K., Serfaty, M., Crawford, M. (2003). Suicide in ethnic minority groups. *British Journal of Psychiatry*, 183, 100-101.

Melhem, N. M., Day, N., Shear, M. K., et al. (2004). Traumatic grief among adolescents exposed to a peer's suicide. *American Journal of Psychiatry*, 161, 1411-1416.

Ploderl, M., Fartacek, R. (2005). Suicidality and associated risk factors among lesbian, gay, and bisexual compared to heterosexual Austrian adults. *Suicide & Life-Threatening Behavior*, 35, 661-670.

Prigerson, H. G., Bierhals, A. J., Kasl, S. V., et al. (1996). Complicated grief as a disorder distinct from bereavement-related depression and anxiety: a replication study. *American Journal of Psychiatry*, 153, 1484-1486.

Rubenowitz, E., Waern, M., Wilhelmson, K., et al. (2001). Life events and psychosocial factors in elderly suicides: a case-control study. *Psychological Medicine*, 31, 1193-1202.

Rudd, D.M. (1990). An integrative model of suicide ideation. *Suicide & Life-Threatening Behavior*, 20, 16-30.

Schneider, S. G., Farberow, N. L., Kruks, G. N. (1989). Suicidal behavior in adolescent and young adult gay men. *Suicide & Life-Threatening Behavior*, 19, 381-94.

Scocco, P., Frasson, A., Costacurta, A., et al. (2005). Interpersonal psychotherapy for suicide survivors. *Bulletin of International Society for Interpersonal Psychotherapy*, 4, 2-8.

Scocco, P., Frasson, A., Costacurta A, et al. (2006). SOPRoxi: a research-intervention project for suicide survivors. *Crisis*, 27, 39-41.

Scocco, P., & Di Munzio, W. (2006). Suicide in ethnic minorities. *Studies on Aggressiveness & Suicide*, 8, 43-49.

Slap, G., Goodman, E., & Huang, B. (2001). Adoption as a risk factor for attempted suicide during adolescence. *Pediatrics*, 108, 30-38.

Smith, J. M., Alloy, L. A., & Abramson, L. Y. (2006). Cognitive vulnerability to depression, rumination, hopelessness and suicide ideation: multiple pathways to self-injurious thinking. *Suicide & Life-Threatening Behavior*, 36, 443-454.

Szanto, K., Prigerson, K., Houck, P., et al. (1997). Suicidal ideation in elderly bereaved: the role of complicated grief. *Suicide & Life-Threatening Behavior*, 27, 194-207.

Weissman, M. M., Markowitz, J. C., & Klerman, G. L. (2000). Comprehensive guide to interpersonal psychotherapy. Albany, NY: Basic Books.

Wexler, L. M. (2006). Inupiat youth suicide and culture loss: changing community conversations for prevention. *Social Science & Medicine*, 63, 2938-2948.

In: Suicide from a Global Perspective: Psychosocial Approaches

Chapter 3

# SELF-DESTRUCTIVE MOTIVATION: AN EVOLUTIONARY PERSPECTIVE

## *R. Michael Brown and Stephanie L. Brown*

Drawing upon the theory of inclusive fitness[1] in evolutionary biology (Hamilton, 1964), Denys deCatanzaro (1986) formulated a mathematical model of the evolution of both self-preservative and self-destructive motivational mechanisms in humans and certain other social species (e.g., social *Hymenopterans*). The model predicts self-destructive motivation for those with low *individual reproductive potential*, for example, due to old age, inadequate heterosexual relationships, poor health, financial hardship, or who feel like a burden to genetic relatives. Under these conditions, staying alive could compromise the individual's *inclusive* fitness. It is important to note that deCatanzaro's model focuses on *past* recurrent evolutionary contingencies, providing an explanation for the *evolution* of self-destructive motivation in humans and some other highly social species. Thus, there is no *a priori* reason to expect that the model should predict all or even most forms of suicidal thinking and behavior in the present. Nevertheless, despite substantial cultural change over time, there is increasing evidence to suggest that the model helps us predict and understand manifestations of self-destructive behavior in *contemporary* environments, as we shall see.

Arguments for the evolutionary plausibility of suicide are not unique to deCatanzaro. For example, Lonergan and Travis (2003) have argued that the evolution of a suicide gene is logically and mathematically plausible, and Mascaro, Korb and Nicholson (2001) used game theoretic methods to show that suicide can become an evolutionarily stable strategy. Such arguments are given additional credence by (a) findings from family correlational studies that are consistent with a genetic basis for suicide and suicidal behavior, independent of related psychopathological disorders (e.g., Kim, Seguin, Therrien, Riopel, Chawky, Lesage & Turecki, 2005; Lieb, Bronisch, Höfler, et al., 2005; Pedersen & Fiske, 2010); (b) well-documented evidence for cell suicide caused by the activation of specific genes (Duke, Ojcius & Young, 1996; Elmore, 2007); (c) evidence suggesting kin-selected suicidal behavior in

---

[1] Inclusive fitness theory established that genes are transmitted to future generations not only through an individual's sexual reproduction, but also through that individual's efforts to help genetic relatives reproduce.

social insects (e.g., Hölldobler & Wilson, 1990; Wilson, 2006; Tofilski, Couvillon, Evison, et al., 2008; Rueppell, et al., 2010); and (d) reports of apparent altruistic suicide in humans (Durkheim, 1897/1951; Leighton & Hughes, 1955; Pape, 2005).

## EVIDENCE IMPLICATING REPRODUCTIVE POTENTIAL AND BURDENSOMENESS

With the exception of our own work (Brown, Dahlen, Mills, Rick & Biblarz, 1999; Brown, Brown, Johnson, et al. 2009), there have been few attempts to directly test deCatanzaro's inclusive fitness model of self-destructive motivation. However, consistent with the model's predictions, data from a variety of other sources show that indicators of low individual reproductive potential, and perceived burdensomeness, are associated with suicidal thinking and behavior, including risk of completed suicide.

### Individual Reproductive Potential

Humans are one among many species in which reproductive value declines with increasing age (Clutton-Brock, 1991). Thus, we might expect suicide rates to increase with age, and indeed there is a global trend in this direction, especially for males (World Health Organization, 2007). Even within an age cohort, individual reproductive potential can be affected by resource availability, health, dominance (social status), and opportunities for successful mating. Each of these factors has been linked to suicide, for example, low family income (Goodman, 1999), and low fertility (Calzeroni, Conte, Pennati & Vita, 1990).

### Perceived Burdensomeness

The hypothesis that perceived burdensomeness might influence self-destructive motivation springs from diverse theoretical and metatheoretical sources. For example, some investigators with a psychoanalytic bent have argued that *expendability* (Sabbath, 1969) or *burdensomeness* (Hendin, 1975; Orbach, 1986; Schrut, 1964) may amplify self-destructive thinking (see Wagner, 1997 for a review). Neo-Darwinists, at best strange bedfellows with psychoanalysts, have also highlighted the link between burdensomeness and self-destructive motivation (deCatanzaro, 1986, 1991). More recently, Joiner, an eclectic clinician and suicidologist, has highlighted perceived burdensomeness as a major contributor to the "desire" for suicide (Joiner, 2005; Van Orden, Witte, Cukrowicz, et al., 2010).

Prior to the millennium, only a handful of studies had explored the hypothesized burden-suicide link empirically, as noted by Joiner, Brown & Wingate (2005). Woznica and Shapiro (1990) reported that clinician ratings of patient burdensomeness constituted a risk factor for adolescent suicidal ideation and attempts, and Motto and Bostrom (1990) reported a similar pattern for completed suicides in adult mental health inpatients. Magne-Invar and Öjehagen (1999) found that nearly 60% of the significant others of a sample of hospitalized suicide attempters stated that providing psychological or practical support to the patient was a burden to them. Consistent with deCatanzaro's inclusive fitness model of self-destructive motivation, survey studies of university students and other populations have demonstrated that self-reported burdensomeness to family predicts not only suicidal ideation and behavior (deCatanzarro, 1995), but also negative affect and hopelessness (Brown, Dahlen, Mills, Rick & Biblarz, 1999).

During the past decade, the empirical case for a link between perceived burdensomeness and self-destructive motivation has been strengthened considerably. This link has been demonstrated in investigations of reasons (self-reported or other-rated) for engaging in suicidal behavior, psychological autopsies, and systematic evaluations of suicide notes (Brown, Comtois & Linehan, 2002; Filiberti, Ripamonti, Totis, Ventafridda, De Conno, Contiero & Tamburini, 2001; Hedberg, Hopkins & Kohn, 2003; Joiner, Pettit, Walker, Voelz, Cruz, Rudd & Lester, 2002; McPherson, Wilson & Murray, 2007). In addition, direct tests of Joiner's theory of suicide have demonstrated that perceived burdensomeness to loved ones predicts measures of suicidal ideation and past attempts in adult outpatients diagnosed with a variety of clinical disorders, independent of measures of depression and hopelessness (Van Orden, Lynam, Hollar & Joiner, 2006; Van Orden, Witte, Gordon, et al., 2008). Finally, direct tests of deCatanzaro's inclusive fitness model of self-destructive motivation have provided preliminary evidence for the model's central prediction - an interaction between perceived burdensomeness and measures of individual reproductive potential (Brown, et al., 2009). Specifically, using university students as participants, Brown, et al. demonstrated for the first time that the positive relationship between perceived burden and suicidal thinking is amplified for participants with low measured health and romantic relationship satisfaction. In the remainder of the present chapter we present additional unpublished *experimental* data that would seem to confirm our initial correlational evidence bearing on deCatanzaro's predicted burden x individual reproductive potential interaction (IRP).

## THE BURDEN X IRP INTERACTION: AN EXPERIMENTAL EVALUATION

A limitation common to investigations linking perceived burdensomeness to measures of self-destructive motivation is the lack of experimental control over the variables of interest. It is just as logical to conclude from the correlational studies that being suicidal makes one a burden, or makes one feel like a burden, or simply makes one more likely to be rated clinically as a burden. It is also conceivable that there is no direct link between burdensomeness and suicide and that some third variable, such as depression or hopelessness, is responsible for the burden-suicide relationship. Of course, it is difficult to imagine an ethically acceptable *experimental* manipulation of participants' burdensomeness. However, it *is* ethically feasible to experimentally manipulate the degree to which a target person in a *scenario* constitutes a burden to family members, and then have participants read the scenarios and rate the target's likelihood of self-destructive behavior. This approach, which we adopted in the present experiment, assumes that there is correspondence between people's responses to scenario events and their responses to real-world events represented by the scenarios (Ellis, 1994).

Our major interest was in evaluating the burden x individual reproductive potential interaction predicted by deCatanzaro's model. Accordingly, we manipulated not only the burdensomeness of the target depicted in our scenarios, but also aspects of the target's IRP. At the same time, we kept the target's described level of depression, and other potentially relevant variables, constant across all conditions of the experiment. We hypothesized that a fictional target's burdensomeness to family, together with indicators of his IRP, would affect participants' ratings of the target's self-destructive motivation. Specifically, these ratings should be highest when the target's reproductive value is low and the burden to family is high. Ratings of the target's self-destructive motivation should be lowest when his reproductive value is high and the burden is low.

## Method

University students (N = 536) were randomly assigned to read different scenarios about a fictional character, "John," and then rate John's mood and suicidal inclinations. In all scenarios, John was described as currently unemployed and depressed. Tragically, fatal accidents claimed not only his parents when he was a child, but also his wife and unborn twins. We held John's level of depression (in response to the death of his wife and children) constant across all scenarios. The scenarios differed in degree of John's burdensomeness to his family (low, high), and his reproductive potential (low, high). These constituted the independent variables of interest, and they were varied in an independent groups factorial MANCOVA design: Participant's Gender x Burden to Family (low, high) x IRP (low, high). The dependent measures, our self-destructive motivation variate, were participants' ratings (on a 6-point scale) of the scenario target's *unhappiness*, *hopelessness*, *suicidal ideation*, and *likelihood of a suicide attempt*. The covariate was the participant's Beck Depression Inventory (BDI) score, which were assessed prior to the start of the experiment.

*Burden Scenarios.* In the high burden scenarios John, following the death of his wife and twins, is described as needing family financial and emotional support, and seeking support from family on a near daily basis. Family reaction, initially sympathetic, turns openly resentful of John's incessantly burdensome behavior. In the low burden scenario John, following the accident, is not depicted as needy, and is described as seeking *occasional* emotional support from family. His family seems happy to provide the support, and John becomes "increasingly aware of how important his own welfare and happiness are" to his family.

*IRP Scenarios.* The individual reproductive potential scenarios varied John's age, health, income, status, capacity for sexual reproduction, perceived attractiveness to females, and past intimate relationships with females. In the low IRP scenario John is depicted as a 40-year old part-time assembly line worker whose income ($20,000 per year) is "barely enough to take care of the essentials." He is further described as an amputee with significant hearing loss and chronic fatigue, a person who "never considered himself attractive to women," a person who "had always experienced difficulties in relating to women on an intimate basis," and who chose to have a vasectomy after learning of his wife's pregnancy, "making it impossible for him to reproduce in the future." In contrast, in the high IRP scenarios John is described as "a handsome, healthy, and physically fit 25-year old . . . corporate executive on the rise," one who is highly marketable. He makes $125,000 a year, leaving considerable discretionary income after expenses. John does not have a vasectomy in the high IRP scenarios.

## Results

Correlational analyses revealed positive and significant correlations among all possible pairings of the dependent participant rating measures, and in the expected directions (all $p$ levels < .001). Results of the MANCOVA revealed significant main effects of burden ($p$ < .001) and IRP ($p$ < .001) on the self-destructive motivation variate. The direction of the main effects was as predicted, with higher values of self-destructive motivation linked to high levels of burden and low levels of IRP. As for the BDI covariate, participants with higher BDI scores were more likely than others to rate the scenario target high on the ideation measure ($p$ < .05). Gender made no significant difference in participant ratings, either as a main effect, or in interaction with the other independent variables.

Planned comparisons (individual contrasts) revealed a significant burden x IRP interaction in the predicted direction ($p$ < .001). As hypothesized, self-destructive motivation attributed to John was highest when he was depicted as someone with low IRP and a burden to his family. Ratings of self-destructive motivation were lowest when John's IRP was high and his burden low. MANCOVA results confirmed the interaction ($p$ < .05), even when participants' own levels of depression were controlled (entered as a covariate).

## Discussion

Our findings suggest that aspects of the scenario target's burdensomeness and reproductive value influenced participants' ratings of his self-destructive motivation. Because we used *multiple* indicators to operationalize burdensomeness and reproductive potential, we cannot tell precisely which aspects of each variable were responsible for the observed effects. Also, we are unable to tell from this experiment whether the scenario findings reveal something about the regulation of self-destructive motivation generally, or whether they apply only to the perception of self-destructive intent in others. Finally, generalizations from these data are limited to a restricted population, namely university students. All that said, results of this experiment are consistent with the model that inspired it, deCatanzaro's (1986, 1991) inclusive fitness account of self-destructive motivation, and with correlational findings from other studies (Brown, et al., 2009; Van Orden, Witte, Gordon, et al., 2008). Findings from these other studies indicate that people respond to questions about their own self-destructive motivation as if, at some level, they are aware of the outcomes dictated by the evolutionary logic. What is most interesting about the findings from the present study is the suggestion that this "awareness" extends to ratings of self-destructive motivation in (a hypothetical) *someone else*.

## IMPLICATIONS

There is mounting evidence to suggest that variables specified by DeCatanzaro's inclusive fitness model of self-destructive motivation should be taken seriously in efforts to understand, predict, and treat suicidality. In particular, there are now sufficient demonstrations, using a variety of samples, to show that patient's perceptions of their burdensomeness to others should be used to assess suicide risk, independent of symptoms of depression or hopelessness (Joiner, Kalafat, Draper, et al., 2007; Van Orden, et al., 2006). Of particular concern may be individuals who show high levels of perceived burden in conjunction with measures of low reproductive value (e.g., failed romantic relationships). As for treating suicidality, cognitive-behavioral interventions in which individuals identify fallacious perceptions of burdensomeness, and focus instead on their contributions to others, may prove effective in reducing levels of perceived burden (Brown, et al., 1999, 2009; Van Orden, et al., 2006). Similar techniques might be used to counter the emotional consequences of recurrent failures in romantic relationships, poor health, financial hardship, and other proxies for low reproductive value. The inclusion of family members in treatment may be especially important, providing them with an opportunity to recognize their own roles in communicating messages of burdensomeness, however unintentionally, to their suicidal relative, spouse, or partner.

## CONCLUSIONS

In conclusion, future intervention efforts should take seriously the possible evolutionary significance of self-destructive thinking and behavior. A better understanding of the adaptive value of suicide may hold the key to a better understanding of suicide prevention.

## REFERENCES

Brown, M. Z., Comtois, K. A., & Linehan, M. M. (2002). Reasons for suicide attempts and nonsuicidal self-injury in women with borderline personality disorder. *Journal of Abnormal Psychology, 111*, 198-202.

Brown, R. M., Dahlen, E., Mills, C., Rick, J., & Biblarz, A. (1999). Evaluation of an evolutionary model of self-destruction. *Suicide & Life-Threatening Behavior, 29*, 58-71.

Brown, R. M., Brown S. L., Johnson, A., Melver, K., Olsen, B., & Sullivan, M. (2009). Empirical support for an evolutionary model of self-destructive motivation. *Suicide & Life-Threatening Behavior, 39*, 1-12.

Calzeroni, A., Conte, G., Pennati, A., & Vita, A. (1990). Celibacy and fertility rates in patients with major affective disorders: the relevance of delusional symptoms and suicidal behavior. *Acta Psychiatrica Scandinavia, 82*, 309-310.

Clutton-Brock, T. H. (1991). *The evolution of parental care*. Princeton, NJ: Princeton University Press.

deCatanzaro, D. (1986). A mathematical model of evolutionary pressures regulating self-preservation and self-destruction. *Suicide & Life-Threatening Behavior, 16*, 166-181.

deCatanzaro, D. (1991). Evolutionary limits to self-preservation. *Ethology & Sociobiology, 12*, 13-28.

deCatanzaro, D. (1995). Reproductive status, family interactions, and suicidal ideation: surveys of the general pubic and high risk groups. *Ethology & Sociobiology, 16*, 385-394.

Durkheim, E. (1951). *Suicide: A study in sociology.* New York: The Free Press. (Original work published 1897).

Duke, R. C., Ojcius, D. M., & Young, J. D. (1996). Cell suicide in health and disease. *Scientific American, 275*, 80-87.

Ellis, L. (1994). *Research methods in the social sciences.* Dubuque, IA: W. C. Brown.

Elmore, S, (2007). Apoptosis: A review of programmed cell death. *Toxicologic Pathology, 35*, 495-516.

Filiberti, A, Ripamonti, C., Totis, A., Ventafridda, V., De Conno, F., Contiero, P., & Tamburini, M. (2001*). Journal of Pain & Symptom Management, 22*, 544-553.

Goodman (1999). The role of socioeconomic status gradients in explaining differences in US adolescents' health. *American Journal of Public Health, 89*, 1522–1528.

Hamilton, W. D. (1964). The genetical evolution of social behavior. *Journal of Theoretical Biology , 7*, 1-16.

Hedberg K, Hopkins D, Kohn M. (2003). Five years of legal physician-assisted suicide in Oregon. *New England Journal of Medicine, 348*, 961-4.

Hendin, H. (1975). Growing up dead: Student suicide. *American Journal of Psychotherapy, 29*, 327-338.

Hölldobler, B., & Wilson, E. O. (1990). *The ants.* Cambridge, MA: Harvard University Press.

Joiner, T. E. (2005). *Why people die by suicide.* Cambridge, MA: Harvard University Press.

Joiner, T. E., Brown, J. S., & Wingate, L. R. (2005). The psychology and neurobiology of suicidal behavior. *Annual Review of Psychology, 56*, 287–314

Joiner, T., Pettit, J.W., Walker, R.L., Voelz, Z.R., Cruz, J., Rudd, M.D., & Lester, D. (2002). Perceived burdensomeness and suicidality: two studies on the suicide notes of those attempting and those completing suicide. *Journal of Social & Clinical Psychology, 21*, 531-545.

Joiner, T., Kalafat, J., Draper, J., Stokes, H., Knudson, M., Berman, A. L., & McKeon, R. (2007). *Suicide & Life-Threatening Behavior, 37*, 353-365.

Kim, C. D., Seguin, M., Therrien, N., Riopel, G., Chawky, N., Lesage, A. D., & Turecki, G. (2005). Familial aggregation of suicidal behavior: a family study of male suicide completers from the general population. *American Journal of Psychiatry, 162*, 1017-1019.

Leighton, A. H., & Hughes, C. C. (1955). Notes on Eskimo patterns of suicide. *Southwestern Journal of Anthropology, 11*, 327-338.

Lieb, R., Bronisch, T., Höfler, M., Schreier, A., Wittchen, H. (2005). Maternal suicidality and risk of suicidality in offspring: findings from a community study. *American Journal of Psychiatry, 162*, 1665–1671.

Lonergan, M., & Travis, J. (2003). On the selective advantage of suicide. *Journal of Gerontology: Biological Science, 58A*, 775.

Magne-Invar, U., & Öjehagen, A. (1999). Significant others of suicide attempters: their views at the time of the acute psychiatric consultation. *Social Psychiatry & Psychiatric Epidemiology, 34*, 73-79.

Mascaro, S., Korb, K. B., & Nicholson, A. E. (2001). Suicide as an evolutionarily stable strategy. In J. Kelemen & P. Sosik (Eds.), *Proceedings of the 6th European Conference on Advances in Artificial Life, Prague, Czech Republic* (pp. 120-132), London: Springer-Verlag.

McPherson, Wilson, & Murray, (2007). Feeling like a burden to others: a systematic review focusing on the end of life. *Palliative Medicine, 21*, 115-128.

Motto, J. A., & Bostrom, A. (1990). Empirical indicators of near-term suicide risk. *Crisis, 11*, 52-59.

Orbach, I. (1986). The "insolvable problem" as a determinant in the dynamics of suicidal behavior in children. *American Journal of Psychotherapy, 40*, 511-520.

Pape, R. A. (2005). Dying to win: The strategic logic of suicide terrorism. New York: Random House.

Pedersen, N. L., & Fiske, A. (2010). Genetic influences on suicide and nonfatal suicidal behavior: Twin study findings. *European Psychiatry, 25*, 264-267.

Rueppell, O., Hayworth, M.K., & Ross, N.P. (2010). Altruistic self-removal of health-compromised honey bee workers from their hive. *Journal of Evolutionary Biology. 23*, 1538-1546.

Sabbath, J. C. (1969). The suicidal adolescent: the expendable child. *Journal of the American Academy of Child Psychiatry, 8,* 272–285.

Schrut, A. (1964). Suicidal adolescents and children. *Journal of the American Medical Association, 188*, 1103-1107.

Tofilski, A., Couvillon, M. J., Evison, S. E. F., Helanterä, H., Robinson, E. J. H., & Ratnieks, F. L. W. (2008). Pre-emptive defensive self-sacrifice by ant workers. *American Naturalist 172*, E239-E243.

Van Orden, K. A., Lynam, M. E., Hollar, D., & Joiner, T. E., Jr. (2006). Perceived burdensomeness as an indicator of suicidal symptoms. *Cognitive Therapy & Research, 30,* 457-467.

Van Orden, K. A., Witte, T. K., Gordon, K. H., Bender, T. W., & Joiner, T. E., Jr. (2008). Suicidal desire and the capability for suicide: tests of the Interpersonal-Psychological Theory of Suicidal Behavior among adults. *Journal of Consulting & Clinical Psychology*, 76, 72-83.

Van Orden, K. A., Witte, T. K., Cukrowicz, K. C., Braithwaite, S. R., Selby, E. A., & Joiner, T. E., Jr. (2010). The interpersonal theory of suicide. *Psychological Review, 117*, 575-600.

Wagner, B. M. (1997). Family risk factors for child and adolescent suicidal behavior. *Psychological Bulletin, 121*, 246-298.

Wilson, E. O. (2006). *Nature revealed: Selected writings 1949-2006.* Baltimore, MD: Johns Hopkins University Press.

World Health Organization. (2007). *Suicide prevention and special programmes.* Retrieved January 27, 2007, from
http://www.who.int/mental_health/prevention/suicide/country_reports/en/.

Woznica, J. G. & Shapiro, J. R. (1990). An analysis of adolescent suicide attempts: the expendable child. *Journal of Pediatric Psychology, 15*, 789-796.

Chapter 4

# SUICIDE AND LIFE EVENTS

*Andrew M. Busch, Michelle M. Cornette, Charles W. Mathias, Dawn M. Marsh and Donald M. Dougherty*

Psychopathology, life-threatening behavior and suicide are influenced, in part, by the life events a person experiences. This chapter provides a broad overview of the relationship between life events and suicidal behavior, including key domains of life events, factors moderating the effects of life events, mechanisms by which life events might impart risk for suicidal behavior and clinical implications for minimizing this risk.

## DOMAINS OF LIFE EVENTS AND THEIR RELATION TO SUICIDAL BEHAVIORS

Life events represent a complex construct for which investigators have used a variety of samples, methods of identifying and classifying, and time-frames for linking antecedent events to later suicide. Despite the diversity of methodologies used in these investigations, three broad domains of life events have been demonstrated as relevant to subsequent suicidal behaviors: traumatic childhood, interpersonal and occupational events.

Trauma, especially those traumatic experiences occurring during the formative childhood years, has significant short and long-term impact on risk for suicidal behavior. The total number of traumatic experiences, abuse (emotional, sexual and physical), parental death, parental mental illness and witnessing domestic violence during childhood have all been linked to suicidal behavior over various time intervals (Dieserud, et al., 2002; Dube, et al., 2001; Yang & Clum, 1996). Given the broad time-frame during which childhood trauma seems to influence suicidal behavior, there are likely multiple mechanisms by which these life events impart risk. For some individuals, childhood trauma acts as an acute risk factor leading to an increased likelihood of suicidal behavior in the near future. For others, traumatic childhood events may facilitate the development of psychopathology (e.g., depressive symptoms or substance use) that can increase cumulative risk and ultimately result in suicidal behavior.

Interpersonal events constitute another important set of life events associated with an increased risk for suicidal behavior. Several studies have linked the overall number of negative interpersonal events to suicide risk (Appleby, et al., 1999; Cavanagh, et al., 1999). More specifically, parental or spousal death (Heikkinen, et al., 1993), serious arguments with a spouse (Paykel, et al., 1975), and social "exit events" (e.g., a family member leaving home) (Slater & Depue, 1981) have been linked to suicide attempts among adults, while parental separation and relationship break-ups have been linked to suicide among adolescents and young adults (Gould, et al., 1996). The interpersonal events most relevant to suicidal behavior appear to be those involving loss or conflict in existing interpersonal relationships, rather than simple social isolation, suggesting that social disintegration may be central to the relationship between interpersonal events and suicide risk.

Negative occupational and academic events is a third domain of life events that contributes to increased risk for suicidal behavior. For instance, occupational loss and major problems at work have been linked to completed suicide (Hagnell & Rorsman, 1980; Thoresen, et al., 2006). In addition, related economic variables such as unemployment and financial strain are common among those who commit suicide (Heikkinen, et al., 1994). For younger individuals, events related to academic pursuits are more central. Among adolescents and young adults, academic difficulties contribute to suicide risk. Failing a grade, suspension from school and dropping out have all been linked to later suicide (Gould, et al., 1996). Occupational and academic events may increase the risk for suicide because they represent a loss of societal role and a diminished sense of effectiveness, which may be important contributors to suicidal ideation (Joiner, 2005; Cornette, et al., 2009; Cornette, et al., 2007).

Some research suggests that objectively neutral or positive life events can also increase the risk for suicide. For example, some findings suggest that change of residence and social "entrance events" (e.g., the birth of child or a new person in the home) may be related to suicidal behavior (Hagnell & Rorsman, 1980; Paykel, et al., 1975). These findings have important clinical implications in that one cannot assume that only objectively negative events increase the risk for suicidal behaviors. Some investigators have identified the value of assessing the valence and relevance of events to individuals and have incorporated these ratings into their research methodologies (Slater & Depue, 1981, Cavanagh, et al., 1999).

## FACTORS MODERATING THE EFFECT OF LIFE EVENTS ON SUICIDE

The influence of life events on suicidal behaviors is not uniformly experienced by all individuals. Individual and group differences in susceptibility to both general and specific life events as risk factors for suicidal behavior must also be considered. Factors that moderate the impact of life events and potentially increase risk for suicidal behavior include stage of development, gender and psychiatric diagnosis.

An individual's age, or stage of development, is important in understanding the type of life events that may increase risk for suicidal behavior. For instance, relationship break-up (non-marital), unwanted pregnancy, social ridicule and academic failure have been identified as possible adolescent specific risk factors (Heikkinen, et al., 1993). In addition, one large-scale study determined that interpersonal loss, family discord, occupational and financial difficulty and residence change were important risk factors for younger adults (20-59) while physical illness was found to be particularly important for understanding suicidal behavior among older adults (60+) (Heikkinen & Lonnqvist, 1995). Collectively, these differences illustrate that life event relevance evolves across the lifetime, suggesting that assessment of risk conferred by life events should include developmental considerations.

Men and women tend to experience life events differently, at least in terms of the extent to which specific life events increase the risk for suicide. For example, abuse perpetrated by parents or a partner more often precedes suicidal behavior among women, while occupational events, bereavement and criminal conviction seem to be more prominent factors influencing suicidality among men (Heikkinen, et al., 1993; Heikkinen, et al., 1994; Osvath, et al., 2004). In addition, some findings suggest that parental mental illness can lead to low self-esteem which contributes to suicide risk in men, and that childhood abuse can lead to depression which contributes to suicide risk in women (Dieserud, et al., 2002). While these are generalities, clinical evaluations need to include consideration of these issues to the extent that particular risk factors may confer differential risk for specific individuals.

Finally, psychiatric diagnosis and profile are also important moderators of the influence of life events on suicidal behaviors. Recent life events do not distinguish among schizophrenic patients with and without suicide attempts (Heikkinen, et al., 1993). However, Baca-Garcia and colleagues (2005) found that life events were more frequent and more influential in patients with depression than in those diagnosed with schizophrenia. Age of onset of psychiatric disorders may also be a moderator that affects the impact of life events. For example, life events of patients who were diagnosed with bipolar disorder early in life were not associated with increased risk for suicide (Pettit, et al., 2006). Finally, some researchers have suggested that suicide among those with more severe mental illness in general may be less influenced by life events (Cooper, et al., 2002).

## HOW DO LIFE EVENTS CONFER RISK FOR SUICIDAL BEHAVIOR?

A critical question regarding the role of life events in suicidal behavior is whether these events function as additive stressors conferring distal risk for suicidal behaviors, or whether they have a direct, proximal role in triggering attempts. Paykel and colleagues (1975) found a sharp spike in the occurrence of life events in the month preceding a suicide attempt, indicating that events can function as proximal triggers. Others have argued that life events influence suicidal behavior as additive stressors, rather than as distinct triggers for attempts. For example, Maris and colleagues (2000) argued that events occurring close to an attempt are not significantly different from those occurring earlier, so an attempt is only "triggered" in the sense that the accumulation of life problems will at times surpass the adaptive threshold of an individual. These two pathways are not mutually exclusive, however, and research supports the possibility that individual differences may explain differing susceptibilities to one or both of these pathways. For instance, those with greater trait impulsivity may be more susceptible to the triggering effects of acute life events (Zouk, et al., 2006).

Several variables have been proposed as possible mediators between life events and suicidal behaviors. For example, Osvath and colleagues (2004) suggest that early life events contribute to biological and cognitive changes that create a vulnerability to later suicidal behavior. Mann (1999) has proposed a stress-diathesis model that suggests drug use and serotonergic function combine with life events and psychiatric states to contribute to risk for suicide attempts. Others have suggested mediators including depression, substance abuse, hopelessness, cognitive dysfunction, and deficient problem solving skills (Dieserud, et al., 2002; Dube, et al., 2001; Konick & Gutierrez, 2005; Yang & Clum 1996).

There is some evidence which suggests that genetic differences may be an important variable in determining whether life events ultimately lead to suicide (Wasserman, et al., 2006). Furthermore, life events do not occur randomly; some are evoked by an individual's behavior. That an individual's behavior functions to influence their environment has received much attention in the psychopathology literature (Scarr & McCartney, 1983) and is important to the study of suicide and life events because of its implications for disentangling the effects of life events and ongoing psychopathology. Certain pathologies result in more life events than others. For example, Heikkinen and colleagues (1997) found that those diagnosed with personality disorders played a greater role in evoking negative life events from their environment, and Brady (2006) concluded that alcohol abuse has a role in promoting the occurrence of stressful life events. Important to note, however, is that several investigators have determined that life events confer risk for suicide even when the effects of ongoing psychopathology have been controlled for (Slater & Depue, 1981).

## CLINICAL IMPLICATIONS AND MINIMIZATION OF IMPACT

When conducting suicide risk assessment, it is imperative that clinicians consider the potential influence of life events. This assessment should include the quality, severity, temporal proximity, number and impact (regardless of the objective valence) of life events. Findings regarding the relevance of life events in general and events specific to particular populations should also be taken into consideration. For example, a clinician could pay particular attention to occupational occurrences in the lives of depressed male patients at risk for suicide. As suicide is notoriously difficult to predict, taking into account environmental factors that have been empirically linked to suicide can serve to improve risk assessment.

There are few empirical findings that provide specific strategies for minimizing the impact of life events. However, findings regarding mediators should provide clinicians with theoretically-based targets for assessment and intervention. Finally, social support may protect against the effects of life events (Heikkinen, et al., 1993; Slater & Depue, 1981; Thoresen, et al., 2006) and, for life events involving the loss of a single interpersonal relationship, having social support available from multiple sources may be especially important. A clinical focus on building social networks and increasing access to social support may be particularly important in protecting vulnerable patients against the effects of life events.

## REFERENCES

Appleby, L., Cooper, J., Amos, T., et al. (1999). Psychological autopsy study of suicides by people aged under 35. *British Journal of Psychiatry*, 175, 168-174.

Baca-Garcia, E., Perez-Rodriguez, M. M., Diaz Sastre, C., et al. (2005). Suicidal behavior in schizophrenia and depression: a comparison. *Schizophrenia Research*, 75, 77-81.

Brady, J. (2006). The association between alcohol misuse and suicidal behaviour. *Alcohol & Alcoholism*, 41, 473-478.

Cavanagh, J. T. O., Owens, D. G. C., & Johnstone, E. C. (1999). Life events in suicide and undetermined death in south-east Scotland: a case-control study using the method of psychological autopsy. *Social Psychiatry & Psychiatric Epidemiology*, 34, 645-650.

Cooper, J., Appleby, L., & Amos, T. (2002). Life events preceding suicide by young people. *Social Psychiatry & Psychiatric Epidemiology*, 37, 271-275.

Cornette, M. M., deRoon-Cassini, T. A., Fosco, G. M., et al. (2009). Application of an interpersonal-psychological model of suicidal behavior to physicians and medical trainees. *Archives of Suicide Research*, 13, 1-14.

Cornette, M. M., deRoon-Cassini, T. A., & Joiner, T.E. (2007). Examination of an interpersonal-psychological model of suicide among returning OEF and OIF veterans: theory and evidence. Unpublished.

Dieserud, G., Forsén, L., Braverman, M., et al. (2002). Negative life events in childhood, psychological problems and suicide attempts in adulthood: a matched case-control study. *Archives of Suicide Research*, 6, 291-308.

Dube, S. R., Anda, R. F., Felitti, V. J., et al. (2001). Childhood abuse, household dysfunction and the risk of attempted suicide throughout the lifespan: findings from the adverse childhood experience study. *Journal of the American Medical Association*, 286, 3089-3096.

Gould, M. S., Fisher, P., Parides, M., et al. (1996). Psychosocial risk factors of child and adolescent completed suicide. *Archives of General Psychiatry*, 53, 1155-1162.

Hagnell, O., & Rorsman, B. (1980). Suicide in the Lundby Study: a controlled prospective investigation of stressful life events. *Neuropsychobiology*, 6, 319-332.

Heikkinen, M., Aro, H., & Lönnqvist, J. (1993). Life events and social support in suicide. *Suicide & Life-Threatening Behavior*, 23, 343-358.

Heikkinen, M., Aro, H., & Lönnqvist, J. (1994). Recent life events, social support and suicide. *Acta Psychiatrica Scandinavica*, 89, 65-72.

Heikkinen, M., Henriksson, M., Isometsä, E., et al. (1997). Recent life events and suicide in personality disorders. *Journal of Nervous & Mental Disease*. 185, 373-381.

Heikkinen, M., & Lönnqvist, J. (1995). Recent life events in elderly suicide: a nationwide study in Finland. *International Psychogeriatrics*, 7, 287-300.

Joiner, T. (2005). *Why people die by suicide*. Cambridge, MA: Harvard University Press.

Konick, L., & Gutierrez, P. (2005). Testing a model of suicide ideation in college students. *Suicide & Life-Threatening Behavior*, 35, 181-192.

Mann, J., Waternaux, C., Haas, G., et al. (1999). Toward a clinical model of suicidal behavior in psychiatric patients. *American Journal of Psychiatry*, 156, 181-189.

Maris, R., Berman, A., & Silverman, M. (2000). *Comprehensive textbook of suicidology*. New York: Guilford.

Osvath, P., Vörös, V., & Fekete, S. (2004). Life events and psychopathology in a group of suicide attempters. *Psychopathology*, 37, 36-40.

Paykel, E., Prusoff, B., & Myers, J. (1975). Suicide attempts and recent life events: a controlled comparison. *Archives of General Psychiatry*, 32, 327-333.

Pettit, J., Paukert, A., Joiner, T., et al. (2006). Pilot sample of very early onset bipolar disorder in a military population moderates the association of negative life events and nonfatal suicide attempt. *Bipolar Disorders*, 8, 475-484.

Slater, J., & Depue, R. (1981). The contribution of environmental events and social support to serious suicide attempts in primary depressive disorder. *Journal of Abnormal Psychology*, 90, 275-285.

Thoresen, S., Mehlum, L., Roysamb, E., et al. (2006). Risk factors for completed suicide in veterans of peacekeeping: repatriation, negative life events, and marital status. *Archives of Suicide Research*, 10, 353-363.

Scarr, S., & McCartney, K. (1983). How people make their own environments: a theory of genotype environment effects. *Child Development*, 54, 424-435.

Wasserman, D., Geijer, T., Sokolowski, et al. (2006). The serotonin 1A receptor C(-1019)G polymorphism in relation to suicide attempt. *Behavioral & Brain Functions*, 2, 14.

Yang, B., & Clum, G. (1996). Effects of early negative life experiences on cognitive functioning and risk for suicide: a review. *Clinical Psychology Review*, 16, 177-195.

Zouk, H., Tousignant, M., Seguin, M., et al. (2006). Characterization of impulsivity in suicide completers: clinical, behavioral and psychosocial dimensions. *Journal of Affective Disorders*, 92, 195-204.

Chapter 5

# STRESS, LIFESTYLE AND SUICIDAL BEHAVIOR

## *Lourens Schlebusch*

There is no identifiable single cause of suicidal behavior. It is understood rather, as a process resulting from a complex interaction of biological, psychological and social variables (Hawton & van Heeringen, 2000; Hawton, 2005; Schlebusch, 2005; Wasserman, 2001a). In this biopsychosocial approach, which is rooted in systems theory, a primary consideration is the reciprocal effect between the individual and the environment. This is important since life events (stressors) impacting the individual's cognitive appraisal, adjustment and coping resources can cause inordinate stress levels (Lazarus & Folkman, 1984; Schlebusch, 2000). An approach that incorporates an understanding of these intricate interactions can assist in the identification, treatment and prevention of suicidal behavior in at risk persons, especially in developing multicultural societies such as many of those in Africa, where there is a paucity of related research.

## THE STRESS RESPONSE

The human stress response can be conceptualised as following two pathways: a psychological and a physiological one (Schlebusch, 2000, 2004). The cognitive model forms the bedrock of the psychological pathway. It posits that difficulty in processing and rationalizing the stressor can precipitate the stress response. Perception and cognitive appraisal are important in this process, and input from the frontal lobes (the higher cognitive centres of the brain) moderates the resultant psychological, emotional and behavioral responses. In the physiological pathway, many neurotransmitter systems are implicated, with the noradrenergic and endogenous opiate systems, as well as the hypothalamic-pituitary-adrenal axis, being found to be hyperactive in individuals with inordinate stress levels who develop stress related disorders (Schlebusch, 2000; van der Kolk, McFarlane & Weissaeth, 1996). The psychological and physiological pathways interact closely, producing a stress cascade (Schlebusch, 2004) that simultaneously involves the endocrine and autonomic nervous systems, thus incorporating a hormonal dimension.

Activated hormonal responses include the corticotropin-releasing factor, the adrenocorticotropic hormone, adrenalin (epinephrine), noradrenalin (norepinephrine), the corticosteroids (aldosterone) and glucocorticoids (cortisol). Simultaneously, the activation of the autonomic nervous system and its sympathetic subsystem results in an immediate stress response, placing the individual in a state of arousal ready for the fight-or-flight response. In summary, the physiological stress response, then, occurs via a dual pathway: a nervous system response, which can be relatively short-lived and an endocrine (hormonal) response, which can last much longer.

## STRESS-DIATHESIS MODELS

A predisposition or vulnerability towards developing a certain disorder is referred to as a diathesis. Inordinate stress in an individual who harbors a diathesis can contribute to the disorder emerging. Not only is a diathesis affected by current stressors that pose adaptive demands, but the factors that contributed to the development of the diathesis can in themselves be powerful stressors (Carson, Butcher & Coleman, 1988). Various stress-diathesis models, with clear advantages for treatment and prevention, have been proposed to provide a better understanding of the interactive dynamics involved, some of which are mentioned here.

Originally a second-order vulnerability model to explain some of the underlying triggers in schizophrenia, a psychologically based stress-diathesis model (Zubin & Spring, 1977) proposed that a genetic vulnerability interacts with the individual's life events (stressors) to trigger this disorder. With lower vulnerability, more stress is required; with greater vulnerability, less stress can act as a trigger. A multidimensional and interactive model, the stress-vulnerability-protective factors model of schizophrenia, has also been proposed (Kopelowicz, et al., 2003). According to this model, protective factors include psychopharmacology (which buffers the psycho-bio-vulnerability of the individual), skills training (such as problem solving), social and communication skills, and the development of support systems.

Globally, studies have shown a strong association between mental illness and suicidal behavior. A meta-analysis of the literature (Harris & Barraclough, 1997) found an increased suicide risk associated with virtually all mental disorders, with the exception of mental retardation and dementia. A review article (Bertolote, et al., 2004) noted that in 98% of completed suicides there had been a diagnosis of at least one mental disorder, with mood disorders, substance use disorders, schizophrenia and personality disorders being common. Depression (associated with impaired serotonergic function) is clinically significant in 60% or more of suicidal behaviors (Lönnqvist, 2000; Mann, 2002), and is considered a final common route toward suicide (van Heeringen, et al., 2000).

A comprehensive stress-diathesis model, which offers a practical, explanatory and predictive model of suicidal behavior, has been advanced to detect suicidal risk (Mann, 2003; Mann, et al., 1999). Here the stress component includes factors such as a psychiatric disorder, as well as life events, while the diathesis includes elements like impulsivity, aggression, pessimism/hopelessness and neurobiological correlates and further reflects a range of other potential variables such as gender, religion, familial and genetic components, traumatic childhood experiences, psychosocial support systems, availability of lethal suicide methods, chronic disease, alcohol and substance abuse, cigarette smoking (Mann, et al., 1999; Oquendo, et al., 2004; Tanskanen, et al., 1998) and even reduced cholesterol levels (Muldoon, et al., 1993). Lowered cholesterol levels are associated with reduced serotonergic activity and increased aggressiveness. Reduced serotonin in the orbital prefrontal cortex plays a role in the pathogenesis of suicidal behavior, with serotonergic hypofunction being related to increasingly lethal suicidal behavior (Mann, 2002).

Additional considerations are sleep deprivation and dietary inefficiency because of potential effects on neurotransmitter functioning (Wasserman, 2001b). The stress-diathesis model can be supplemented by a stress-vulnerability model that involves the development of the suicidal process (Wasserman, 2001b). Factors that play a role here include the suicidal individual's cognitive style, personality, environmental factors, stress that contributes to the diathesis, psychosocial and cultural support, and protective factors against individual vulnerability.

## NEUROPSYCHOLOGICAL CONSIDERATIONS

The importance of the prefrontal cortex of the brain in explaining suicidal behavior is clear from biological and psychological studies (van Heeringen, et al., 2000). The prefrontal cortex is concerned with, among other things, cognitive, emotional and motivational responses and, if functioning appropriately, it facilitates the individual's capacity to formulate and initiate goal-directed behavior, as well as playing a critical role in impulse control. Impairment of this region through head injury or other causes can result in personality changes and adverse repercussions over the entire behavioral repertoire of the affected individual, including disinhibition, impulsivity, aggression, impaired executive functioning and decision making, and an inability to be guided by the consequences of one's action and suicide risk (Jollant, et al., 2005; Kelp, et al., 2001; Lezak, et al., 2004; Lishman, 1998; Mann, et al., 1999).

Negative stress can cause micronutrient deficiencies with adverse psycho-physiological consequences, leading to more stress-related symptoms and progressively reduced stress tolerance (Schlebusch, et al., 2000). It also has adverse impacts on brain structures and memory (Newcomer, et al., 1999; Schlebusch, 2000) which in turn may impair appropriate coping strategies in a suicidal person (Schlebusch, 2000, 2005; Wasserman, 2001b). Severe stress that results in the secretion of endogenous stress hormones affects how memories are laid down. For example, elevated cortisol levels are known to be toxic to the hippocampus (van der Kolk, et al., 1996). The hippocampus constitutes a major component of the memory system with a primal role in learning, retention and rapid association of information received from different cortical areas (Lezak, et al., 2004).

## STRESS, LIFESTYLE AND SUICIDE RISK FACTORS

Not only do chronic and acute stress have implications for disturbances in various neurotransmitters (Wasserman, 2001b) and neurohormones (van der Kolk, et al., 1996), they are also critical comorbid etiological considerations in suicidal behavior. This is especially significant in developing countries in Africa where society is often less stable (Schlebusch, 2005). Research findings on suicidal behavior across Africa vary. The continent is not a religious, cultural or ethnic entity, and generalizations are difficult to make, particularly as there is a paucity of research into suicide in many parts of Africa. Considerable research data has come, however, from South Africa (Schlebusch, 2005).

In addition to the usual risk factors for suicidal behavior, research in South Africa (Schlebusch, 2005) has found the following as having the potential to create high stress levels with suicidal implications: rapid movement from traditional roles and values to a more western lifestyle; the stress of urbanization; after a history of human rights violations; rising expectations which might not be fulfilled; competition for education and employment; academic-related problems; socioeconomic difficulties; high crime, violence and trauma rates; and dysfunctional family dynamics, including exposure to family violence, child abuse, incest, partner problems, a family member's suicide, and a personal history of suicidal behavior. The HIV/AIDS pandemic in sub-Saharan Africa (UNAIDS, 2006) has implications for suicidal behavior, and various related risk factors have been identified (Schlebusch, 2005). These include, among other things, stress-related relationships, social and work difficulties, and potential psychiatric and neurocognitive complications (Schlebusch, 2006).

In certain occupational subgroups (for example, the police services in South Africa), posttraumatic stress disorder has been found to be a predominant risk factor (Schlebusch, 2005). South African investigations reported that the common diagnosis of mood disorders (depression) was applicable in nearly two-thirds of nonfatal suicidal patients, followed by substance abuse, schizophrenia and substance-induced psychosis (Schlebusch, 2005). In South Africa, depression is commonly found in general medical practice (Schlebusch, 2005), where depressed patients present at the doctor's office frequently lacking the clear-cut symptoms of the various subgroups of mood disorders described in the professional literature. Many of these patients present with a whole spectrum of somatic, psychological, social, occupational and other problems, but infrequently complain directly of depression or suicidal tendencies. Cultural and subcultural influences on prevalence rates have yet to be resolved, but there is evidence that culture can modify the expression of depressive symptomatology associated with suicidality, resulting in under-diagnosis.

In South Africa, substance abuse as a comorbid factor in suicidal behavior is cause for concern, particularly with alcohol, household poisons and medical substances (especially analgesics, benzodiazepines and antidepressants) being implicated (Schlebusch, 2005). The use of these substances is often a method of choice in overdose and in attempts to cope with the ravages of stress. South African alcohol abuse figures are consistently high, and some studies (Schlebusch, 2005) have found up to 45% of fatal suicides had high levels of blood alcohol concentrations (BACs). Furthermore, in 50% or more, BACs of 0.08 g/100 ml or higher were present in nonfatal injuries due to homicide and motor vehicle accidents; 61% of patients admitted to trauma units in major centres had a mean BAC level of 0.12 g/100 ml; and in instances of violence, 74% of cases showed significant elevated alcohol levels. All of these factors combine to produce a breeding ground for potential suicidality. (The legal limit for driving a vehicle is a BAC of less that 0.05 g/ml and for a professional driver it is 0.02 g/ml [Kalinski, 2006].)

## MANAGEMENT AND PREVENTION

There is extensive international literature on the management and prevention of suicidal behavior (Hawton, 2005; Hawton & van Heeringen, 2000; Vijayakumar, 2003; Wasserman, 2001a). Not only mental health experts, but also family practitioners, other primary healthcare workers and the public should play a role in prevention of suicide. The importance of cross-cultural sensitivity is indispensable in this regard, and the value of a structured and systematic treatment and prevention approach in developing societies has been shown (Schlebusch, 2005). Follow-up treatment attendance after discharge from hospital for nonfatal suicidal behavior is generally poor in developing communities. Thus, the importance of initial consultations must be emphasized, as well as the need to establish a protocol regarding the referral of suicidal patients, especially within large hospital structures (Schlebusch, 2005).

## CONCLUSION

Suicidal behavior is a highly complex phenomenon that cannot readily be attributed to a single cause as it involves intricate interactions between many variables, including biological/genetic factors ("nature") and life experiences ("nurture"). As such, we know that suicidal behavior is a process. Stress-diathesis models have been proposed in order to understand and explain the development and dynamics of suicidal behavior. A bio-psycho-social approach and cultural sensitivity are also important considerations.

## REFERENCES

Bertolote, J. M., Fleischmann, A., De Leo, D., et al. (2004). Psychiatric diagnoses and suicide: revisiting the evidence. *Crisis,* 25,147-55.

Carson, R. C., Butcher, J. N., & Coleman, J. C. (1988). *Abnormal Psychology and Modern Life. 8th Ed.* New York: Harper Collins.

Harris, E. C., & Barraclough, B. (1997). Suicide as an outcome for mental disorders: a meta-analysis. *British Journal of Psychiatry,* 170: 205-228.

Hawton, K. (Ed.) (2005). Prevention and treatment of suicidal behaviour: from science to practice, Oxford, UK: Oxford University Press.

Hawton, K., & van Heeringen, K. (2000). *The international handbook of suicide and attempted suicide.* Chichester, UK: Wiley.

Jollant, F., Bellivier, F., Leboyer, M., et al. (2005). Impaired decision making in suicide attempters. *American Journal of Psychiatry,* 162, 304-310.

Kalinski, S. (2006). *Psycholegal assessment in South Africa.* Cape Town, South Africa: Oxford University Press.

Kelp, J. G., Sackeim, H. A., Brodsky, B. S., et al. (2001). Neuropsychological dysfunction in depressed suicide attempters. *American Journal of Psychiatry,* 158, 735-741.

Kopelowicz, A., Liberman, R. P., & Wallace, C. J. (2003). Psychiatric rehabilitation for schizophrenia. *International Journal of Psychology & Psychological Therapy,* 3, 283-298.

Lazarus, R. S., & Folkman, S. (1984). *Stress, appraisal and coping*. New York, NY: Springer.

Lezak, M. D., Howieson, D. B., & Loring, D. W. (2004). *Neuropsychological assessment*. 4$^{th}$ Ed. Oxford, UK: Oxford University Press.

Lishman, W. A. (1998). Organic psychiatry: the psychological consequences of cerebral disorder. 3$^{rd}$ Ed. Oxford, UK: Blackwell Publishing.

Lönnqvist, J. K. (2000). Psychiatric aspects of suicidal behaviour: depression. In K. Hawton & K. van Heeringen (Eds.) *The international handbook of suicide and attempted suicide*, pp.107-120. Chichester, UK: Wiley.

Mann, J. J. (2002). A current perspective of suicide and attempted suicide. *Annals of Internal Medicine*, 136, 302-311.

Mann, J. J. (2003). Neurobiology of suicidal behaviour. *Nature Reviews/Neuroscience*, 4, 819-828.

Mann, J. J., Waternaux, C., Haas, G. L., et al. (1999). Toward a clinical model of suicidal behavior in psychiatric patients. *American Journal of Psychiatry*, 156, 181-189.

Muldoon, M. F., Rossouw, J. E., Manuck, S. B., et al. (1993). Low or lowered cholesterol and risk of death from suicide and trauma. *Metabolism*, 42, 45-56.

Newcomer, J. W., Selkeg, G., Nelson, A. K., et al. (1999). Decreased memory performance in healthy humans induced by stress-level cortisol treatment. *Archives of General Psychiatry*, 56, 527-533.

Oquendo, M. A., Galfalvy, H., Russo, S., et al. (2004). Prospective study of clinical predictors of suicidal acts after a major depressive episode in patients with major depressive disorder or bipolar disorder. *American Journal of Psychiatry*, 161, 1433-1441.

Schlebusch, L. (2000). *Mind shift: stress management and your health*. Pietermaritzburg, South Africa: University of Natal Press.

Schlebusch, L. (2004). The development of a stress symptom checklist. *South African Journal of Psychology*, 34, 3, 327-349.

Schlebusch, L. (2005). *Suicidal behaviour in South Africa*. Pietermaritzburg, South Africa: University of Kwa-Zulu Natal Press.

Schlebusch, L. (2006). HIV/Aids og risikoen for selvmordsatferd (trans. HIV/AIDS and the risk for suicidal behaviour). *Suicidologi*, 11, 30-32.

Schlebusch, L., Bosch, B. A., Pillay, B. J., et al. (2000). A double-blind, placebo-controlled, double-centre study of the effects of an oral multivitamin-mineral combination on stress. *South African Medical Journal*, 90, 12, 1216-1223.

Tanskanen, A., Viinamäki, H., Hintikka, J., et al. (1998). Smoking and suicidality among psychiatric patients. *American Journal of Psychiatry*, 155, 129-130.

UNAIDS. (2006). *Uniting the world against AIDS*. Fact Sheets. http://www.unaids.org/en/MediaCentre/PressMaterials/FactSheets.asp

van der Kolk, B. A., McFarlane, A. C., & Weisaeth, L. (1996). Traumatic stress: the effects of overwhelming experience on mind, body and society. New York: Guilford.

van Heeringen, K., Hawton, K., & Williams, J. M. G. (2000). Pathways to suicide: an integrative approach. In K. Hawton & K. van Heeringen (Eds.) *The international handbook of suicide and attempted suicide*, pp.223-234. Chichester, UK: Wiley.

Vijayakumar, L. (2003). *Suicide prevention: meeting the challenge together*. Chennai, India: Orient Longman.

Wasserman, D. (2001a). *Suicide: an unnecessary death*. London, UK: Martin Dunitz.

Wasserman, D. (2001b). A stress-vulnerability model and the development of the suicidal process. In D. Wasserman (Ed.) *Suicide: an unnecessary death*, pp.13-27. London, UK: Martin Dunitz.

Zubin, J., & Spring, B. (1977). Vulnerability-a new view of schizophrenia. *Journal of Abnormal Psychology*, 86,103-126.

*Chapter 6*

# WHAT CAN WE LEARN FROM SUICIDE NOTES? A STUDY IN INDIA

*Antoon A. Leenaars, T.D. Dogra,*
*Shalina Girdhar and Lindsey Leenaars*

Suicide is strongly forbidden in India. The *Dharmashastras* (a book on the codes of living in ancient India) is explicit in the condemnation of suicide (Thakur, 1963). In India, assisting suicide is a punishable offence under the legal code (Leenaars, et al., 2001). There are strong taboos toward suicide in India, even toward research into suicide. Indeed, there is a silence, not only about self-directed violence, but also about violence in general (World Health Organization (WHO), 2002).

India is the second most populous country in the world. The vast majority of India's almost one billion people still live in rural villages. Jawaharlal Nehru, India's first Prime Minister (India became independent in 1947) noted, "Poverty and uttermost misery have long been the inseparable companions of the people" (Ward, 1997). Suicide is a pervasive problem (Thakur, 1963; Leenaars, et al., 2001; Vijayakumar, 2003). Over 100,000 people die by suicide each year in India. The available data on suicide in India show an increasing trend. The rates (all rates are crude rates per 100,000) for a sample of years are as follows: 1975, 7.2; 1980, 6.3; 1985, 7.1; 1990, 8.9; 1993, 9.5; 1997, 10.0; 1999, 11.2; 2000, 10.8 (Girdhar, Dogra, & Leenaars, 2003; Lester, Aggarwal, & Natarajan, 1999).

Despite some increase in the study of suicide in India, further research is needed. This is equally true for other nations on the Indian subcontinent. Indeed, many countries lag behind India, especially Bangladesh, Nepal and Afghanistan (Khan, 2002). To date, there have been only a few studies of suicide in India, even at a population (macro) level. Those few studies indicate the following. Male suicides are more prevalent than female suicides, but the gap is relatively small by international comparisons (Banerjee, et al. 1990; Mayer, 2003; Mayer & Ziaian, 2002; Steen & Mayer, 2003). (China is the only exception to the male/female difference [Phillips, et al., 1999]). Marital and interpersonal problems are present in over half of the suicides (Girdhar, et al., 2004; Rao & Mahendran, 1989), and this is an especially true for young female suicides (Mayer & Ziaian, 2002). Rural factors are strong (Hedge, 1980), education is a protective factor (Girdhar, et al., 2004), while being married is not a protective factor unlike many places in the world (Girdhar, et al., 2004). Despite this limited research, it is also easy to conclude, following Rao and Mahendran (1989) and Vijayakumar and Rajkumar (1999), that suicide in India is complex. Suicide is a multidimensional malaise (Leenaars, 1996; WHO, 2002), and greater in-depth studies of the complexity of suicide are needed in India. The study of suicide in India needs to move to more micro-based level rather than the study of macro-level (national mortality) data (Vijayakumar & Rajkumar, 1999), a proposal in keeping with priorities for suicide research around the world (Leenaars, et al., 1997; WHO, 2002).

## SUICIDE NOTES

The main problem for the study of suicide in India is the lack of reliable and available data (Mayer & Ziaian, 2002; Vijayakumar & Rajkumar, 1999). How then can we study suicide? Shneidman and Farberow (1957), Maris (1981) and others have suggested the following avenues: statistics, third-party interviews (often called psychological autopsies), the study of nonfatal suicide attempters, and the study of documents (including personal documents such as suicide notes). All of these have their limitations, and there are problems in obtaining these data in India (Vijayakumar & Rajkumar, 1999). One of these methods, suicide note analysis, is the focus here. A suicide note is, in fact, the closest that we can get to the suicidal mind, since it is often written moments before the death.

Girdhar, Leenaars, Dogra, Leenaars and Kumar (2004) reported the first study of suicide notes in India. Following Ho, et al. (1998), we investigated content and descriptive characteristics of suicide notes. The study was conducted at All India Institute of Medical Sciences, New Delhi, from February 2001 to August 2002 (Girdhar, et al., 2004). The Forensic Deptartment of this institute is responsible for post-mortem examinations in the New Delhi area. During an eighteen-month period, 1,943 postmortems were conducted. Out of the 1,943 cases, 320 (16.5%) were suicides. Of these, 235 were men and 85 were women, and 51 (15.9%) left a suicide note, with 50 available for analysis. A comparison sample of 50 was selected from the non-note writers, and data from the official records for the two groups were compared.

The most important finding of the study was that note writers did *not* differ greatly from non-note writers. This finding is consistent with Stengel's (1964) assertion that there are essentially no meaningful differences between note writers and non-note writers who commit suicide, except maybe that they are better communicators. Males were more represented in the note writers; the illiterate and poorly educated were less likely to write a note, as were the non-salaried group; and divorced/separated/widowed people were more likely to leave a note. Despite the few differences, overall it would appear that one can cautiously generalize from note writers to suicides in general.

The suicide notes indicated that social and interpersonal factors were central, mainly family problems and problems associated with medical illness, but so were more intrapsychic factors such as psychopathology, consistent with the results of earlier studies in India using different data sources (Bhatia, et al., 2000; Panally, 1986; Vijayakumar & Rajkumar, 1999). There appeared to be no *single* reason given for the suicide in the suicide notes. Over half of the note writers gave a reason for their self-chosen death, but the reasons were diverse. In keeping with India's religious tradition, there were a few people who gave rebirth and reunion as the reason for their suicide in their note. Some key characteristics emerged beyond whether there was a mental illness or not. When affect (emotion) was examined in the notes, asking for forgiveness seemed most prevalent (56%), followed by low mood/hopelessness (36%) and anger (26%). Most notes, consistent with previous analyses in other nations (Leenaars, 1988), expressed more than one affect.

Results from this sample in India agree with the findings of the complexity of suicide in a Hong Kong sample from Ho, et al. (1998) who said, "Most suicide notes are characterized by some concrete and specific instructions, a fairly rich emotional state, and some explanation of the suicide victim's difficulties" (p. 472). This was true for this Indian sample of suicides.

Suicide notes indicate a *malaise* (Shneidman & Farberow, 1957), and this was true for this Indian sample. To explore this further, Leenaars, Dogra, Girdhar, Wenckstern and Leenaars (2010) undertook a thematic or theoretical/conceptual analysis of the Indian suicide notes. Leenaars and his colleagues studied seventy-two suicide notes (36 Indian notes and 36 notes from the USA) matched for age (plus or minus two years) and sex. They were analyzed for the presence of the following theoretical protocol sentences/clusters: unbearable pain, mental constriction, indirect expressions (e.g., ambivalence, redirected aggression and unconscious dynamics), inability to adjust or psychopathology, weakened ego, problematic interpersonal relationships, and rejection/aggression. The results indicate that all the clusters or themes were present in both samples in roughly equal numbers. However, there was one difference: the notes from India scored higher than the American notes for indirect expressions. When one examined the specific protocol sentences in this cluster, the notes from India more often expressed statements of aggression turned inwards and statements indicating unconscious processes. Thus, it appears that the suicidal mind is the suicidal mind, whether in India or elsewhere.

The fact that Indian notes contained more indirect expressions was unexpected on the basis of previous cross-cultural research (Leenaars, 1996, 2004). Perhaps Indian society's taboo about suicide reinforces secrecy. People in India, in fact, take pride in their passive, introverted, silent style, and so their suicidal state may be veiled, clouded or guarded. This is called dissembling or masking and is a significant factor for suicide risk (Leenaars, 2004). In the notes, the Indian writers expressed humility, submission, devotion, subordination and self-criticism, but they also were angry. Anger was one of the most predominant moods classified in the notes (Girdhar, et al., 2004). Aggression is a commonality in suicide (Leenaars, 1988; 2004). The person may turn the rage upon the self as well as towards others. Consistent with Girdhar, et al.'s study (2004), we can conclude that these dynamics stem from the person's relationships, consistent with Rao and Mahendran's (1989) finding of the centrality of marital and interpersonal factors in suicide in India. Much of the suicidal process appears to be unconscious or hidden. This again may be a result of the taboo or the passivity of Indians.

The problem for clinicians in India is how can they break through this indirect mask? How do they break the reinforced silence, not only about self-directed violence, but also about aggression and violence in general in India?

## CONCLUDING THOUGHTS

As Vijayakumar and Rajkumar (1999) noted, further study of suicide is urgently needed in India. By the year 2000, over 100,000 people were dying by suicide each year in India, and this number has increased by 5,000 every year since then. There is, as Nehru pointed out, far too much "uttermost misery," a malaise. Suicide becomes an *escape* for too many people in India from this *misery*.

Despite the increase in the study of suicide in India, more research is needed. However, suicide and anything associated with it, such as research, praxis and publications, remains a taboo, although there are many people, ranging from crisis workers to doctors, breaking the silence in India. Not only are there taboos, there are laws reinforcing the taboo in India. It is a crime to be suicidal. One can be imprisoned for attempting suicide. One can understand the secrecy, yet the silence is *lethal*, and the same is true for domestic violence and violence in general in India.

Finally, we agree with Vijayakumar and Rajkumar (1999) that the study of suicide in India needs to move to more micro-based level rather than focusing only on macro-level (national mortality) statistics. This is in keeping with priorities for suicide research around the world (Leenaars, et al., 1997). It is imperative that this research take place in the most populous nations, such as India and China, as these countries contribute in most to the needless self-directed violent deaths around the world (WHO, 2002). Our studies have attempted to break the silence. They are some of the first micro-based studies in India and the first on suicide notes. We believe that recent studies on suicide in India have allowed us to come to a better understanding of the suicidal Indian mind and, if we know the suicidal Indian mind better, we can better prevent suicide in India.

## REFERENCES

Banerjee, G., Nandi, P., Nandi, S., et al. (1990). The vulnerability of Indian women to suicide: a field study. *Indian Journal of Psychiatry,* 32, 305-308.

Bhatia, M., Aggarwal, N., & Aggarwal, B. (2000). Psychosocial profile of suicide ideators, attempters, and completers. *International Journal of Social Psychiatry*, 46, 155-163.

Girdhar, S., Dogra, T., & Leenaars, A. (2003). Suicide in India, 1995-1999, *Archives of Suicide Research,* 7, 389-393.

Girdhar, S., Leenaars, A., Dogra, T., et al. (2004). Suicide notes in India: what do they tell us? *Archives of Suicide Research,* 8, 179-185.

Hedge, R. (1980). Suicide in rural communities. *Indian Journal of Psychiatry*, 22, 368-370.

Ho, T., Yip, P., Chiu, C., et al. (1998). Suicide notes: what to do they tell us? *Acta Psychiatrica Scandinavica*, 98, 467-473.

Khan, M. (2002). Suicide on the Indian subcontinent. *Crisis,* 23, 104-107.

Leenaars, A. (1988). *Suicides notes.* New York: Human Sciences Press.

Leenaars, A. (1996). Suicide: a multidimensional malaise. *Suicide & Life-Threatening Behavior,* 26, 221-236.

Leenaars, A. (2004). *Psychotherapy with suicidal people.* Chichester, UK: John Wiley & Sons.

Leenaars, A., Connolly, J., Cantor, C., et al. (2001). Suicide, assisted suicide, and euthanasia: international perspectives. *Irish Journal of Psychological Medicine*, 18, 33-37.

Leenaars, A., Girdhar, S., Dogra, T.D., Wenckstern, S., & Leenaars, L. (2010) Suicide notes from India and the United States: a thematic comparison. *Death Studies*, 34, 426-440.

Leenaars, A., De Leo, D., Diekstra, R., et al. (1997). Consultations for research in suicidology. *Archives of Suicide Research*, 3, 139-151.

Leenaars, A., De Wilde, E., Wenckstern, S., et al. (2001). Suicide notes of adolescents: a life-span comparison. *Canadian Journal of Behavioural Sciences*, 33, 47-57.

Lester, D., Aggarwal, K., & Natarajan, M. (1999). Suicide in India. *Archives of Suicide Research*, 5, 91-96.

Maris, R. (1981). *Pathways to suicide*. Baltimore, MD: John Hopkins University Press.

Mayer, P. (2003). Female equality and suicide in the Indian states. *Psychological Reports*, 92, 1022-1028.

Mayer, P., & Ziaian, T. (2002). Suicide, gender and age variations in India: are women in Indian society protected from suicide? *Crisis*, 23, 98-103.

Panally, R. (1986). Suicide and social structure in India. *Social Defense*, 21, 5-29.

Phillips, M., Liu, H., & Zhang, Y. (1999). Suicide and social change in China. *Culture, Medicine & Psychiatry*, 22, 368-370.

Rao, V., & Mahendran, N. (1989). One hundred female burn cases: a study in suicidology. *Indian Journal of Psychiatry*, 31, 43-50.

Shneidman, E. (1985). *Definition of suicide*. New York: Wiley.

Shneidman, E., & Farberow, N. (Eds.). (1957). *Clues to suicide*. New York: McGraw-Hill.

Siegel, E. (1956). *Nonparametric statistics*. New York, NY: McGraw-Hill.

Steen, D., & Mayer, P. (2003). Patterns of suicide by age and gender in the Indian states: a reflection of human development? *Archives of Suicide Research*, 7, 247-267.

Stengel, E. (1964). *Suicide and attempted suicide*. Baltimore, MD: Penguin.

Thakur, U. (1963). *History of suicide in India*. Munshi, India: Ron Manahar La.

Vijayakumar, L. (Ed.) (2003). *Suicide prevention: meeting the challenge together*. Chennai, India: Orient Longman.

Vijayakumar, L., & Rajkumar, S. (1999). Are risk factors for suicide universal? A case-control study in India. *Acta Psychiatrica Scandinavica*, 99, 407-411.

Ward, G. (1997). India: turning fifty. *National Geographic*, 191, 2-57.

World Health Organization (WHO). (2002). *World report on violence and health*. Geneva, Switzerland: World Health Organization.

*Chapter 7*

# CHILDHOOD TRAUMA IN SUICIDAL BEHAVIOR

## *Marco Sarchiapone, Vladimir Carli and Alec Roy*

Childhood trauma is common. For example, one community study found that 31% of males and 21% of females reported childhood physical abuse (Thombs, et al., 2006). Over the past two decades, many studies have demonstrated a strong link between traumatic experiences during childhood and adult psychopathology, including suicide attempts. Childhood trauma has been found to be associated with increased odds of depression and anxiety (Heim & Nemeroff, 2001), dissociative symptoms (Schafer, et al., 2006), substance use disorders (Roy, 2004) and personality disorders (Lee, 2006). Many different kinds of childhood trauma have been described. These include physical and sexual abuse, physical and emotional neglect, witnessing domestic violence, family members with substance abuse, mental disorders or suicidal behavior, loss or separation from parents and socioeconomic disadvantage (Felitti, et al., 1998). The impact of childhood trauma on the development of mental disorders is much higher if we consider that childhood trauma is underestimated and underreported. Generally only the more severe and substantiated cases of child maltreatment are reported to the authorities. Furthermore, forgetting, stigma, relation to the perpetrator and repression play a relevant role in underreporting traumatic childhood experiences. It has been reported that 80% of abuse victims did not report the abuse to anyone (Edgardh & Ormstad, 2000).

## CHILDHOOD TRAUMA AS A DISTAL SUICIDE RISK FACTOR

The generally accepted model of suicide risk is the stress-diathesis risk factor model (Moscicki, 1997). Risk factors may be either distal or proximal. Distal risk factors create a predisposing diathesis and determine an individual's response to a stressor. They include biological and genetic variables such as a family history and impulsive aggressive personality traits. Developmental factors, such as childhood trauma, have also been shown to be distal risk factors for suicide. Distal risk factors affect the threshold for suicide and indirectly increase an individual's risk when he or she experiences a proximal risk factor. Proximal, or trigger, factors are more closely related to the suicidal behavior and act as precipitants. They include life events, stress, acute episodes of depression and acute alcohol or substance abuse. Suicidal individuals differ from nonsuicidal individuals in distal risk factors (e.g., impulsivity and childhood trauma), and may be moved toward suicidal behaviors by proximal risk factors (Moscicki, 1997).

Evidence that childhood trauma is a distal risk factor for suicidal behavior comes from general population and clinical studies. For example, Davidson, et al. (1996) examined respondents in the Epidemiologic Catchment Area (ECA) Study and found a strikingly increased risk for a suicide attempt in women sexually abused before 16 years of age. Using data from the US National Comorbidity Survey, Molnar, et al. (2001) concluded that a strong association exists between childhood sexual abuse and suicidal behavior. Similarly, an Australian community study of twins found that a history of childhood trauma significantly increased the risk for a suicide attempt (Nelson, et al., 2002). A review of ten years of clinical studies also concluded that patients who have experienced childhood trauma are more vulnerable to suicidal behavior (Santa Mina & Gallop, 1998). We studied the role of childhood trauma in the suicidal behavior of a large sample of cocaine and opiate addicts, and alcoholics (Roy, 2004). After dividing the patients into those who had attempted suicide and those who had not, we showed that attempters had significantly higher childhood trauma scores for emotional abuse, physical abuse, sexual abuse, emotional neglect and physical neglect than non-attempters.

It is also noteworthy that, in the stress-diathesis model, childhood trauma may not only be a distal risk factor for suicide but may also be a predisposing risk factor for conditions that may trigger suicide, that is, abused children more frequently develop a substance abuse disorder or a depressive disorder as adults.

## POSSIBLE PATHWAYS

There are several pathways that may lead from childhood traumatic events to suicidal behavior. First, childhood trauma is associated with the development of mental disorders, substance abuse and certain psychopathological traits, such as impulsivity and aggression, all of which predispose to suicide. Second, some studies suggest the possibility that childhood trauma is a strong and independent risk factor for suicidal behavior. Third, childhood trauma may impact neurobiological variables.

The psychological effects of childhood trauma include low self-esteem and disrupted attachment mechanisms which may also account for increased odds of suicidal behavior. Low self-esteem may have significant cognitive consequences, and recent studies have reported significant associations between poor decision making and suicidal behavior (Jollant, et al., 2005). A profile of cognitive vulnerability to suicidal behaviors has been outlined in which rigid thinking was observed as a characteristic feature of suicidal subjects, together with a reduced ability in problem-solving (Pollock & Williams, 2004). Jollant and colleagues (2005) also found an impairment in the decision-making process among both violent and non-violent suicide attempters, which was largely independent from the underlying affective disorder and from other variables such as age, intelligence, education and features of the attempt. Largely consistent with this cognitive paradigm of a suicide attempter are the neuropsychological steps suggested by Van Heeringen in the formulation of the Process Model of suicidal behaviors (Van Heeringen, 2001). In this model, the trait-dependent predisposition to suicide may be determined by the perception of "defeat," "no escape" and "no rescue," with each feature lying upon a phenomenological, neuropsychological, neuroanatomical, temperament and neurobiological foundation.

Exposure to trauma can affect the developing brain with potentially lifelong alterations in the physiological stress response system and in brain neurotransmitters. Some authors have reported significant negative correlations between childhood emotional neglect and CSF levels of 5-HIAA and HVA, suggesting the possibility that childhood trauma may have an effect on central monoamine function (Roy, 2002a). Childhood sexual abuse has also been associated with lower urinary-free cortisol output (Roy, 2002b), suggesting that childhood trauma may have an effect on HPA-axis function and on stress response systems.

## RELATIONSHIP TO AGGRESSION

Aggressive behavior has also been found to be related to childhood abuse and has been suggested as a possible mediator between childhood trauma and suicidal behavior. Brodsky, et al. (2001) reported that both childhood abuse and impulsivity and aggression scores were associated with suicide attempts in depressed patients, and they concluded that childhood abuse may be an environmental risk factor for the development of impulsivity and aggression as well as for suicide attempts. Osvath, et al. (2004) noted a significant relationship between childhood trauma and trait anger in suicide attempters. Studying suicidal populations, we have noted positive relationships between Childhood Trauma Questionnaire (CTQ) scores and scores on the Brown-Goodwin Lifetime Assessment of Aggression interview. Anger associated with being abused may play a role in the transformation of the passive victimized child into an adult with active aggressive tendencies, who also develops a predisposition to commit violent acts. These violent acts are not necessarily committed against others, but may be directed towards the self and expressed as self-harm behaviors.

## STUDIES ON DEPRESSED PATIENTS

We conducted a study on a sample of depressed patients in order to evaluate the prevalence of childhood trauma and to test the hypothesis that suicide attempters would report more childhood trauma than depressed patients who had never attempted suicide. In our sample, patients who had attempted suicide (43.5%) had significantly higher scores for emotional abuse and emotional neglect as well as a higher weighted total score on the CTQ. Significant correlations were also found between Brown-Goodwin Life History of Aggression (BGLHA) scores and CTQ scores for emotional abuse and physical neglect, as well as with the weighted total CTQ score (Sarchiapone, et al., 2007).

A logistic regression model was used in order to evaluate the independent contribution of the study variables and childhood trauma. This showed significantly increased odds of suicide attempts independently associated with being female, unemployed, having suffered emotional neglect and high scores on the BGLHA. Suicide attempters reported a significantly higher total CTQ score and significantly higher CTQ scores for both emotional abuse and emotional neglect than depressed patients who had never attempted suicide. Another result of our study was that depressed patient who had attempted suicide had significantly higher lifetime scores for aggression on the BGLHA than depressed patients who had never attempted suicide. High BGLHA scores were independently associated with significantly increased odds of suicidal behavior.

Similarly, Malone, et al. (1995) reported significantly higher BGHA scores in unipolar patients who had attempted suicide. A similar finding was also reported in bipolar patients who had attempted suicide (Oquendo, et al., 2000). More recently, Dumais, et al.(2005) found that impulsive-aggressive personality disorders were an independent predictor of completed suicide in patients with major depression. The data from these four studies all suggest that impulsive aggression traits might play a role in suicidal behavior in depressed patients. Garno, et al. (2005) similarly reported that among bipolar patients, Cluster B personality disorder diagnoses were significantly associated with CTQ scores for emotional abuse, physical abuse and emotional neglect. These findings are consistent with a large body of research that reports associations of childhood trauma with specific behavioral and social patterns. Adults that were abused as children more often abuse alcohol and drugs and may develop a substance abuse disorder (Mulvihill, 2005). Childhood maltreatment is also associated with aggression and delinquency (Smith, et al., 2005; Grogan-Kaylor & Otis, 2003).

## RELATIONSHIP WITH AGE AT FIRST ATTEMPT AND NUMBER OF ATTEMPTS

Research suggests that childhood trauma impact not only the risk of attempting suicide but also important characteristics of the suicidal behavior. For example, Brown, et al. (1999), in studying adolescents and young adults, found that those with a history of sexual abuse had an eight times greater risk of repeated suicide attempts. Physical abuse alone contributed to repeated suicide attempts. Among 214 inpatients with borderline personality disorder, Brodsky et al. (2005) found that the mean number of previous suicide attempts was significantly higher for those who reported a history of childhood abuse, while among 136 depressed inpatients they found that the mean age of first attempt was lower in the group with childhood abuse than in the non-abused group.

In a study of 1,280 abstinent substance dependent patients, the CTQ was used to measure patients self-report of childhood trauma (Roy, 2004). The results showed that patients who had made three or more attempts had significantly higher CTQ scores than patients who had made two attempts, who had higher scores than patients who had made one attempt, who had higher scores than patients who had never attempted suicide. Furthermore, patients who first attempted suicide before the age of 20 had significantly higher CTQ scores than patients who first attempted after 20 years of age. Dube, et al. (2001) reported a powerful graded relationship between adverse childhood experiences and the risk of attempting suicide throughout the life span among 17,337 adults attending a primary care clinic. As the number of adverse childhood experiences increased, the likelihood of childhood/adolescent and adult suicide attempts increased. Similarly, Post, et al. (2003), noted that the frequency of physical and sexual abuse was positively related to an increased incidence of suicide attempts among 676 bipolar patients, suggesting a "stress or dose-response" relationship.

## RELATIONSHIP WITH GENDER

Women attempt suicide more than men. Clinical studies based on hospital admissions show a higher frequency of admissions for a suicide attempt by women than men, with gender ratios ranging from 1.3 to 3.0. Weissman, et al. (1999) reported cross-national epidemiological data and found that, in all nine countries examined, females had higher rates for suicide attempts than males, reaching a two to three-fold increase in most countries. The reason for this is not completely understood.

We examined two competing hypotheses about gender differences in relation to childhood sexual abuse and suicidal behavior (Roy & Janal, 2006). As women report more childhood trauma than males, we decided to examine whether the higher rates of suicide attempts in women might be due to either their higher incidence of childhood sexual abuse or from possible gender differences in the impact of sexual abuse on suicidal behavior. To do this we examined a large sample of 1,889 patients. The results showed higher rates of suicide attempts in women than men, higher CTQ scores in women than men, and higher CTQ scores in attempters than non-attempters.. However, logistic regression indicated that gender and abuse did not interact to determine attempter status. Thus the results supported the first hypothesis that the greater frequency of suicide attempts in women may partly be attributable to the higher prevalence of childhood sexual abuse in girls. Therefore, although many factors are involved in females attempting suicide more than males, the possibility exists that one factor is that women have experienced more childhood sexual abuse.

## RELATIONSHIP WITH GENES

Research suggests the possibility that the effect of childhood trauma as a distal risk factor for suicide attempts may be impacted by genetic predisposition. Caspi, et al., (2003) were the first to examine the gene-environment interaction in this regard. They reported an interaction between a serotonin transporter promoter (5-HTTLPR) polymorphism and stressful life events for depression, suicidal ideation and suicide attempts. They carried out a prospective longitudinal study of 1,037 children assessed at regular intervals up until the age of 26 years. They measured stressful life events occurring between the ages of 21 to 26 years. Individuals with an s allele of the 5-HTTLPR and with stressful life events after 21 years had an increase in depressive symptoms and suicidal behavior/ideation whereas l/l homzygotes did not. Relevant to childhood trauma, when Caspi, et al. (2003) examined childhood maltreatment that occurred during the first ten years of life, they found that childhood trauma predicted depression as an adult but again only among individuals with the s allele and not among l/l homozygotes.

We administered the CTQ to 306 patients and genotyped them for the 5-HTTLPR genotypes. Although the distribution of 5-HTTLPR genotypes did not differ between patients who had or had not attempted suicide, we did find evidence of a CTQ-gene interaction.

Patients with the combination of a low expression 5-HTTLPR genotype and above–median CTQ scores were more likely to have attempted suicide than the rest of the patients. Logistic regression showed an increasing risk of a suicide attempt with increasing reports of childhood trauma scores. In addition, the increase was exaggerated among those with low expression forms of the 5-HTTLPR genotype. These gene-environment results suggest that childhood trauma interacts with low expressing 5-HTTLPR genotypes to increase the risk of suicidal behavior.

## THE RELEVANCE OF PRIMATE STUDIES

Relevant to the studies outlined above, and to how childhood trauma may predispose individuals to suicide attempts, are the studies of Higley, et al (1997). They reported that an interaction of 5-HTTLPR genotype with early experience had an impact on central serotonin functioning in primates. Bennett, et al. (2002) compared monkeys reared with their mothers with monkeys separated from their mothers at birth and peer-reared. The measure of central serotonin function used was cisternal CSF 5-HIAA concentrations. They found that CSF 5-HIAA concentrations were significantly influenced by genotype, but only in the peer-reared monkeys. Peer-reared s/l heterozygous monkeys had significantly lower CSF 5-HIAA concentrations than peer -reared homozygous monkeys with two l alleles. However, there was no difference in CSF 5-HIAA concentrations between the s/l or l/l genotypes in mother-reared monkeys. Only monkeys with early deleterious rearing experiences showed the genotype-predicted difference in CSF 5-HIAA concentrations. These CSF 5-HIAA data are relevant since low CSF 5-HIAA concentrations are found among patients attempting suicide impacted by childhood trauma.

Also relevant are earlier findings that monkeys with low CSF 5-HIAA concentrations were significantly more impulsive and aggressive than monkey with high CSF 5-HIAA concentrations (Higley, et al., 1996; Westergaard, et al., 2003; Mehlman, et al., 1994). These data are relevant since the trait of impulsive-aggression is associated with low CSF 5-HIAA concentrations in humans, is thought to be an intermediate phenotype for suicidal behavior, and is impacted by childhood trauma (Higley & Linnoila, 1997; Roy & Linnoila, 1988; Williams, et al., 2003; Zhou, et al., 2005).

## METHODOLOGICAL ISSUES IN CLINICAL STUDIES

The major methodological limitations of research on long-term effects of childhood trauma are (1) the retrospective design of most studies and (2) the childhood trauma data were mostly derived from self-report questionnaires. The CTQ, however, has been shown to have high reliability and validity (Bernstein, et al., 1997). Furthermore, Bifulco, et al.(1997) found a high correlation between 87 community-based sister pairs, selected for high rates of neglect or abuse, on independent assessment of what childhood trauma had happened to each. Bifulco, et al. concluded that it was possible to collect retrospective accounts of childhood neglect and abuse with some degree of confidence. Also, Goodman, et al., (1999) observed good reliability in the longitudinal assessment of the history of childhood trauma given by patients with serious psychiatric disorders.

## CONCLUSION

There is strong evidence in the literature that childhood trauma plays a significant role as a distal risk factor for suicidal behavior. Childhood trauma appears to be independently associated with suicidal behavior and at the same time may lead to a cascade of life events, each of which increases the risk of suicide. Traumatic experiences during childhood may have a wide range of effects in adulthood. These include cognitive, behavioral, social, psychopathological and neurobiological consequences. These findings have important implications for suicide treatment and prevention. Individuals who have undergone traumatic experiences during childhood should be considered a high risk group for suicidal behavior and might be considered for specific intervention strategies, particularly if they have attempted suicide previously. Ultimately, preventive measures should be used to try to prevent childhood trauma as well as limit its various long-term effects, including suicidal behavior.

## REFERENCES

Bennett, A. J., Lesch, K. P., Heils, A., et al. (2002). Early experience and serotonin transporter gene variation interact to influence primate CNS function. *Molecular Psychiatry*, 7, 118-122.

Bernstein, D. P., Ahluvalia, T., Pogge, D., et al. (1997). Validity of the Childhood Trauma Questionnaire in an adolescent psychiatric population. *Journal of the American Academy of Child & Adolescent Psychiatry*, 36, 340-348.

Bifulco, A., Brown, G. W., Lillie, A., et al. (1997). Memories of childhood neglect and abuse: corroboration in a series of sisters. *Journal of Child Psychology & Psychiatry*, 38, 365-374.

Brodsky, B. S., Oquendo, M., Ellis, S. P., et al. (2001). The relationship of childhood abuse to impulsivity and suicidal behavior in adults with major depression. *American Journal of Psychiatry*, 158, 1871-1877.

Brown, J., Cohen, P., Johnson, J. G., et al. (1999). Childhood abuse and neglect: specificity of effects on adolescent and young adult depression and suicidality. *Journal of the American Academy of Child & Adolescent Psychiatry*, 38, 1490-1496.

Caspi, A., Sugden, K., Moffitt, T. E., et al. (2003). Influence of life stress on depression: moderation by a polymorphism in the 5-HTT gene. *Science*, 301, 386-389.

Davidson, J. R., Hughes, D. C., George, L. K., et al. (1996). The association of sexual assault and attempted suicide within the community. *Archives of General Psychiatry*, 53, 550-555.

Dube, S. R., Anda, R. F., Felitti, V. J., et al. (2001). Childhood abuse, household dysfunction, and the risk of attempted suicide throughout the life span: findings from the Adverse

Childhood Experiences Study. *Journal of the American Medical Association*, 286, 3089-3096.

Dumais, A., Lesage, A. D., Alda, M., et al. (2005). Risk factors for suicide completion in major depression: a case-control study of impulsive and aggressive behaviors in men. *American Journal of Psychiatry,* 162, 2116-2124.

Edgardh, K., & Ormstad, K. (2000). Prevalence and characteristics of sexual abuse in a national sample of Swedish seventeen-year-old boys and girls. *Acta Paediatrica*, 89, 310-319.

Felitti, V. J., Anda, R. F., Nordenberg, D., et al. (1998). Relationship of childhood abuse and household dysfunction to many of the leading causes of death in adults: the Adverse Childhood Experiences (ACE) Study. *American Journal of Preventive Medicine*, 14, 245-258.

Garno, J. L., Goldberg, J. F., Ramirez, P. M., et al. (2005). Impact of childhood abuse on the clinical course of bipolar disorder. *British Journal of Psychiatry,* 186, 121-125.

Goodman, L. A., Thompson, K. M., Weinfurt, K., et al. (1999). Reliability of reports of violent victimization and posttraumatic stress disorder among men and women with serious mental illness. *Journal of Traumatic Stress*, 12, 587-599.

Grogan-Kaylor, A., & Otis, M. D. (2003). The effect of childhood maltreatment on adult criminality: a tobit regression analysis. *Child Maltreatment*, 8, 129-137.

Heim,, C. & Nemeroff, C. B. (2001). The role of childhood trauma in the neurobiology of mood and anxiety disorders: preclinical and clinical studies. *Biological Psychiatry* 49, 1023-1039.

Higley, J. D., & Linnoila, M. (1997). Low central nervous system serotonergic activity is traitlike and correlates with impulsive behaviour: a nonhuman primate model investigating genetic and environmental influences on neurotransmission. *Annals of the New York Academy of Sciences,* 836, 39-56.

Higley, J. D., Mehlman, P. T., Poland, R. E., et al. (1996). CSF testosterone and 5-HIAA correlate with different types of aggressive behaviors. *Biological Psychiatry*, 40, 1067-1082.

Jollant, F., Bellivier, F., Leboyer, M., et al. (2005). Impaired decision making in suicide attempters. *American Journal of Psychiatry,* 162, 304-310.

Lee, R. (2006). Childhood trauma and personality disorder: toward a biological model. *Current Psychiatry Reports*, 8, 43-52.

Malone, K. M., Haas, G. L., Sweeney, J. A., et al. (1995). Major depression and the risk of attempted suicide. *Journal of Affective Disorders*, 34, 173-185.

Mehlman, P. T., Higley, J. D., Faucher, I., et al. (1994). Low CSF 5-HIAA concentrations and severe aggression and impaired impulse control in nonhuman primates. *American Journal of Psychiatry,* 151, 1485-1491.

Molnar, B. E., Berkman, L. F., & Buka, S. L. (2001). Psychopathology, childhood sexual abuse and other childhood adversities: relative links to subsequent suicidal behaviour in the US. *Psychological Medicine*, 31, 965-977.

Moscicki, E. K. (1997). Identification of suicide risk factors using epidemiologic studies. *Psychiatric Clinics of North America*, 20, 499-517.

Mulvihill, D. (2005). The health impact of childhood trauma: an interdisciplinary review, 1997-2003. *Issues in Comprehensive Pediatric Nursing*, 28, 115-136.

Nelson, E. C., Heath, A. C., Madden, P. A., et al. (2002). Association between self-reported childhood sexual abuse and adverse psychosocial outcomes: results from a twin study. *Archives of General Psychiatry*, 59, 139-145.

Oquendo, M. A., Waternaux, C., Brodsky, B., et al. (2000). Suicidal behavior in bipolar mood disorder: clinical characteristics of attempters and nonattempters. *Journal of Affective Disorders*, 59, 107-117.

Osvath, P., Voros, V., & Fekete, S. (2004). Life events and psychopathology in a group of suicide attempters. *Psychopathology*, 37, 36-40.

Pollock, L. R., & Williams, J. M. (2004). Problem-solving in suicide attempters. *Psychological Medicine*, 34, 163-167.

Post, R. M., Leverich, G. S., Altshuler, L. L., et al. (2003). An overview of recent findings of the Stanley Foundation Bipolar Network (Part I). *Bipolar Disorders*, 5, 310-319.

Roy, A. (2002a). Self-rated childhood emotional neglect and CSF monoamine indices in abstinent cocaine-abusing adults: possible implications for suicidal behavior. *Psychiatry Research*, 112, 69-75.

Roy, A. (2002b). Urinary free cortisol and childhood trauma in cocaine dependent adults. *Journal of Psychiatric Research*, 36, 173-177.

Roy, A. (2004). Relationship of childhood trauma to age of first suicide attempt and number of attempts in substance dependent patients. Acta *Psychiatrica Scandinavica*, 109, 121-125.

Roy, A., & Janal, M. (2006). Gender in suicide attempt rates and childhood sexual abuse rates: is there an interaction? *Suicide & Life-Threatening Behavior*, 36, 329-335.

Roy, A., & Linnoila, M. (1988). Suicidal behavior, impulsiveness and serotonin. *Acta Psychiatrica Scandinavica*, 78, 529-535.

Santa Mina, E. E., & Gallop, R. M. (1998). Childhood sexual and physical abuse and adult self-harm and suicidal behaviour: a literature review. *Canadian Journal of Psychiatry*, 43, 793-800.

Sarchiapone, M., Carli, V., Cuomo, C., et al. (2007). Childhood trauma and suicide attempts in patients with unipolar depression. *Depression & Anxiety*, 24, 268-272.

Schafer, I., Harfst, T., Aderhold, V., et al. (2006). Childhood trauma and dissociation in female patients with schizophrenia spectrum disorders: an exploratory study. *Journal of Nervous & Mental Disease*, 194, 135-138.

Smith, C. A., Ireland, T. O., & Thornberry, T. P. (2005). Adolescent maltreatment and its impact on young adult antisocial behavior. *Child Abuse & Neglect.*, 29, 1099-1119.

Thombs, B. D., Bernstein, D. P., Ziegelstein, R. C., et al. (2006). An evaluation of screening questions for childhood abuse in 2 community samples: implications for clinical practice. *Archives of Internal Medicine*, 166, 2020-2026.

van Heeringen, C. (2001). The suicidal process and related concepts. In C. Van Heeringen (Ed.) *Understanding suicidal behaviour: The suicidal process approach to research, treatment and prevention*, pp. 3-15. Chichester, UK: Wiley.

Weissman, M. M., Bland, R. C., Canino, G. J., et al. (1999). Prevalence of suicide ideation and suicide attempts in nine countries. *Psychological Medicine*, 29, 9-17.

Westergaard, G. C., Suomi, S. J., Chavanne, T. J., et al. (2003). Physiological correlates of aggression and impulsivity in free-ranging female primates. *Neuropsychopharmacology*, 28, 1045-1055.

Williams, R. B., Marchuk, D. A., Gadde, K. M., et al. (2003). Serotonin-related gene polymorphisms and central nervous system serotonin function. *Neuropsychopharmacology,* 28, 533-541.

Zhou, Z., Roy, A., Lipsky, R., et al. (2005). Haplotype-based linkage of tryptophan hydroxylase 2 to suicide attempt, major depression, and cerebrospinal fluid 5-hydroxyindoleacetic acid in 4 populations. *Archives of General Psychiatry,* 62, 1109-1118.

*Chapter 8*

# SUICIDE PROTECTORS

## *Leo Sher*

Clinicians and researchers frequently write about risk factors for suicidal behavior, an important topic. At the same time, it is reasonable to discuss factors that improve resilience to suicide. An understanding of risk and vulnerability to suicidal behavior still outweighs our knowledge of protective factors and resilience. Knowledge of protective factors for suicide, however, may also help prevent and/or predict suicidal behavior. Because risk and protective factors are interrelated, it is necessary to discuss risk factors when we discuss suicide protectors.

## THE STRESS-DIATHESIS MODEL OF SUICIDAL BEHAVIOR

Most patients with psychiatric disorders do not commit suicide, indicating that other factors influence risk. Risk factors may be thought of as leading to or being associated with suicide, that is, people "possessing" the risk factor have a greater potential for suicidal behavior (Móscicki, 1997; Mann, 1998; Sher, et al., 2001). Protective factors, on the other hand, reduce the likelihood of suicide. They enhance resilience and may serve to counterbalance risk factors. Risk and protective factors may be biopsychosocial, environmental or sociocultural in nature. Although this division is somewhat arbitrary, it provides the opportunity to consider these factors from different perspectives.

Understanding the interactive relationship between risk and protective factors in suicidal behavior and how this interaction can be modified are challenges for suicide prevention. Unfortunately, the scientific studies that demonstrate the suicide prevention effect of altering specific risk or protective factors remain limited in number. The impact of some risk factors, however, can clearly be reduced by certain interventions including providing lithium for bipolar disorder or strengthening social support in a community (Baldessarini, et al., 1999; Sher, et al., 2001; Sher & Mann, 2003).

Suicide is not simply a logical response to extreme stress. This conclusion led to the hypothesis of a stress-diathesis model of suicidal behavior (Mann, 1998; Sher, et al., 2001).

The diathesis or predisposition to suicidal behavior is a key element that differentiates psychiatric patients who are at high risk from those at lower risk. The objective severity of the psychiatric illness or number of recent life events do not assist in identifying patients at high risk for suicide attempt. Instead it is the impact of the illness or life events on the person that varies greatly and is correlated with suicidal behavior.

Resilience determines how an individual reacts to a given stressor, and it depends on factors that mold the personality including environmental and genetic factors such as parenting, psychiatric and medical illnesses, especially those affecting the brain, such as epilepsy, migraine, Huntington's disease, alcoholism and substance abuse, and cholesterol level (Schulsinger, et al., 1979; Schoenfeld, et al., 1984; Breslau, 1992; Kaplan, et al., 1994; Brent, et al., 1996; Mann, 1998; Ghosh & Victor, 1999; Sher, et al., 2001; Sher & Mann, 2003; Conner & Duberstein, 2004; Sher, et al., 2005; Sher, 2006). Some of these factors may be interrelated.

## DEMOGRAPHIC CHARACTERISTICS AND SUICIDAL BEHAVIOR

### Gender

In the general population, the rate of suicide is about four times higher in males compared with females, and yet females attempt suicide three times more than males (Canetto, 1997; Ghosh & Victor, 1999; Sher, et al., 2001). Part of the reason for the higher suicide rate in men is accounted for by the more violent means they use. Qin, et al. (2001) suggested that gender differences could not be explained by differential exposure to known risk factors. In some countries, such as China, the suicide rate in women is similar to that of men, perhaps, due to the use of highly lethal methods by women (Sher, et al., 2001). Overall, however, being female is a protective factor against completed suicide.

### Age

Suicide rates in females are generally stable with age after mid-teens until the very oldest age groups (85+) where there is usually a slight drop-off (Sher, et al., 2001). Elderly white males have a big increase in suicide rates beginning in their 70s (Canetto, 1997; Sher, et al., 2001). In the USA, the adolescent suicide rate tripled from 1950 until 1980, but then began to fall. The suicide rate for the entire population has fallen about 9% from 1988 to 1998. Generally, among males, being younger is a protective factor against suicide.

### Race

About 90% of all suicides in the U.S. are committed by whites (Ghosh & Victor, 1999; Sher, et al., 2001). Most studies indicate that Caucasians are at highest risk for suicide, followed by Native Americans, African Americans, Hispanic Americans, and Asian Americans. For example, in community sample studies, Anglo bipolar patients have higher rates of suicide attempt (32% are attempters versus 68% nonattempters), than African Americans (21% are attempters) or Hispanic Americans (13% are attempters) (Chen & Dilsaver, 1996). The reasons for ethnic differences in suicide rates are unknown.

## Marital Status

In general, people who are unmarried, divorced or widowed are at higher risk of suicide (Ghosh & Victor, 1999; Sher, et al., 2001). Highest to lowest rates in the United States are found in the following order: widowed, divorced, single or never married, married, and married with children. The protective effect of marriage against suicide is especially marked among males and whites. Studies suggest that having children may serve as a protective factor against suicide in patients with mood disorders and in the general population (Fawcett, et al., 1990; Hoyer & Lund, 1993).

## Education and Social Status

Most studies that have examined associations between measures of social disadvantage and completed and attempted suicide have reported an increased risk of suicidal behavior among individuals from socially disadvantaged backgrounds characterized by such features as low socioeconomic status, limited educational achievement, low income and poverty (Bucca, et al., 1994; Gould, et al., 1996; Beautrais, 2000). Higher socioeconomic status protects against suicide. This underlines the importance of social improvements in preventing suicides both in developed and in developing countries.

## Religion

Suicide rates are lower in religious countries than in secular ones (Stack, 1983; Dervic, et al., 2004). Some of this difference may be due to under-reporting in religious countries because of concerns over stigma. Although some of the difference may be real, it is not known whether the negative association between religion and suicide is due to its integrative benefits, such as social cohesion as proposed by Durkheim (1951) or to the moral imperatives of religious belief, given its prohibitions against suicidal behavior (Stack, 1983; Stack & Lester, 1991; Dervic, et al., 2004).

# Clinical Characteristics and Suicidal Behavior

## Role of Psychiatric and Medical Disorders

Conditions associated with a high risk for attempted suicide and completed suicide include mood disorders, alcohol and substance abuse and Cluster B personality disorders (Sher, et al., 2001; Conner & Duberstein, 2004; Sher, et al., 2005; Sher, 2006). Angst and Preisig (1995), in a follow-up study, found no difference in rates of suicide in patients with unipolar depression compared to patients with bipolar disorder. There is, however, disagreement in the literature regarding the role of relationship of mood disorder subtype to suicide (Rihmer, et al., 1990; Bulik, et al., 1990; Buchholtz-Hansen, et al., 1993; Sher, et al., 2001). Unlike the study by Angst and Preisig (1995), most studies do not involve long-term follow-up, but instead are based on psychological autopsies of completed suicides or are short-term follow-up studies. For example, Rihmer, et al. (1990) studied 100 consecutive suicides with major depression and found that 46% of them had bipolar II disorder. Bulik, et al. (1990), studying recurrent major depression in patients without Axis II pathology, noted that the presence of alcohol abuse was significantly more common in suicide attempters. The association between comorbid substance abuse and suicide attempts was found in both genders and in all age groups. Research in psychiatric populations suggests that substance abuse, alcoholism and smoking may increase the risk for suicide, or may directly contribute to suicide risk through facilitating disinhibition, depressed mood or other neurochemical effects on the brain (Ballenger, et al., 1979; Sher, et al., 2005; Sher, 2006). Physical illness has also been found to increase the risk for suicide and suicidal behavior (Schoenfeld, et al., 1984; Breslau, 1992; Mann, 1998; Ghosh & Victor, 1999; Sher, et al., 2001; Sher & Mann, 2003).

## Presence of Specific Symptoms and Personality Traits

The presence of specific components may play a role in suicidal behavior. As a result of the National Institute of Mental Health Collaborative Depression study, three groups of symptoms have been put forward as more predictive of suicide than either diagnoses or syndromes (Fawcett, et al., 1997): (1) anhedonia and hopelessness; (2) anxiety, agitation and panic; and (3) aggression and impulsivity. Beck (1986) suggested that cognitive dysfunctions (particularly hopelessness) are a strong predictor of suicidal behavior in persons with affective disorders.

The role of psychotic symptoms in suicidal behavior in persons with mood disorders remains controversial (Sher, et al., 2001). Several studies have reported no support for increased suicidality in persons with psychosis and affective disorder (Sher, et al., 2001). However, some studies support the association of the symptoms of delusional thinking and other psychotic features in major depression and suicide (Roose, et al., 1983; Wolfersdorf, et al., 1987; Sher, et al., 2001).

## Childhood Stressors

A family history of parental separation or divorce is associated with an increase risk of completed and attempted suicide (Fergusson & Lynskey, 1995; Gould, et al., 1998; Beautrais, 2000). Suicides, for example, have been found to be more likely than control subjects to come from a non-intact family of origin, even after controlling for demographic factors (Gould, et al., 1998). Positive childhood experiences may increase resilience to suicidal behavior in adulthood.

# THE NEUROBIOLOGY OF SUICIDAL BEHAVIOR

## Genetic and Familial Effects

Family, twin, adoption, and molecular genetic studies suggest that suicidal behavior can be inherited (Schulsinger, et al, 1979; Roy, et al., 1995; Sher & Mann, 2003; Baldessarini & Hennen, 2004). There is evidence that a predisposition to suicidal behavior can be transmitted independently of psychiatric disorders. The contribution of genetic factors is indicated by a higher average concordance rate for suicidal behavior among co-twins of suicidal identical twins compared to fraternal twins or to relatives of other suicidal subjects. Therefore, some individuals may be "genetically protected" from suicidal behavior while others are not.

## Changes in the Serotonergic System

5-Hydroxyindolacetic acid (5-HIAA) is the major metabolite of serotonin. A number of research groups have studied cerebrospinal fluid (CSF) 5-HIAA levels in the CSF of psychiatric patients (Åsberg, et al., 1986; Oquendo & Mann, 2000; Sher, et al., 2001; Sher & Mann, 2003; Sher, 2007). Most studies that have looked at suicide attempters with mood disorders compared with nonattempters with mood disorders have found that suicide attempters have lower levels of CSF 5-HIAA.

Fenfluramine causes the release of serotonin and inhibits serotonin reuptake. A history of a highly lethal suicide attempt is associated with a blunted prolactin response to fenfluramine (Sher & Mann, 2003). Like low CSF 5-HIAA, a blunted prolactin response to fenfluramine may be a biochemical trait. Both are low in those with a lifetime history of aggression and impulsivity. This suggests that low serotonergic activity is a correlate of serious suicidal behavior, aggression, and impulsivity. Normal serotonergic function protects against suicidal behavior. This underlines the importance of biological treatments of psychiatric disorders.

## The Relationship between Cholesterol Levels and Suicidal Acts

Low levels of cholesterol or cholesterol-lowering treatments (particularly diet) increase the probability of suicidal behavior (Neaton, et al., 1992; Kaplan, et al., 1994; Kunugi, et al., 1997). Cholesterol levels appear to have an effect on behavior involving aggression and suicidality. It remains to be determined by what pathway cholesterol influences suicide risk. In primates, low cholesterol is associated with greater aggressive behavior (Kaplan, et al., 1994), but it is not known if a similar mechanism operates in man. It appears that normal cholesterol level is a suicide protector.

## SUICIDE PROTECTORS IN ADOLESCENTS

Parent-family connectedness is an important protective factor for suicidal behavior that cuts across the gender and racial/ethnic groups of adolescents (Borowsky, et al., 2001). Other studies have also found a protective effect of family connectedness and cohesion on suicidal behavior among American Indian and Alaska Native youth, Mexican American teenagers and a largely white sample of adolescents (Rubenstein, et al., 1989; Guiao & Esparza, 1995; Borowsky, et al., 1999). Emotional well-being is also a significant protective factor for suicidal behavior (Borowsky, et al., 2001). The majority of adolescent suicides are characterized by psychopathology, primarily depression. These findings support a twofold role for schools, proposed by Resnick, et al. (1993) - nurturing both academic proficiency as well as a sense of connectedness among students, a connectedness that includes the student's perceptions that teachers care about them and treat them fairly, feeling they are close to people at school, and feeling a sense of belonging, happiness and safety at school.

## CONCLUSION

Protective factors are quite varied and include an individual's biological and behavioral characteristics, as well as attributes of the environment and culture. Important suicide protectors include effective clinical care for psychiatric disorders (including substance abuse) and physical disorders; easy access to a variety of clinical interventions and support for help seeking; restricted access to highly lethal means of suicide; strong connections to family and community support; good problem-solving and conflict resolution skills; and cultural and religious beliefs that discourage suicide and support self preservation (USDHHS, 2006).

## FUTURE DIRECTIONS

To prevent suicidal behavior we need to develop new approaches to suicide prevention by enhancing our understanding of

a) the biological and behavioral characteristics of children that increase their risk of growing up to commit suicidal acts;
b) protective factors, that is, conditions, events, and processes in families and communities that prevent the development of high potentials for suicidal behavior in high-risk individuals; and
c) preventive interventions grounded in knowledge of protective factors.

# REFERENCES

Åsberg, M., Nordström, P., & Träskman-Bendz, L. (1986). Cerebrospinal fluid studies in suicide: an overview. *Annals of the New York Academy of Sciences,* 487, 243-255.

Angst, J., & Preisig, M. (1995). Outcome of a clinical cohort of unipolar, bipolar and schizoaffective patients. Results of a prospective study from 1959 to 1985. *Schweizer Archiv fur Neurologie und Psychiatrie,* 146, 17-23.

Baldessarini, R. J., & Hennen, J. (2004). Genetics of suicide: an overview. *Harvard Review of Psychiatry,* 12, 1-13.

Baldessarini, R., Tondo, L., & Hennen, J. (1999). Effects of lithium treatment and its discontinuation on suicidal behavior in bipolar manicdepressive disorders. *Journal of Clinical Psychiatry,* 60 (Suppl. 2), 77-84.

Ballenger, J. C., Goodwin, F. K., Major, L. F., et al. (1979). Alcohol and central serotonin metabolism in man. *Archives of General Psychiatry,* 36, 224-227.

Beautrais, A. L. (2000). Risk factors for suicide and attempted suicide among young people. *Australian & New Zealand Journal of Psychiatry,* 34, 420-436.

Beautrais, A. L., Joyce, P. R., & Mulder, R. T. (1996). Risk factors for serious suicide attempt among youths aged 13 through 24 years. *Journal of the American Academy of Child & Adolescent Psychiatry,* 35, 1174-1182.

Beck, A. T. (1986). Hopelessness as a predictor of eventual suicide. *Annals of the New York Academy of Sciences,* 487, 90-96.

Borowsky, I. W., Ireland, M., & Resnick, M. D. (2001). Adolescent suicide attempts: risks and protectors. *Pediatrics,* 107, 485-493.

Borowsky, I., Resnick, M.D., Ireland, M., et al. (1999). Suicide attempts among American Indian and Alaska Native youth: risk and protective factors. *Archives of Pediatrics & Adolescent Medicine,* 153, 573-580.

Brent, D. A. (1986). Overrepresentation of epileptics in a consecutive series of suicide attempters seen at a Children's Hospital, 1978-1983. *Journal of the American Academy of Child & Adolescent Psychiatry,* 25, 242-246.

Breslau, N. (1992). Migraine, suicidal ideation, and suicide attempts. *Neurology,* 42, 392-395.

Bucca, M., Ceppi, M., Peloso, P., et al. (1994). Social variables and suicide in the population Genoa, Italy. *Comprehensive Psychiatry,* 35, 64-69.

Buchholtz-Hansen, P. E., Wang, A. G., & Danish University Antidepressant Group (1993). Mortality in major affective disorder: relationship to subtype of depression. *Acta Psychiatrica Scandinavica,* 87, 329-335.

Bulik, C. M., Carpenter, L. L., Kupfer, D. J., et al. (1990). Features associated with suicide attempts in recurrent major depression. *Journal of Affective Disorders,* 18, 29-37.

Canetto, S. S. (1997). Gender and suicidal behavior: theories and evidence. In R. W. Maris, M. M. Silverman & S. S. Canetto (Eds.) *Review of suicidology,* pp.138-164. New York: The Guilford.

Chen, Y. W., & Dilsaver, S. C. (1996). Lifetime rates of suicide attempts among subjects with bipolar and unipolar disorders relative to subjects with other Axis I disorders. *Biological Psychiatry,* 39, 896-899.

Conner, K. R., & Duberstein, P. R. (2004). Predisposing and precipitating factors for suicide among alcoholics: empirical review and conceptual integration. *Alcoholism: Clinical & Experimental Research,* 28(5 Supplement), 6S-17S.

Dervic, K., Oquendo, M. A., Grunebaum, M. F., et al. (2004). Religious affiliation and suicide attempt. *American Journal of Psychiatry,* 161, 2303-8.

Durkheim, E. (1951). *Suicide.* New York: Free Press.

Fawcett, J., Busch, K., Jacobs, D., et al. (1997). Suicide: a four-pathway clinical biochemical model. In D. Stoff, & J. J. Mann (Eds.) *The neurobiology of suicide: From the bench to the clinic,* pp.288-301. New York: New York Academy of Sciences.

Fawcett, J., Scheftner, W.A., Fogg, L., et al. (1990). Time-related predictors of suicide in major affective disorder. *American Journal of Psychiatry,* 147, 1189-1194.

Guiao, I. Z., & Esparza, D. (1995). Suicidality correlates in Mexican American teens. *Issues in Mental Health Nursing,* 16, 461-479.

Fergusson, D. M., & Lynskey, M. T. (1995). Suicide attempts and suicidal ideation in a birth cohort of 16 year old New Zealanders. *Journal of the American Academy of Child & Adolescent Psychiatry,* 34, 1308-1317.

Ghosh, T. B., & Victor, B. S. (1999). Suicide. In R. E. Hales, S. C. Yudofsky & J. A. Talbott (Eds.) *The American psychiatric press textbook of psychiatry. 3$^{rd}$ Ed.* pp. 1383-1404.Washington, DC: American Psychiatric Press,

Gould, M. S., Fisher, P., Parides, M., et al. (1996). Psychosocial factors for child and adolescent completed suicide. *Archives of General Psychiatry,* 53, 1155-1162.

Gould, M. S., Shaffer, D., Fisher, P., et al. (1998). Separation/divorce and child and adolescent suicide. *Journal of the American Academy of Child & Adolescent Psychiatry,* 37, 155-162.

Hoyer, G., & Lund, E. (1993). Suicide among women related to number of children in marriage. *Archives of General Psychiatry,* 50, 134-137.

Kaplan, J. R., Shively, C. A., Fontenot, M. B., et al. (1994). Demonstration of an association among dietary cholesterol, central serotonergic activity, and social behavior in monkeys. *Psychosomatic Medicine,* 56, 479-484.

Kunugi, H., Takei, N., Aoki, H., et al. (1997). Low serum cholesterol in suicide attempters. *Biological Psychiatry,* 41, 196-200.

Mann, J. J. (1998). The neurobiology of suicide. *Nature Medicine,* 4, 25-30.

Moscicki, E. K. (1997). Identification of suicide risk factors using epidemiologic studies. *Psychiatric Clinics of North America,* 20, 499-517.

Neaton, J. D., Blackburn, H, Jacobs, D, et al. (1992). Serum cholesterol level and mortality findings for men screened in the Multiple Risk Factor Intervention Trial. Multiple Risk Factor Intervention Trial Research Group. *Archives of Internal Medicine,* 152, 1490-1500.

Oquendo, M. A., & Mann, J. J. (2000). The biology of impulsivity and suicidality. *Psychiatric Clinics of North America,* 23, 11-25.

Qin, P., Agerbo E., Westergard-Nielsen, N., et al. (2000). Gender differences in risk factors for suicide in Denmark. *British Journal of Psychiatry,* 177, 546-550.

Resnick, A. D., Harris, L. J., & Blum, R. W. (1993). The impact of caring and connectedness on adolescent health and well-being. *Journal of Paediatrics & Child Health,* 29, S3-S9.

Rihmer, Z., Barsi, J., Arató, M., et al. (1990). Suicide in subtypes of primary major depression *Journal of Affective Disorders,* 18, 221-225.

Roose, S. P., Glassman, A. H., Walsh, B. T., et al. (1983). Depression, delusions, and suicide. *American Journal of Psychiatry,* 140, 1159-1162.

Schoenfeld, M., Myers, R. H., Cupples, L. A., et al. (1984). Increased rate of suicide among patients with Huntington's disease. *Journal of Neurology, Neurosurgery & Psychiatry,* 47, 1283-1287.

Schulsinger, F., Kety, S. S., Rosenthal, D., et al. (1979). A family study of suicide. In M. Schou & E. Stromgren (Eds.) *Origin, prevention and treatment of affective disorders.* New York: Academic Press.

Sher, L. (2006). Alcoholism and suicidal behavior: a clinical overview. *Acta Psychiatrica Scandinavica,* 113, 13-22.

Sher, L., & Mann, J. J. (2003). Neurobiology of suicide. In J. C. Soares, & S.Gershon (Eds.) *Textbook of medical psychiatry,* pp. 701-711. New York: Marcel Dekker.

Sher, L., Oquendo, M. A., Galfalvy, H. C., et al. (2005). The relationship of aggression to suicidal behavior in depressed patients with a history of alcoholism. *Addictive Behaviors,* 30, 1144-1153.

Sher, L., Oquendo, M. A., Grunebaum, M. F., et al. (2007). CSF monoamine metabolites and lethality of suicide attempts in depressed patients with alcohol dependence. *European Neuropsychopharmacology,* 17, 12-15.

Stack, S. (1983). The effect of religious commitment on suicide: a cross-national analysis. *Journal of Health & Social Behavior,* 24, 362–374.

Stack S., & Lester, D. (1991). The effect of religion on suicide ideation. *Social Psychiatry & Psychiatric Epidemiology,* 26,168–170.

U.S. Department of Health and Human Services (USDHHS) (2006). *National Strategy for Suicide Prevention.* http://www.mentalhealth.samhsa.gov/suicideprevention/strategy.asp (Accessed September 17, 2006.)

Wolfersdorf, M., Keller, F., Steiner, B., et al. (1987). Depressional delusion and suicide. *Acta Psychiatrica Scandinavica,* 76, 359-363.

# Part 2: Environmental Approaches to Suicide

In: Suicide from a Global Perspective: Psychosocial Approaches   ISBN 978-1-61470-965-7
Editors: A. Shrivastava, M. Kembrell et al. pp. 69-74   © 2012 Nova Science Publishers, Inc.

*Chapter 9*

# SOCIOLOGICAL PERSPECTIVES ON SUICIDE

## *Masahito Fushimi*

In general, social factors associated with suicide may be defined as those that are the result of the interaction between the individual and external situations. Durkheim (1897) was one of the first scholars to view suicide as a result of social factors, examining the role of these factors using data from several European countries and, following Durkheim's groundbreaking study, social relationships were included in suicidology. Many subsequent studies have explored suicide as a social phenomenon, especially as a form of social pathology.

Individuals live in society and, therefore, it is natural that their behaviors are affected by their social situations or circumstances. Suicidal behavior creates anxiety in the society, as well as seriously affecting families and communities. As the number of suicides increase in a society, members of the society are influenced by those who kill themselves, resulting in chain reactions of suicide, suicide contagion, imitation and clusters of suicidal acts (Gould, 1994; Stack, 2005). Another example of the impact of social forces is that, in the past, suicide was taboo in society and viewed as deviant behavior, with some religions strictly forbidding it. Devoutly religious societies, therefore, typically have low rates of suicide.

## A THEORY TO EXPLAIN THE RELATION BETWEEN SUICIDE AND ITS SOCIAL FACTORS

Suicidal behavior can result from a series of stressful experiences, and the process of committing suicide can be explained by the stress-vulnerability hypothesis, using the mediating variable of coping skills (Cohen, 1988). When applying this hypothesis to suicide from a sociological perspective, for example, social isolation is an important stressor and social support can be a coping resource. The relationship between suicide and its social factors is illustrated by Figure 9.1. Biological, genetic or psychological individual variables are excluded from this figure. The social factors are classified into two types: negative social factors and positive social factors. Furthermore, this figure shows that, depending on the degree of the relative forces of each factor, social factors cause an increase in the suicide rate or a decrease in the suicide rate. Social indicators such as age, divorce and marital status affect the strength of both of these social forces.

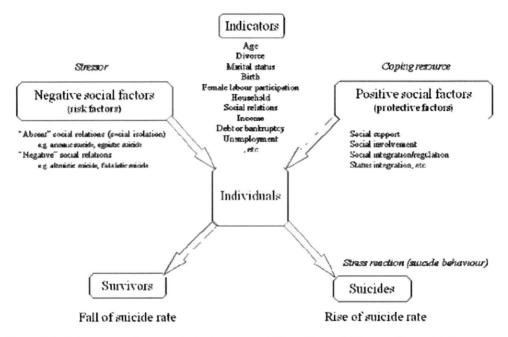

Figure 9-1. A theory to explain the relation between suicide and its social factors. The social factors are classified into two: negative and positive social factors. This figure depicts that, depending on the degree of the relative forces of each factor, social factors cause either the rise or the fall of suicide rate. In addition, indicators predicting the condition of the forces of both factors are illustrated.

## SOCIAL FACTORS THAT INFLUENCE SUICIDE

Variables which are often analyzed as indicators of social factors include age, divorce, marital status, birth rates, female labor force participation, household composition, social relationships (social integration), income (economic inequality), debt or bankruptcy, and unemployment. Divorce rates, marital status, birth rates and household composition could be considered as indicators of family integration. Durkheim argued that one of the most important factors in high suicide rates, along with modernization, is low levels of family integration.

### Age

A general tendency described in many studies is that the greater the age, the higher the suicide rate (Hamermesh & Soss, 1974). Furthermore, males are more likely to commit suicide than females, indicating that males are more influenced by aging than are females (Chuang & Huang, 1997).

## Divorce

A positive correlation between divorce and suicide appears to be a general worldwide finding (Leenaars, et al., 1993; Burr, et al., 1997; Brainerd, 2001; West, 2003). Divorce is a serious crisis in family relationships and lowers social integration, both of the society as a whole and of the divorced individuals. Regarding the differences by gender, the impact of divorce seems to increase the rate of suicidal behavior more in males than in females (Chuang & Huang, 1997; Neumayer, 2003).

## Marital Status

It has been observed that countries or regions with higher marriage rates have lower suicide rates (Leenaars, et al., 1993), presumably because a high marriage rate indicates a high level of family integration. The lower suicide rate in married individuals is greater for men than for women, indicating that marriage has a greater protective effect for men with regard to suicide (Neumayer, 2003).

## Birth Rates

The presence of children in a family is regarded as an indicator of greater social integration (Leenaars, et al., 1993). An increase in the birth rate is, therefore, expected to result in a decrease in the rate of suicide, in particular, the form of suicide labeled by Durkheim as egoistic suicide. Studies indicate that suicide rates are, in fact, lower in countries with high birth rates (Leenaars, 1993; Neumayer, 2003).

## Female Labor Force Participation

It is assumed that individuals who have a wider social circle are at a lower risk of suicide compared with those with few social contacts. There are two contradictory hypotheses regarding whether female labor force participation correlates positively or negatively with the suicide rate. One hypothesis states that female labor force participation results in increased stress for family members and higher suicide rates, particularly among females. An alternative hypothesis asserts that the increased social participation by females who go to work increases their social relationships and enhances their lives and, rather than causing stress, results in a decrease in suicide rates, particularly among females. Research on which of these two hypotheses is true has produced conflicting results (Lester, et al., 1992; Burr, et al., 1997; Chuang & Huang, 1997; Neumayer, 2003).

## Household Composition

According to one study, the larger the size of the household, the higher the suicide rate (Burr, et al., 1997). Another study found, however, that the male suicide rate was not associated with the number of household members while the female suicide rate correlated negatively with the number of household members (Neumayer, 2003). Research has been conducted on the correlation between the proportion of people living alone in the society and the suicide rate (Burr, et al., 1997), again with conflicting results.

## Income and Economic Inequality

Several studies have investigated income as a factor in suicide. It has been reported that the higher the level of income, the lower the risk of suicide. However, in areas where there are a large number of people with an income that is above a certain level, the higher the level of income, the higher the risk of suicide (Neumayer, 2003). Therefore, it is difficult to reach a simple conclusion. Furthermore, income is found to be a more important risk factor for suicide in men than in women (Chuang & Huang, 1997; Brainerd, 2001), but income is not found to be a risk factor for young people (Hamermesh & Soss, 1974).

Research indicates that economic inequality affects the level of health and mortality rate in individuals in a society (Kawachi, et al., 1997), but there is no significant association between income inequality in nations (the Gini coefficient) and their suicide rates (Lester, 1987).

## Debt or Bankruptcy

Suicide rates are reportedly high in areas where the debt is high, especially for men. Moreover, an increase in the number of individual bankruptcies is found to be positively correlated with a rise in the suicide rate, although this correlation is weak (West, 2003).

## Unemployment

Unemployment reduces the level of income and the standard of living of the members of a society. In addition, unemployment also results in a loss of social status, one's role in society and personal relationships, and this can weaken social integration. There exists a positive correlation between unemployment and suicide rates in some studies (Hamermesh & Soss, 1974; Lewis & Sloggett, 1998), but other studies have found no significant association between unemployment and suicide rates (Burr, et al., 1997; Chuang & Huang, 1997). Unemployment appears to be a more important suicide risk factor for males than for females (Neumayer, 2003; West, 2003), and unemployment is a risk factor for suicide in adults, but not for youths (Hamermesh & Soss, 1974).

## CONCLUSIONS

This brief review indicates that both the societal suicide rate and the risk of suicide for individuals are impacted by social factors. Although there has been criticism of the reliability and validity of officially reported suicide rates at the national level (Douglas, 1967), the results of research on the social correlates of suicide have found consistent and important correlates of societal suicide rates. This demonstrated impact of social factors on suicide suggests that large-scale programs at the societal level may have an impact on the suicide rate of a society, and several nations have now formulated and implemented national suicide prevention programs (Hakanen & Upanne, 1996; Taylor, et al., 1997).

## REFERENCES

Brainerd, E. (2001). Economic reform and mortality in the former Soviet Union: a study of the suicide epidemic in the 1990s. *European Economic Review*, 45, 1007-1019.

Burr, J. A., McCall, P. L., & Powell-Griner, E. (1997). Female labor force participation and suicide. *Social Science & Medicine*, 44, 1847-1859.

Chuang, H., & Huang, W. (1997). Economic and social correlates of regional suicide rates: a pooled cross–section and time–series analysis. *Journal of Socio-Economics*, 26, 277-289.

Cohen, S. (1988). Psychosocial models of the role of social support in the etiology of physical disease. *Health Psychology*, 7, 269-297.

Cutler, D. M., Glaeser, E. & Norberg, K. (2000). Explaining the rise in youth suicide. *NBER Working Paper* 7713.

Douglas, J. D. (1967). *The social meanings of suicide*. Princeton, NJ: Princeton University Press.

Durkheim, E. (1951) [1897] *Suicide: a study of* sociology. New York: Free Press.

Gould, M. S., Petrie, K., Kleinman, M. H., et al. (1994). Clustering of attempted suicide: New Zealand national data. *International Journal of Epidemiology*, 23, 1185-1189.

Hakanen, J., & Upanne, M. (1996). Evaluation strategy for Finland's suicide prevention project. *Crisis*, 17, 167-174.

Hamermesh, D. S., & Soss, N. M. (1974). An economic theory of suicide. *Journal of Political Economy*, 82, 83-98.

Kawachi, I., Kennedy, B. P., Lochner, K., et al. (1997). Social capital, income inequality and mortality. *American Journal of Public Health*, 87, 1491-1498.

Leenaars, A. A., Yang, B., & Lester, D. (1993). The effect of domestic and economic stress on suicide rates in Canada and the United States. *Journal of Clinical Psychology*, 49, 918-921.

Lester, D. (1987). Relation of income inequality to suicide and homicide rates. *Journal of Social Psychology*, 127, 101-102.

Lester, D., Motohashi, Y., & Yang, B. (1992). The impact of the economy on suicide and homicide rates in Japan and the United States. *International Journal of Social Psychiatry*, 38, 314-317.

Lewis, G., & Sloggett, A. (1998). Suicide, deprivation, and unemployment: record linkage study. *British Medical Journal*, 317, 1283-1286.

Mann, J. J., Apter, A., Bertolote, J., et al. (2005). Suicide prevention strategies: a systematic review. *Journal of American Medical Association*, 294, 2064-2074.

Maris, R. W., Berman, A. L., & Silverman, M. M. (2000). *Comprehensive textbook of suicidology*. New York: Guilford.

Neumayer, E. (2003). Are socioeconomic factors valid determinants of suicide? Controlling for national cultures of suicide with fixed–effects estimation. *Cross-Cultural Research*, 37, 307-329.

Stack, S. (2005). Suicide in the media: a quantitative review of studies based on non-fictional stories. *Suicide & Life-Threatening Behavior*, 35, 121-133.

Taylor, S. J., Kingdom, D., & Jenkins, R. (1997). How are nations trying to prevent suicide? An analysis of national suicide prevention strategies. *Acta Psychiatrica Scandinavica*, 95, 457-463.

West, M. (2003). *Dying to get out of debt: Consumer insolvency law and suicide in Japan*. The John M. Olin Center for Law & Economics Working Paper Series 21 Ann Arbor, MI: University of Michigan Law School.

Chapter 10

# ADVANCES IN SOCIOLOGICAL APPROACHES TO UNDERSTANDING SUICIDE

*Augustine J. Kposowa*

In the past three decades, social science research on suicide and suicidal behavior has made advances in two main areas. There have been theoretical developments and significant advances in study design and methodology. There have also been advances in interdisciplinary overtures designed to incorporate what is known in the biomedical sciences, including psychiatry and public health. The purpose of this chapter is to describe the progress that has been made and to suggest pathways for future work.

## THEORETICAL ADVANCES

Research on suicide in the past two decades has documented the continuing influence of Emile Durkheim on theoretical development in the social sciences. His seminal work, *Le Suicide,* first published in 1897 remains the starting point of most discussions of suicidal behavior both in sociology and related sciences (Cutchin & Churchill, 1999; Baller & Richardson, 2002; Tubergen, et al., 2005). The bulk of research since the 1990s attempt to modify and test variations of Durkheim's original proposition, namely that suicide rates increase in direct proportion to the level of *social integration* prevailing among social groups. Social integration has been understood in different terms, but it is generally used in reference to the quantity and quality of ties that bind individuals to others, to their community, and to the wider society. It indexes the degree of cohesion in social and interpersonal ties (Breault & Kposowa, 1987). In his original formulation of the social integration perspective, Durkheim (1897/1951) suggested that social integration can be either excessive or insufficient and that, in both cases, it increases suicide rates. In its excessive state, social integration results when group interests dominate individual interests, resulting in altruistic suicide. Some analysts propose, however, that in modern nation states, it is rare for social integration to be excessive. Hence, researchers have increasingly focused on reduced or insufficient social integration

(Breault, 1986; Kposowa, et al., 1995; Baller & Richardson, 2002; Stockard & O'Brien, 2002).

According to social integration theory, suicide rates tend to be high among groups that have lower levels of domestic integration, while communities with low levels of integration exhibit high suicide rates. As Durkheim (1897/1951, p. 209) explained, "Suicide varies inversely with the degree of integration of the social groups of which the individual forms a part...As collective force is one of the obstacles best calculated to restrain suicide, its weakening involves a development of suicide." Social integration has also been expanded upon by some analysts to incorporate networks. As Tubergen, et al. (2005, p. 802) recently observed, "...social networks in general, provide social and emotional support to their members, which prevents people from committing suicide." Regardless of conceptualization, most sociological work has found support for the social integration perspective, with the variable of marital status offering the most consistent results (Kposowa, 2000; Stack 2000; Luoma & Pearson, 2003).

While acknowledging the contribution of Durkheim to theory development, there have also been substantial attempts within the past three decades to point out shortcomings in his views. One of the more severe challenges is with regard to Durkheim's insistence that suicide can be explained only by social facts or sociological variables. In this regard, he either downplayed or dismissed the role of mental states, including insanity and alcoholism or substance use. Some more critical authors point out for instance that Durkheim made statements that were contrary to his own data. Skog (1991) noted that, while the French data used by Durkheim showed a strong correlation between alcohol consumption and suicide, Durkheim concluded that there was no such link. In a more critical work, Norström (1995) argued that alcohol abuse increases reckless behavior which in turn reduces social integration by weakening personal ties and, thereby, elevates suicide risk. Thus, Norstrom incorporated alcohol use within Durkheim's original social integration theory.

In addition to dismissing alcohol abuse and mental health (including insanity, depression, psychosis and anxiety) as contributing factors to suicidal behavior, Durkheim did not have much regard for imitation. He wrote, "It is one thing to share a common feeling, another to yield to the authority of opinion, and third to repeat automatically what others have done" (Durkheim, 1897/1951, p. 129). Yet social science research, especially since the groundbreaking work of Phillips (1974, 1982), has incorporated *imitation theory* as a perspective for understanding suicide. The essential argument in imitation theory is that widely publicized suicide stories on television and in newspapers and other mass media could increase suicide rates by triggering copycat suicidal behavior. Support for the theory has been found in numerous studies, for example Jonas (1992) for Germany, Ishii (1991) and Stack (1996) for Japan, and Stack (1992) for the USA.

In the last two decades, some sociologists have borrowed criminological theories to explain suicide. Paramount among these is *opportunity theory*. As applied to suicidal behavior, it is argued that individuals differ in structured opportunities that are available for committing suicide and, accordingly, where opportunities are high, suicide rates will increase. The stream of research testing opportunity theory and suicide typically focuses on methods of death. For example, availability of firearms in the home increases suicide risk because of opportunity (Stack, 2000). Many studies, both in and outside sociology, confirm that firearm availability is a significant risk factor for suicide (Kellerman, et al., 1996; Kposowa & McElvain, 2006).

Efforts by sociologists to acknowledge and bring in variables dismissed by Durkheim, and yet found in other disciplines to explain suicide rates, constitute one of the strongest areas of advancement to date in social science research on suicide. There have also been significant strides in formulating new sociological theories to explain suicidal behavior.

## ADVANCES IN METHODOLOGY

In the area of methodology, perhaps the main advance has occurred in study designs. Prior to the 1990s, most sociological work on suicide was based on ecological data. In the United States, studies typically used units ranging from counties (Breault, 1986; Pope & Danigelis, 1981), standard metropolitan statistical areas (Ellison, et al., 1997) and states (Cutchin & Churchill, 1999). The practice of using aggregate data was based in part on Durkheim's influence on suicide research within sociology. Some have argued that, although Durkheim proposed his social integration theory in terms of micro (individual) units, he tested its various propositions with aggregated data (Tubergen, et al., 2005; Poppel & Day, 1996; Breault, 1986). Since the 1990s, however, there have been calls for the use of micro-level data, and quite a few analysts have answered (Stack, 1990; Kposowa, 2000; Kposowa & McElvain, 2006).

In the past decade, there has emerged an important innovation whereby researchers have moved to multi-level modeling strategies to acknowledge the impact of contextual variables on suicide, and to avoid inference problems with regard to the ecological fallacy (Robinson, 1950). Some studies have tested contextual effects by studying lower level units, such as counties, within larger level units, such as regions or states (Ellison, et al., 1997; Cutchin & Churchill, 1999; Pescosolido, 1990). Others have embedded individual level data within aggregate units (Tubergen, et al., 2005). The multilevel design using individuals and ecological units is perhaps the most promising method for analyzing suicide data. The analyst can ascertain individual risk factors, especially in the case of longitudinal data, and can also take into account the fact that individual suicide risk may be influenced by the social, economic and other contexts in which persons are located. A major challenge that has to be overcome, especially in the USA, is the paucity of individual-level data on suicides. Although there are mortality data from state and federal sources, they are frequently not available to academic researchers in a manner that lends itself to productive analysis. For example, due to confidentiality concerns, data that are made available to academic researchers (so-called public-use files) lack important variables that could be potentially important risk factors for suicide.

## CONCLUSION

It is apparent that substantial progress has been made in the social sciences, especially in sociology, in suicide research over the past three decades. While acknowledging their debt to Durkheim's 1897 work, sociologists have been bold to point out shortcomings and break new ground in theory construction and development. This trend will likely grow, especially as the discipline becomes less dominated by American scholars. Efforts at interdisciplinary work are commendable as there appears to be increasing recognition that suicide can be explained, not only by social facts, but by psychological, psychiatric and perhaps even economic and political factors. In other words, the phenomenon is complex, and a full explanation is beyond the scope of one discipline. Sociological work has generally lagged behind in terms of suicide prevention. It is expected that, with the greater use of individual-level data and the use of hierarchical modeling approaches, sociologists will focus not only on explaining suicide risk, but also will contribute more toward public policy policies for suicide prevention.

## REFERENCES

Baller, R. D., & Richardson, K. K. (2002). Social integration, imitation, and the geographic patterning of suicide. *American Sociological Review,* 67, 873-888

Breault, K. D. (1986). Suicide in America: a test of Durkheim's theory of religious and family integration, 1933-1980. *American Journal of Sociology*, 92, 628-656.

Breault, K. D., & Kposowa, A. J. (1987). Explaining divorce in the United States: a study of 3,111 counties, 1980. *Journal of Marriage & the Family*, 49, 549-558.

Cutchin, M. P., & Churchill, R. (1999). Scale, context, and causes of suicide in the United States. *Social Science Quarterly*, 80, 97-114.

Durkheim, E. (1897/1951). *Suicide: a study in sociology*. Translated by Spaudlin J. A. & Simpson, G.. New York: Free Press.

Ellison, C. G., Burr, J. A., & McCall, P. L. (1997). Religious homogeneity and metropolitan suicide rates. *Social Forces*, 76, 273-279.

Fossion, P., Servais, L., Rejas, M. C., et al. (2004) Psychosis, migration and social environment: an age-and-gender controlled study. *European Psychiatry*, 19, 338-343.

Ishii, K. (1991). Measuring mutual causation: effects of suicide news on suicides in Japan. *Social Science Research*, 20,188-195.

Jonas, K. (1992). Modeling and suicide: a test of the Werther effect. *British Journal of Social Psychology*, 31, 295-306.

Kposowa, A. J. (2000). Marital status and suicide in the National Longitudinal Mortality Study. *Journal of Epidemiology & Community Health*, 54, 254-261.

Kposowa, A. J., & McElvain J. P. (2006). Gender, place, and method of suicide. *Social Psychiatry & Psychiatric Epidemiology*, 41, 435-443.

Luoma, J. B., & Pearson, J. L. (2003). Suicide and marital status in the United States, 1991-1996: is widowhood a risk factor? *American Journal of Public Health*, 92, 1518-1522.

Norström, T. (1995). The impact of alcohol, divorce, and unemployment on suicide: a multilevel analysis. *Social Forces*, 74, 293-314.

Phillips, D. P. (1974). The influence of suggestion on suicide: substantive and theoretical implications of the Werther Effect. *American Sociological Review*, 39, 340-354.

Pescosolido, B. A. (1990). The social context of religious integration and suicide: pursuing the network explanation. *Sociological Quarterly*, 31, 337-357.

Phillips, D. P. (1982). The impact of fictional television stories on U.S. adult fatalities: new evidence on the effect of the mass media on violence. *American Journal of Sociology*, 87, 1340-1359.

Pope, W., & Danigelis, N. (1981). Sociology's one law. *Social Forces*, 60, 495-516.

Poppel, F. V., & Day, L. H. (1996). A test of Durkheim's theory of suicide without committing the "ecological fallacy." *American Sociological Review*, 61, 500-507.

Robinson, W. S. (1950). Ecological correlations and the behavior of individuals. *American Sociological Review*, 15, 351-357.

Skog, O. (1991). Alcohol and suicide: Durkheim revisited. *Acta Sociologica*, 34, 193-206.

Stack, S. (1990). New micro level data on the impact of divorce on suicide *Journal of Marriage & the Family*, 52, 119-127

Stack, S. (1992). Media and suicide: the great depression. *Suicide & Life-Threatening Behavior*, 22, 255-267.

Stack, S. (1996). The effect of the media on suicide: evidence from Japan. *Suicide & Life-Threatening Behavior*, 26, 132-142.

Stack, S. (2000). Suicide: a 15-year review of the sociological literature Part II: modernization and social integration perspectives. *Suicide & Life-Threatening Behavior*, 30, 163-176.

Stockard, J., & O'Brien, R. M. (2002). Cohort effects on suicide rates: international variations. *American Sociological Review*, 67, 854-872.

Tubergen, V. F, Grotenhuis, M. T., & Ultee, W. (2005). Denomination, religious context, and suicide: Neo-Durkheimian multilevel explanations tested with individual and contextual data. *American Journal of Sociology*, 111, 797-823.

Chapter 11

# SUICIDE AND UNEMPLOYMENT

*Steven Stack*

The effect of unemployment on suicide risk has been studied with a variety of research methodologies including those at both the aggregate and individual levels of analysis. There are many convincing research findings linking unemployment to suicidality. For example, for the period 1900-2000, the suicide rate in the USA peaked in 1932-33, the point at which the unemployment rate reached its highest level in the 20th Century. However, there are investigations that fail to find a link between unemployment rates and suicide rates, especially those that are based on aggregated data (Platt, 1984; Platt & Hawton, 2000). The present review is limited to a survey of investigations of unemployment and completed suicide at the individual level of analysis.

## INDIVIDUAL LEVEL RESEARCH

Research following a cross sectional design compares the incidence of suicide among members of the unemployed to that for employed persons at one point in time. A total of 26 such studies exist. Studies comparing suicide rates in a variety of nations and a variety of periods tend to demonstrate a link between unemployment and suicide. In French society in the 1990's, among men, the suicide rate among unemployed was 74.9 per 100,000 per year, more than double that of employed men (32.3). In Hong Kong the unemployed had a suicide rate nearly three times that of the employed (37.2 vs. 13.2). In Austria the suicide rate of the jobless was nearly four times higher than that of the employed (98.3 vs. 25.0). A recent investigation determined that the suicide rate of the unemployed was double that of the local population in Newcastle upon Tyne (20.5 vs. 10.28). However, there are some exceptions. These include a study of Indianapolis (USA) where the unemployed had a suicide rate significantly less than that of the employed (13.7 vs. 19.2).

Other recent cross-sectional investigations report other measures of risk such as odds ratios. For example, a study based in India determined that the risk of suicide was 6.15 times greater among the unemployed than among the employed (Gururaj, et al., 2004). A study of

Italy during 1977-1987 determined that the relative risk of suicide among unemployed men was 3.2 times that of employed men.

It should be noted that the results of these studies are often difficult to compare rigorously. The definition of unemployment (e.g., labor market surveys, union members only surveys, data based only on those registered for unemployment benefits) varies across studies.

## EXPLANATIONS OF UNEMPLOYMENT AND SUICIDE

### Causal Thesis

Unemployment can directly affect suicide risk of unemployed persons by decreasing the income and general economic welfare of the jobless. However, unemployment also has psychological and social consequences. Psychologically it often reduces self-esteem, increases anxiety and increases a sense of hopelessness and depression. These psychological states increase suicide risk. For example, a cohort study over time determined that unemployment at baseline predicted an enduring high level of hopelessness. Unemployed persons were seven times more apt than their counterparts to be marked by a consistent high level of hopelessness over the study period. Hopelessness is a key predictor of suicide risk. Furthermore, job loss can increase alcohol consumption and marital turmoil which, in turn, can elevate suicide risk.

Unemployment affects physical health. Controlling for covariates, unemployment has been associated with a 73% elevation in the odds of poor health. Unemployment often reduces social ties, especially bonds with former co-workers. An unemployed person may also migrate to another locality to find a job. Migration can increase the risk of suicide by breaking social bonds.

### Selection Bias Thesis

As Platt (1984) correctly cautions, suicidal people may lose or quit their jobs because their psychological problems prevent them from being productive workers. Hence, psychological problems may be the root cause of job loss and, in turn, eventual suicide. Part of the possible association between unemployment and suicide is due to preexisting psychiatric problems of the unemployed. Research based on psychiatric outpatients often finds extraordinarily high rates of unemployment among both eventual suicides and non-suicides. For example, in a study in Philadelphia, 22% of the controls and 49% of the suicides were unemployed at baseline. This level of unemployment matches or exceeds that found in the Great Depression of the 1930

## REVIEW OF LONGITUDINAL INVESTIGATIONS

In order to assess the issues of selection versus causality, research based on longitudinal designs are necessary. With longitudinal research we can determine to what extent psychiatric morbidity is a cause or a consequence of unemployment.

There are 27 research investigations that follow a longitudinal, individual level design. These vary in the characteristics of their methodologies, which may explain some variability in their findings. For example, the sample size varies from 23 to over 9,011 suicides; some control for psychiatric morbidity at baseline and others do not; only a few involve multiple follow-ups from baseline; the interval from baseline to follow-up varies from less than a year to over twenty years; and few measure employment status after baseline.

The 27 studies contain a total of 55 findings. A total of 42 out of 55 (76.4%) of the findings provide evidence that those persons who were unemployed at baseline had a greater chance of having died from suicide than those persons who were employed at baseline. Kposowa (2001) determined that unemployed men at baseline were 2.3 times more apt to have died from suicide at the two-year follow-up than were employed men. Kposowa's findings controlled for a variety of socio-economic covariates of unemployment including age, education and living arrangements, but not for psychiatric morbidity. However, unemployment at baseline did not predict suicide at the five-year follow-up, possibly since many of those unemployed had found new employment by that time.

In order to test the selection hypothesis, we need to focus on those studies that control for psychiatric morbidity level at baseline. These studies tend to support a causal hypothesis in which unemployment increases the suicide risk independently of psychiatric morbidity.

The best designed investigation that controlled for psychiatric disorders at baseline is from Denmark. It consisted of all persons aged 25-60 who completed suicide during 1982-1997 (n=9011) and 180,220 controls. It determined that, without controls for psychiatric morbidity and related factors, persons who had been unemployed in the year preceding death were between 1.69 to 2.38 times more likely to die from suicide than were employed persons (Agerbo, 2005). However, Agerbo found that, after controlling for psychiatric history and numerous socio-economic factors, persons who were unemployed at some point during the last year of life were between 1.31-1.39 times more likely than employed persons to complete suicide (depending on the duration of their joblessness). Hence, while psychiatric morbidity was related to unemployment status at baseline, unemployment had an impact on suicide risk that was independent of psychiatric disorder. This latter impact was, however, relatively small.

A twenty-year prospective study of 6,891 Philadelphia area outpatients controlled for major depressive disorder, bipolar disorder, psychiatric hospitalization, and other contributing factors. Nevertheless, unemployed persons were still 2.56 times more apt to die from suicide than employed persons.

A retrospective study of 73 suicides and matched controls in Hong Kong, controlling for baseline psychiatric morbidity and other predictor variables, determined that patients who were unemployed after release were 12.2 times more apt to complete suicide than were patients who gained employment. However, a cohort study of 185,000 employed and unemployed persons over two years in Taiwan did not support a positive link between unemployment and suicide.

## POLICY IMPLICATIONS

The nations of the world vary considerably over time in the scope and intensity of their economic safety nets for the unemployed. Macro-economic policies have consequences for a host of social problems including suicide. Weyerer and Weidenmann (1995) found that the business cycle predicted swings in German suicide rates from 1881-1919, but not for other periods. They argue that enhanced government-provided assistance for the unemployed may account for the lack of a relationship between the business cycle and suicide trends in Germany from 1949-1989. The relationship between unemployment rates and suicide rates is affected by the amount and duration of economic supports or safety nets for the unemployed.

For example, one study determined that only 39% of unemployed American workers versus 89% of the unemployed German workers received unemployment benefits. Furthermore, American workers could generally collect benefits for only six months whereas Germans could collect benefits for 32 months in stage-one of benefits, and collect indefinitely after 32 months if they qualified for stage-two of the unemployment coverage plan (Gangl, 2004). In nations without national health insurance, it becomes more difficult for the unemployed to seek treatment for any psychiatric or physical morbidity. In the USA, a 1% rise in unemployment was associated with an increase of 1.2 million more people not covered by health insurance. It can be argued that, in nations lacking strong safety nets for the unemployed (e.g., Greece, Italy, Japan, the UK and the USA all rate low for benefit entitlements, OECD 1997), one would be more apt to find consistent and positive associations between unemployment and suicide.

## REFERENCES

Agerbo, E. (2005). Middle life suicide risk, partner's psychiatric illness, spouse and child bereavement by suicide or other means of death: a gender specific study. *Journal of Epidemiology & Community Health,* 59, 407-412.

Dooley, D. (2004). *The social costs of unemployment.* Cambridge, UK: Cambridge University Press.

Dooley, D., Prause, J., & Ham-Rowbottom, K. A. (2000). Underemployment and depression: longitudinal relationships. *Journal of Health & Social Behavior,* 41, 421-436.

Gangl, M. (2004). Welfare state and the scar effects of unemployment: a comparative analysis of the United States and West Germany. *American Journal of Sociology,* 109, 1319-1364.

Gururaj, G., Issac, M. K., Subbakrishna, D. K., et al. (2004). Risk factors for completed suicide: a case control study from Bangalore, India. *Injury Control & Safety Promotion,* 11, 183-191.

Kposowa, A. K. (2001). Unemployment and suicide: a cohort analysis of social factors predicting suicide in the US national longitudinal mortality study. *Psychological Medicine,* 31, 127-138.

Lester, D. (2000). Why people kill themselves: a 2000 summary of research on suicide. 4th Ed. Springfield, IL: Charles C. Thomas.

Organization for Economic Cooperation and Development. (1997). *Making work pay: taxation, benefits, employment and unemployment.* Paris, France: OECD.

Platt, S. (1984). Unemployment and suicidal behavior: a review of the literature. *Social Science & Medicine*, 19, 93-115.

Platt, S., & Hawton, K. (2000). Suicidal behavior and the labour market. In K. Hawton & K. van Herrington (Eds.) *The international handbook of suicide and attempted suicide,* pp. 309-384. New York: John Wiley.

Stack, S. (2000a). Work and the economy. In R. Maris, A. Berman, & M. Silverman, (Eds.) *Comprehensive textbook of suicidology,* pp. 193-221. New York: Guilford.

Stack, S. (2000b) Suicide: a fifteen-year review of the sociological literature. Part I: Cultural and economic factors. *Suicide & Life-Threatening Behavior*, 30, 145-162.

Tsai, S. L, Lan, C. F., Lee, C. H., et al. (2004). Involuntary unemployment and mortality in Taiwan. *Journal of the Formosa Medical Association*, 103, 900-907.

Weyerer, S., & Wiedenmann, A. (1995). Economic factors and the rates of suicide in Germany between 1881 and 1989. *Psychological Reports*, 76, 1331-1341.

Chapter 12

# SUICIDE AND ECONOMIC STATUS

## *Augustine J. Kposowa*

This chapter reports research to investigate the association between economic status and suicide. One of the earliest proponents of a connection between economic status and suicide was Emile Durkheim who in 1897 argued that being in the labor force is a form of economic integration which reduces suicide risk. While employment is integral to economic integration, Durkheim (1897/1951, p. 250) also emphasized the negative consequences of social stratification or class position in society because "the economic ideal assigned each class of citizens is itself confined to certain limits within which … desires have free range." He suggested a positive relationship between social class and suicide since higher class location leads to unlimited aspirations on the part of individuals. These aspirations could prove suicidogenic if they are not fulfilled, which might occur during economic disasters that bring about sudden change in fortunes or reclassification. Durkheim (1897/1951, p. 254) argued that poverty reduces suicide risk because it is a restraint. This implies that the less one has, say in material comfort, the lower one's aspirations and ambitions. On the other hand, wealth increases suicide risk because it "deceives us into believing that we depend on ourselves only." According to him, wealth reduces any resistance that its holders encounter from daily living, thereby leading them to believe that success is unlimited. Accordingly, wealthier or higher class individuals are less capable of withstanding any limitations placed upon them by social or economic circumstances, and hence their higher propensity to suicide.

## PAST RESEARCH

The relationship between economic status and suicide remains a subject of research interest across various disciplines in many countries. Contrary to Durkheim's arguments about the dangers of wealth and higher social class location, research findings have consistently shown a negative association between economic status and suicide (Cubin, LeClere & Smith, 2000; Kposowa, 2001; Page, et al., 2006; Agerbo, Sterne & Gunnell, 2006; Strand & Kunst, 2006). In an Australian study, Page, et al. (2006) reported significantly higher suicide rates in lower compared to higher socioeconomic status areas. Among males, for example, in 1999-2003, the suicide rate ratio (low versus high SES) was 1.44 (CI=1.38-1.49). The corresponding rate ratio for females was 1.33 (CI=1.27-1.40). A recent Danish study based on 9,011 suicides and 180,220 matched controls (Agerbo, Sterne & Gunnell, 2006) found that the suicide risk increased as income levels declined. Similarly, unemployed persons along with individuals not in the labor force experienced a higher risk of suicide than the employed.

In a cross-national study based on ten countries (Norway, Finland, England and Wales, Denmark, Belgium and Switzerland), and three cities (Turin, Barcelona and Madrid), Lorant, et al. (2005) found that, for all male populations, the suicide rate was significantly higher in the group with lower educational attainment. They observed, however, that lower education provided immunity from suicide among women in Norway, Denmark and Switzerland. A British study utilizing 103 electoral wards in Oxfordshire County found that areas with high levels of socio-economic deprivation had high suicide rates, which were especially marked among middle-aged and younger males (Hawton, et al., 2001). Despite the remarkable consistency in findings showing an inverse association between economic status and suicide risk, there are some exceptions. Stack (1996) found that some high status occupations have high suicide rates. Using American data, he reported that dentists had suicide risks that were over six times greater than those in the rest of the working age population. Employing Australian data, Hassan (1995) observed that, for men, those in blue collar occupations tend to have higher suicide rates than those in white collar occupations. The pattern was reversed for women for whom white-collar professions experienced elevated suicide rates.

## METHODS

To examine the impact of economic status on suicide, the U.S. National Longitudinal Mortality Study (1979-1989) was used (National Heart, Lung, Blood Institute 1995). The NLMS is a prospective study of mortality among the non-institutionalized population of the United States. The public use data-file employed in the present study consisted of a cohort of five national samples derived from the Current Population Surveys conducted in March 1979, April, August, and December 1980, and March 1981. The mortality experiences of the cohort members were studied until 1989. Due to space constraints, the NLMS is not described here, but a more detailed description of the data has been presented elsewhere (Kposowa, 2001; Rogot, et al., 1992).

### Variables and Measures

The dependent variable was the risk of suicide. Deaths resulting from suicide were identified using cause of death codes E950-E959 from the *International Classification of Diseases* (*Ninth Revision*). In estimating the risk of suicide, all persons surviving beyond the 9-year follow-up and those dying during the follow-up from causes other than suicide were treated as right-censored observations. Analysis was based on 538,319 persons 10 years of age and above at the beginning of the study, of whom 582 committed suicide during the 9-year follow-up period.

There were two indicators of economic status: education and annual family income. *Education* was measured using five dummy variables, 0-8 years of schooling, 9-11 years, 12 years of schooling (high school graduates), 13-15 years of schooling, and persons with missing information. Individuals with 16 or more years of schooling constituted the reference group. *Annual family income* (adjusted for inflation to 1980 dollars) was indexed by five dummy variables, less than $5,000, $5,000-$9,999, $10,000-$19,999, $20,000-$24,999, and unknown income. Those with family incomes of $25,000 or more were the reference group.

The control variables were sex (men coded 1), age, marital status and race/ethnicity. Marital status was measured by dividing the sample into persons not married (coded 1) with the married as the reference group. *Race/ethnicity* was defined in terms of one dummy variable for non-Hispanic Whites, with non-whites as the reference category.

## Statistical Modeling

Cox's proportional hazards model was applied to the NLMS data to assess the impact of economic status on suicide while controlling for confounders including age, sex, marital status and race/ethnicity. The proportionality of the hazards was ascertained by inspecting relevant plots, which showed the hazards to form a parallel step function.

## Results

Preliminary analysis revealed that economic status had no significant effect on suicide among women. Therefore, results of the multivariate proportional hazards regression analysis shown in Table 12-1 are for men only. As may be seen, the lower the educational attainment, the higher the suicide risks. Men with 8 or less years of schooling were 67% more likely to commit suicide than their counterparts with over 15 years of schooling. Men with 9-11 years of education were over 1.5 times as likely to commit suicide as those with 16 or more years of education. High school graduates experienced a suicide risk that was over 52% higher than their counterparts with 16 or more years of schooling. Finally, men with 13-15 years of education were 53% more likely to kill themselves as those with 16 years or more of schooling.

Furthermore, men at the lowest income levels experienced much higher suicide risks than those in the highest income bracket. For instance, men with household incomes below $5,000 were 55% more likely to commit suicide than men in households making $25,000 or more. Similarly, men with household incomes $5,000-$9,999 were 1.6 times (or 60%) as likely to commit suicide as their counterparts from households making $25,000 or more.

**Table 12-1. Proportional Hazards Regression Results of the Effect of Economic Status on Suicide Risk: The U.S. National Longitudinal Mortality Study (N=257,323)**

| Covariate | β | RR | 95% CI |
|---|---|---|---|
| **Education** | | | |
| 16+ years | | 1.000 | Reference |
| 0-8 years | 0.513** | 1.671 | 1.155-2.417 |
| 9-11 years | 0.419* | 1.522 | 1.060-2.183 |
| 12 years | 0.423** | 1.527 | 1.098-2.124 |
| 13-15 years | 0.426* | 1.532 | 1.059-2.216 |
| Unknown/missing | -0.427 | 0.653 | 0.334-1.272 |
| **Annual Household Income** | | | |
| $25,000 + | | 1.000 | Reference |
| < $5,000 | 0.440** | 1.553 | 1.078-2.237 |
| $5,000-$9,999 | 0.472** | 1.604 | 1.195-2.152 |
| $10,000-$19,999 | -0.016 | 0.984 | 0.757-1.279 |
| $20,000-$24,999 | 0.249 | 1.283 | 0.953-1.726 |
| Unknown/missing | -0.242 | 0.785 | 0.480-1.282 |
| **Marital Status** | | | |
| Married | | 1.000 | Reference |
| Not Married | 0.479** | 1.614 | 1.309-1.991 |
| **Race/Ethnicity** | | | |
| Not White | | 1.000 | Reference |
| White | 0.590** | 1.804 | 1.348-2.414 |
| **Age** | 0.012** | 1.012 | 1.007-1.018 |
| -2 Log Likelihood | 11,240.87 | | |
| Likelihood Ratio Statistic | 126.21 | | |
| Df | 13 | | |
| Number of Suicides | 458 | | |
| Population at Risk | 257,323 | | |

*Significant at p < .05.
**Significant at p < .01.

# DISCUSSION

Results from the U.S. National Longitudinal Mortality Study did not confirm Durkheim's proposition that the higher the economic status the higher the suicide risk. Indicators of economic status (education and income) were inversely associated with suicide. These findings provide evidence to suggest that stressors or strains may be at work. Low education may elevate suicide risk because it reduces opportunities for employment, thereby diminishing chances for self-fulfillment. Low income produces financial strain which could influence suicide indirectly through factors such as alcohol consumption, depression or other mental distress. Stress stemming from low income could also indirectly promote suicide because of its possible connection with suicidogenic conditions, such as marital instability, drug use, poor physical health and job dissatisfaction. As Stack (2000) observes, groups faced with greater terror in life and, therefore, elevated suicide rates are those under economic stress, including the poor, the unemployed and the less educated.

The findings from this study are generally consistent with others that have found an inverse relationship between economic status and suicide. The consistency of results across different disciplines and countries provides a rare opportunity for suicide prevention policies. Since low education and low income are risk factors for suicide, a public policy aimed at suicide prevention would not only encourage education, but also provide the means by which the less fortunate might pay for tuition. A related policy directive is to encourage or mandate that employers provide living wages. A society that fails or refuses to uplift all of its citizens through education, decent job creation and living incomes will likely abandon a substantial proportion of its members to suicide.

## REFERENCES

Agerbo, E., Sterne, J. A. C., & Gunnell, D. J. (2006). Combining individual and ecological data to determine compositional and contextual socio-economic risk factors for suicide. *Social Science & Medicine*, 64, 451-461.

Cubbin, C., LeClere, F. B., & Smith, G. S. (2000). Socioeconomic status and the occurrence of fatal and nonfatal injury in the United States. *American Journal of Public Health*, 90, 70-77.

Durkheim, E. (1897/1951). *Suicide: a study in sociology*. Translated by Spaudlin J. A. & Simpson, G. New York: Free Press.

Hassan, R. (1995). *Suicide explained*. Melbourne, Australia: Melbourne University Press.

Hawton, K., Harriss, L, Hodder, K., et al. (2001). The influence of the economic and social environment on deliberate self-harm and suicide: an ecological and person-based study. *Psychological Medicine*, 31, 827-836.

Kposowa, A.J. (2001). Unemployment and suicide: a cohort analysis of social factors predicting suicide in the US National Longitudinal Mortality Study. *Psychological Medicine*, 31, 127-138.

Lorant, V., Kunst, A.E., Huisman, M., et al. (2005). Socio-economic inequalities in suicide: a European comparative study. *British Journal of Psychiatry*, 187, 49-54.

National Heart, Lung, and Blood Institute. (1995). *National Longitudinal Mortality Study, 1979-1989 (Machine Readable Public Use Data Disk)*. Bethesda, MD: National Institutes of Health.

Page, A., Morrell, S., Taylor, R., et al. (2006) Divergent trends in suicide by socio-economic status in Australia. *Social Psychiatry & Psychiatric Epidemiology*, 41, 911-917.

Rogot, E., Sorlie, P. D., Johnson, N. J., et al. (1992). *A mortality study of 1.3 million persons by demographic, social, and economic factors: 1979-1985 follow-up*. Washington, D.C.: National Institutes of Health.

Stack, S. (1996). Suicide risk among dentists. *Deviant Behavior*, 1, 107-117.

Stack, S. (2000). Suicide: a 15-year review of the sociological literature. Part I: cultural and economic factors. *Suicide & Life-Threatening Behavior*, 30, 145-162.

In: Suicide from a Global Perspective: Psychosocial Approaches   ISBN 978-1-61470-965-7
Editors: A. Shrivastava, M. Kembrell et al. pp. 93-99   © 2012 Nova Science Publishers, Inc.

*Chapter 13*

# SUICIDE IN RURAL AND URBAN COMMUNITIES

## *Ping Qin*

Suicide rates exhibit great variation in many aspects, with place of residence being one of the well-known sources for this variation. Rural-urban differences in suicide rates have been noticed for a long time, although the pattern of the differences may vary from one community to another. In many countries, suicide rates are generally higher in urban areas than in rural areas, but there are also countries where there is a higher suicide rate in rural areas (World Health Organization, 1989). At the same time, the rural-urban disparity of suicide displays significant differences by sex and age.

Studies from a number of Western countries, both at the aggregate and individual levels, have consistently demonstrated that people living in large urban communities have an increased risk for suicide when compared with those living in rural areas (Heikkinen, et al., 1994; Johansson, et al., 1997; Mortensen, et al., 2000). Recent Danish studies that used data from Danish national population registers indicate that risk of suicide in the general population increased progressively with increasing degree of urbanicity of living place (Qin, 2005; Qin, et al., 2003; Qin, et al., 2000). The highest risk ratio of suicide was 1.58 (95% CI: 1.51-1.65) for people living in the capital compared with those living in the rural areas (Qin, 2005). Studies from Sweden (Johansson, et al., 1997) and Italy (Micciolo, et al., 1991) have also shown higher suicide rates for people living in urban areas relative to people living in rural communities.

At the same time, a reversed direction of rural-urban differences in the suicide rate is seen in some other countries. For instance, in China, both men and women living in rural communities have a more than three-fold higher suicide rate than their urban counterparts (Phillips, et al., 2002; Qin & Mortensen, 2001), with such rural versus urban differences being most noticeable in elderly people (Phillips, et al., 2002). In the USA, data from the Centres for Disease Control (2006) indicates that, in every region in the United States and for the country as a whole, the rate of suicide is higher in non-metropolitan areas compared to metropolitan areas. Other countries, such as Greece, have also reported rural suicide rates twice as high as urban rates (Zacharakis, et al., 1998).

Moreover, in some countries or regions, the urban-rural disparity differs for men and women. For instance, in Australia, suicide rates for males, but not for females, at all ages are significantly higher in rural areas compared to urban areas, with the rate for 15-24 years old being about 1.4 times higher among rural males compared to urban males (Taylor, et al., 2005). In the UK, female suicide rates are significantly higher in densely populated districts while male suicide rates are highest in the most rural areas (Saunderson, et al., 1998). Similar results of higher male suicide rates in rural rather than urban areas is also noted in a study using local data in Finland (Pesonen, et al., 2001).

However, the observed urban-rural differences in the suicide rate seem to be modified by factors such as socioeconomic status, access to health care and social support, a result of their inequality in distribution between urban and rural communities. The study using data from Danish longitudinal population registers (Qin, 2005) demonstrated that, on an individual level, the excess risk of suicide associated with living in more urbanized areas was largely eliminated when adjusted for marital status, income and ethnicity. It was even reversed when further adjusted for psychiatric status. Stratified analyses by age show that, after taking the effects of socioeconomic and psychiatric factors into account, living in urban areas raised the suicide risk in women across all age groups, with a particularly strong effect for women aged 25-34 and above 65 years of age. However, it reduced the risk for suicide in men across all age groups except for those 75 years and older while the protective effect seemed more pronounced for young men.

Similarly, but on a community level, a study from Australia (Taylor, et al., 2005) found that the higher male suicide rate in rural areas in Australia, compared to urban areas, was rendered non-significant after adjustment for migrant and area socioeconomic status. Adjusting for mental disorder prevalence, in addition to migrant and socioeconomic status, reduced the excess suicide risk in rural areas. The excess risk was reduced even further with the addition of mental health service utilization.

These findings suggest that socioeconomic, and probably cultural circumstances, contribute, to a large degree, to the urban-rural differences in suicide rates. The disparities in urban-rural suicide can be largely explained by the urban-rural disparities of factors such as marital status, ethnic composition, income and, in particular, by psychiatric status and relevant services. This suggests that these factors, rather than place of residence per se, are likely to be more fundamental risk factors for suicide.

## CHANGES IN RURAL-URBAN DIFFERENCES IN THE SUICIDE RATE

Suicide rates fluctuate over time. However, the changes in rural and urban communities are not always consistent with each other. The growing pace of urbanization or social transition has led to research on corresponding changes in suicide rates associated with place of residence. For instance, studies from Australia (Dudley, et al., 1992), the UK (Middleton, et al., 2003), the USA (Singh, and Siahpush, 2002), Norway (Mehlum, et al., 1999), Finland (Pesonen, et al., 2001) and Denmark (Qin, 2005) have demonstrated significant changes in the urban-rural disparity of suicide rates in contemporary society. A Danish study that used individual data to address the development of suicide risk in relation to urbanicity from 1981 to 1997 (Qin, 2005) indicated that the suicide risk associated with urbanicity during the study period was rather constant in women, but it changed significantly in men, with a declining trend of the urban-rural disparities. After adjusting for the effect of personal socioeconomic and psychiatric status, the reduced risk for suicide among men living in urbanized areas became more prominent over time, especially for the effect related to living in the capital. The study from the USA (Singh & Siahpush, 2002), using data at a community level, showed that the rural-urban gradient of the suicide rate increased consistently, suggesting widening rural-urban differentials in male suicides over time during the period of 1970 through 1997 when controlling for geographic variation in divorce rate and ethnic composition. At the same time, the observed rural-urban differential for women diminished over time. Comparable results have been noted in reports using population data from Norway (Mehlum, et al., 1999), Australia (Dudley, et al., 1992) and the UK (Middleton, et al., 2003) that highlight an increase of rural suicide rates relative to the rates in urbanized communities.

## CONTRIBUTING FACTORS TO URBAN-RURAL DIFFERENCES

Relative to numerous studies investigating the rural-urban differences in suicide rates, less research has examined the mechanisms underpinning these variations. According to the literature, contributing factors may comprise the following three groups (Judd, et al., 2006; Macintyre, et al., 2002): characteristics of individual residents in particular places (compositional effects), opportunity structures and characteristics in the local physical and social environment (contextual effects), and sociocultural and historical features of communities (collective effects).

Compositional differences of residents between residential areas are important contributors to rural-urban disparities of suicide rates. Composition may vary across residents in various communities with regard to the prevalence of some mental disorders, physical illnesses and socioeconomic status, as well as preceding life situations such as exposure to risk behaviors and psychological stressors.

It has been postulated that cities have a deleterious effect on people's health due to the increased density and diversity of populations in cities. Psychological autopsy studies have shown that urban suicides more frequently had various disorders and psychiatric comorbidity and more often had experienced stressful life events such as separation, whereas rural suicides more often had physical problems (Isometsa, et al., 1997). A number of population studies, although not all, have even demonstrated a dose-response relationship between level of urbanicity and prevalence of, for example, schizophrenia (McGrath, et al., 2004; Mortensen, et al., 1999), psychotic disorders (Sundquist, et al., 2004; van Os, et al., 2001), depression (Sundquist, et al., 2004; Wang, 2004) as well as the incidence of admissions to psychiatric hospitals (Dekker, et al., 1997). Risky behaviors (e.g., alcohol and drug abuse) (James, et al., 2002; Paykel, et al., 2000) and stressors (e.g., neighborhood relationships and job competition) (Marsella, 1998) are encountered more frequently and more severely by residents in more urbanized areas. Meanwhile, people with lower socioeconomic status and minorities are often over-represented in urban areas (Denmarks Statistik, 1997), although internal migration may have resulted in a selection of more healthy and competent people moving to cities for education and jobs. After the adjustment for inequalities in personal socioeconomic and psychiatric status, as demonstrated in studies, for example, from Denmark (Qin, 2005), it is found that these compositional factors largely eliminated the excess risk for suicide associated with urban living. At the same time, the findings regarding significant sex and age differences in rural-urban disparities (Qin, 2005) suggest that men, especially young men, may benefit more from the advantages of living in big cities, whereas women may be more vulnerable in a competitive environment than their male counterparts.

Contextual and collective effects are defined as community level variables that are associated with individual suicide but are independent of association at the individual level (composition). Strong evidence has suggested that geographic variation in access to lethal methods for suicide is of great importance for the observed rural-urban disparities of suicide, especially for the high suicide rate in the rural communities. Access to firearms is much more common in rural than in urban areas, which is an important contributing factor to the very high suicide rate among farmers and ranchers as reported from England and Wales (Kelly, et al., 1995), Australia (Judd, et al., 2006), and the USA (Stallones, 1990). At the same time, the common use of highly toxic poisons, such as pesticides in the countryside, may be, to a large extent, responsible for the high suicide in some rural communities. A multicenter study including sites in eight low and middle income countries (Fleischmann, et al., 2005) showed that self-poisoning by pesticides played a particularly important role in Yuncheng, China (71.6% females, 61.5% males), in Colombo, Sri Lanka (43.2% males, 19.6% females), and in Chennai, India (33.8% males, 23.8% females), and that more than 65% of suicide attempts resulted in danger to life in the patients in Yuncheng and in Chennai. Therefore, it is postulated that the high suicide rate, for instance, in rural China and Sri Lanka, is not due to higher levels of mental illness or rates of self-harm, but to a higher lethality of self-harm acts (Eddleston & Gunnell, 2006). The strong lethality of methods used for suicide, as well as the lack of well trained medical personnel who can manage pesticide poisoning in the countryside, result in high rates of mortality among people who impulsively ingest pesticides but who do not intend to die. This situation leads to an overall increase in the rate of completed suicides in rural areas and, since deliberate self-harm is much more common in women than in men, a relative increase in the rates of completed suicide among women, particularly among young rural women (Phillips, et al., 2002; Qin & Mortensen, 2001).

Service utilization, which reflects service availability and accessibility, is another important contextual factor to consider. The accessibility to psychiatric services differs greatly from urban to rural areas, especially in developing countries (Quine, et al., 2003). The lack of access to mental health services and the shortages of specialized mental health practitioners in rural areas may result in substantially more untreated patients with psychiatric problems in rural than urban regions.

Other contextual or collective explanations of the rural-urban gradient of suicide include socioeconomic disadvantages, job opportunities, social cohesion and isolation, concern about stigma and discrimination, and religious affiliation. For example, a few studies have consistently demonstrated that the suicide rate was higher in areas of socioeconomic disadvantage, with the excess rate being even greater in males than in females and greatest among those aged 30-54 years (Cantor, et al., 1995; Taylor, et al., 2005). A USA study indicated that stigma in rural communities is a much stronger deterrent to seeking mental health care as compared to urban areas (Rost, et al., 1998).

Taken together, it would be difficult to disentangle the complexity of explanations as to whether the rural-urban suicide differences are due to the composition of resident population or to the features of region. It is likely that compositional, contextual and collective effects interact with one another. Individuals with personal risk factors may then be even more vulnerable to suicide if they are living in a community with more disadvantages.

It is not easy to fully capture reasons for rural-urban differences in suicide risk related to temporal trends. During the past few decades, both rural and urban areas have experienced profound social and demographic changes. However, these changes may have affected rural areas much more adversely than urban areas. For instance, divorce rates, household crowding, female participation in the labor force and income inequality have changed more in the most rural areas than in the most urban areas. In addition, the general improvement in psychiatric services, reduction in the availability of lethal compounds often used for suicide, as well as new effective treatment of intoxications, may have not been equally propagated across communities. At the same time, the process of urbanization or modernization may have resulted in a decline in rural areas, loss of social infrastructure and reduction of social cohesion and community participation. It may have also led to migration-selection such that persons moving away from rural areas are more likely to be better educated and have greater job prospects, while persons moving into or staying in rural areas are more often from low-income groups. Other factors such as changes in socioeconomic conditions and life-style may also play a role in the secular changes of rural-urban suicide disparities in contemporary society.

## CLINICAL CONSIDERATIONS

To help reduce suicide rates in both rural and urban communities and eliminate the rural–urban gradient, public health researchers and policy-makers need to have a broad knowledge of the compositional, contextual and collective factors contributing to the disparities, as well as closely monitoring residential and temporal trends in these measures. Social and public policies that emphasize investment in social integration or social capital through job creation, provision of gainful employment and social services, and improved social support and networks through community organization and involvement, especially for the rural young and elderly, may lower suicide rates. Restricting access to lethal methods, such as pesticides and firearms, may also reduce suicide rates to a certain extent, particularly the excess rate in rural areas. Such restrictions should be implemented by integrating the efforts of different sectors, such as health, agriculture, education and justice (Fleischmann, et al., 2005). Improving the availability and accessibility of mental health services and psychological consultation is essential to reducing suicide in remote areas. Efforts targeting the specific needs of people in different sex and age groups may also be of great help to those at-risk individuals in the community.

## REFERENCES

Centers for Disease Control. (2006). *Suicide fact sheet*. (www.cdc.gov/ncipc/factsheets/suifacts.htm)

Cantor, C. H., Slater, P. J., & Najman, J. M. (1995). Socioeconomic indices and suicide rate in Queensland. *Australian Journal of Public Health*, 19, 417-420.

Dekker, J., Peen, J., Gardien, R., et al. (1997). Urbanisation and psychiatric admission rates in The Netherlands. *International Journal of Social Psychiatry*, 43, 235-246.

Denmarks Statistik. (1997). Statistisk årbog [Statistical yearbook].

Dudley, M., Waters, B., Kelk, N., et al. (1992). Youth suicide in New South Wales: urban-rural trends. *Medical Journal of Australia,* 156, 83-88.

Eddleston, M., & Gunnell, D. (2006). Why suicide rates are high in China. *Science,* 311, 1711-1713.

Fleischmann, A., Bertolote, J. M., De Leo, D., et al. (2005). Characteristics of attempted suicides seen in emergency-care settings of general hospitals in eight low- and middle-income countries. *Psychological Medicine,* 35, 1467-1474.

Heikkinen, M., Aro, H., & Lonnqvist, J. (1994). Recent life events, social support and suicide. *Acta Psychiatrica Scandinavica, Supplementum,* 377, 65-72.

Isometsa, E., Heikkinen, M., Henriksson, M., et al. (1997). Differences between urban and rural suicides. *Acta Psychiatrica Scandinavica,* 95, 297-305.

James, K. E., Wagner, F. A., & Anthony, J. C. (2002). Regional variation in drug purchase opportunity among youths in the United States, 1996-1997. *Journal of Urban Health,* 79, 104-112.

Johansson, L. M., Sundquist, J., Johansson, S. E., et al. (1997). Ethnicity, social factors, illness and suicide: a follow-up study of a random sample of the Swedish population. *Acta Psychiatrica Scandinavica,* 95, 125-131.

Judd, F., Cooper, A. M., Fraser, C., et al. (2006). Rural suicide: people or place effects? *Australian & New Zealand Journal of Psychiatry,* 40, 208-216.

Judd, F., Jackson, H., Fraser, C., et al. (2006). Understanding suicide in Australian farmers. *Social Psychiatry & Psychiatric Epidemiology,* 41, 1-10.

Kelly, S., Charlton, J., & Jenkins, R. (1995). Suicide deaths in England and Wales, 1982-92: the contribution of occupation and geography. *Popular Trends,* 16-25.

Macintyre, S., Ellaway, A., & Cummins, S. (2002). Place effects on health: how can we conceptualise, operationalise and measure them? *Social Science & Medicine,* 55, 125-139.

Marsella, A. J. (1998). Urbanization, mental health, and social deviancy: a review of issues and research. *American Psychologist,* 53, 624-634.

McGrath, J., Saha, S., Welham, J., et al. (2004). A systematic review of the incidence of schizophrenia: the distribution of rates and the influence of sex, urbanicity, migrant status and methodology. *BMC Medicine,* 2, 13.

Mehlum L., Hytten K., & Gjertsen F. (1999). Epidemiological trends of youth suicide in Norway. *Archives of Suicide Research,* 5, 193-205.

Micciolo, R., Williams, P., Zimmermann-Tansella, C., et al. (1991). Geographical and urban-rural variation in the seasonality of suicide: some further evidence. *Journal of Affective Disorders,* 21, 39-43.

Middleton, N., Gunnell, D., Frankel, S., et al. (2003). Urban-rural differences in suicide trends in young adults: England and Wales, 1981-1998. *Social Science & Medicine,* 57, 1183-1194.

Mortensen, P. B., Agerbo, E., Erikson, T., et al. (2000). Psychiatric illness and risk factors for suicide in Denmark. *Lancet,* 355, 9-12.

Mortensen, P. B., Pedersen, C. B., Westergaard, T., et al. (1999). Effects of family history and place and season of birth on the risk of schizophrenia. *New England Journal of Medicine,* 340, 603-608.

Paykel, E. S., Abbott, R., Jenkins, R., et al. (2000). Urban-rural mental health differences in Great Britain: findings from the national morbidity survey. *Psychological Medicine*, 30, 269-280.

Pesonen, T. M., Hintikka, J., Karkola, K. O., et al. (2001). Male suicide mortality in eastern Finland--urban-rural changes during a 10-year period between 1988 and 1997. *Scandinavian Journal of Public Health*, 29, 189-193.

Phillips, M. R., Li, X., & Zhang, Y. (2002). Suicide rates in China, 1995-99. *Lancet*, 359, 835-840.

Qin, P. (2005). Suicide risk in relation to level of urbanicity--a population-based linkage study. *International Journal of Epidemiology*, 34, 846-852.

Qin, P., Agerbo, E., & Mortensen, P. B. (2003). Suicide risk in relation to socioeconomic, demographic, psychiatric, and familial factors: a national register-based study of all suicides in Denmark, 1981-1997. *American Journal of Psychiatry*, 160, 765-772.

Qin, P., & Mortensen, P. B. (2001). Specific characteristics of suicide in China. *Acta Psychiatrica Scandinavica*, 103, 117-121.

Qin, P., Mortensen, P. B., Agerbo, E., et al. (2000). Gender differences in risk factors for suicide in Denmark. *British Journal of Psychiatry*, 177, 546-550.

Quine, S., Bernard, D., Booth, M., et al. (2003). Health and access issues among Australian adolescents: a rural-urban comparison. *Rural & Remote Health*, 3, 245.

Rost, K., Zhang, M., Fortney, J., et al. (1998). Rural-urban differences in depression treatment and suicidality. *Medical Care*, 36, 1098-1107.

Saunderson, T., Haynes, R., & Langford, I. H. (1998). Urban-rural variations in suicides and undetermined deaths in England and Wales. *Journal of Public Health Medicine*, 20, 261-267.

Singh, G. K. and Siahpush, M. (2002). Increasing rural-urban gradients in US suicide mortality, 1970-1997. *American Journal of Public Health*, 92, 1161-1167.

Stallones, L. (1990). Suicide mortality among Kentucky farmers, 1979-1985. *Suicide & Life-Threatening Behavior*, 20, 156-163.

Sundquist, K., Frank, G., and Sundquist, J. (2004). Urbanisation and incidence of psychosis and depression: follow-up study of 4.4 million women and men in Sweden. *British Journal of Psychiatry*, 184, 293-298.

Taylor, R., Page, A., Morrell, S., et al. (2005). Social and psychiatric influences on urban-rural differentials in Australian suicide. *Suicide & Life-Threatening Behavior*, 35, 277-290.

van Os, J., Hanssen, M., Bijl, R. V., et al. (2001). Prevalence of psychotic disorder and community level of psychotic symptoms: an urban-rural comparison. *Archives of General Psychiatry*, 58, 663-668.

Wang, J. L. (2004). Rural-urban differences in the prevalence of major depression and associated impairment. *Social Psychiatry & Psychiatric Epidemiology*, 39, 19-25.

World Health Organization (1989). *World health statistics annual*. Geneva, Switzerland: WHO.

Zacharakis, C. A., Madianos, M. G., Papadimitriou, G. N., et al. (1998). Suicide in Greece 1980-1995: patterns and social factors. *Social Psychiatry & Psychiatric Epidemiology*, 33, 471-476.

Chapter 14

# SUICIDE, ENVIRONMENT AND ECOLOGY

### Mark S. Kaplan and Stacey A. Sobell

> The victim's acts which at first seem to express only his personal temperament are really the supplement and prolongation of a social condition which they express externally.
> 
> Émile Durkheim, *Suicide: A Study in Sociology* (1897/1951, p. 299)

Suicide is an important cause of death worldwide. According to the World Health Organization (WHO, 2002a), nearly one million deaths are attributed to suicide each year. The real number is thought to be higher because of misclassification and under-reporting. Suicide is the thirteenth leading cause of mortality and accounts for approximately 1.6% of all deaths (WHO, 2002a; Desjarlais, et al., 1995). Global suicide rates have risen steadily for men since 1950, whereas the rates for women have remained much more stable (WHO, 2002b). The burden of suicide includes national economic costs (e.g., lost productivity), as well as the trauma experienced by survivors whose lives are profoundly affected emotionally, socially and economically (WHO, 2002a).

There are many theories concerning the underlying causes of suicide. Two dominant perspectives are discussed here: the biomedical (the primary underlying orientation in contemporary suicidology) and the socioecological (derived from the emerging population-health perspective). Writing in another context, the medical anthropologists Arthur Kleinman and Joan Kleinman (1997) argued that opposing views dominate studies of health and mental health as well as their social sources and consequences. In contrast, the biomedical perspective, focused on individual level influences on health, increasingly reduces complex etiological factors into objective biological structures that underlie bodily processes (e.g., biological psychiatry). In comparison, the sociopolitical orientation holds that diseases are caused by major social changes and require similar societal transformations for their prevention. Kleinman and Kleinman observed that the immense political and economic dislocations of recent times (e.g., the effects of globalization) and their powerful impact on local cultural traditions have created a pandemic of behavioral, social and mental health problems involving rising rates of alcohol and drug abuse and related self-inflicted violence in Western and non-Western societies alike.

The social realism just discussed, embodying a wide range of social environmental influences, can be traced back to the pioneering work of the French sociologist Émile Durkheim. Although Durkheim's sociological perspective has been subjected to much criticism in the contemporary literature on suicidology, his main thesis remains remarkably important for understanding the social anatomy of suicide. In his monumental work, *Suicide: A Study in Sociology*, Durkheim (1897/1951) delineated four types of suicide: egoistic, altruistic, anomic, and fatalistic. He organized his typology around two independent explanatory variables: social integration and social regulation. Social integration referred to the degree to which individuals in the society were bound by social ties and relationships, while social regulation referred to the degree to which individuals had their desires and emotions controlled by the social values of the society (Lester, 1994). Furthermore, Durkheim examined integration in three spheres of society: religious, domestic, and political. In each case, he attributed lower suicide rates to higher levels of societal integration. Durkheim also held that the etiology, nature and incidence of suicide reflect the quality, meaning and value of life, as produced by the organization and conditions of society and as perceived and experienced in the private lives of individuals (Moller, 1996). In the following sections we review research that has explicitly related suicidal behavior to a range of social and environmental factors. Many of the studies reflect the growing interest in the social determinants of suicide and underscore the current relevance of Durkheim's social research on suicide. The most prevalent themes to emerge in our review are the effects of rapid social change and economic instability on suicide rates.

## SOCIETIES IN TRANSITION: THE EFFECTS OF SOCIAL AND CULTURAL CHANGE ON SUICIDE MORTALITY

The forces of globalization have reached most corners of the world, shifting social norms and changing the conditions and status of many populations. The resulting societal changes experienced by members of these populations can have significant impacts on social integration and quality of life, leading to differential rates of suicide.

In the past two decades, Europe has undergone rapid social change, in addition to increases and decreases in suicide mortality. Some of the highest suicide rates in the world are now found in Eastern Europe, in a group of countries that share similar historical and sociocultural traits (Bertolote & Fleischmann, 2002; WHO, 2002a). Makinen (2000) found evidence of a relationship between suicide and social processes in 16 of 28 former Eastern Bloc countries from 1984 to 1994. Evidence from numerous studies show that in the past thirty years, as a result of the social instability that occurred following the breakup of the former Soviet Union, many countries in Eastern Europe, including Latvia, Lithuania, Poland, Hungary, Croatia and the Ukraine, have experienced pronounced fluctuations in suicide rates that correlate with periods of societal transition and changing political and economic conditions (Udrasa & Logins, 2004; Gailiene, 2004; Jarosz, 1999; Zonda, et al., 2005; Jakovljevic, et al., 2004; Mokhovikov & Donets, 1996). Rapid social transformation may affect some population subgroups more than others. Varnik, et al. (2005) suggested that, after the dissolution of the Soviet Union, the dramatic rise in suicide rates among members of the Russian minority in Estonia reflected their radically changed status and may have been a reaction to stress caused by the loss of their privileged position many years after immigration.

Studies from elsewhere in Europe also provide evidence of the correlation between rapid societal transformation and suicide mortality. A sharp and steady rise in male suicides in Ireland in the past two decades may be due to rapid social change that the country has experienced in terms of urbanization, decreased religiosity and the weakening of familial bonds (Corcoran, et al., 2004). Furthermore, rapid sociocultural change in Greenland in the past fifty years has led to disrupted social networks and a steadily increasing suicide rate (Leineweber, et al., 2001).

Westernization and marginalization can influence societal rates of suicide. Indigenous groups in both Canada and Australia have experienced profound cultural change, accompanied by sharp increases in suicide rates in the past century (WHO, 2002). For example, Tester and McNicoll (2004) found high rates of suicide among Inuits in the newly created Nunavut Territory of Canada, particularly among male youths. They proposed that, while low self-esteem is an important factor in Inuit suicide, it is not a psychological problem, but rather one that can be traced to a history of colonialism and paternalism.

The effects of modernization and globalization can also be seen in China, where a high suicide rate, particularly among young rural women, is found in association with a low prevalence of mental illness (Chan, et al. 2001). This association, in contrast to Western countries, where psychiatric disorders are more prevalent and suicide rates are lower, challenges traditional individualistic approaches to suicide prevention. While there is a lack of reliable data on suicide rates in China prior to 1987, making it difficult to tell whether and how the prevalence of suicide in China has changed over the past century, anecdotal and contemporary evidence from analyses of suicide rates and case studies shows fairly strong support for the effects of macro-level social changes on suicide (Yip, et al., 2005; Lester, 2005; Phillips, et al., 1999). It is important to note that, while processes of modernization may lead to an increase in suicide for certain populations, they can have a protective effect on other populations. For example, an analysis of suicide mortality data in Japan revealed that urbanization was associated with a decline in suicide deaths among men (Otsu, et al., 2004).

## VOLATILE ECONOMIES: THE EFFECTS OF ECONOMIC INSTABILITY, UNEMPLOYMENT AND SOCIOECONOMIC STATUS ON SUICIDE

There is a large body of evidence to suggest that the effects of socioeconomic variables, particularly levels of unemployment and economic uncertainty, have an impact on suicide mortality rates. Macrosocial causes of economic instability can threaten individual identity, leading to unmet expectations, barriers to the attainment of desired roles, and social and economic exclusion.

The recent sharp increase in suicides among farmers in India's main cotton belt illustrates the consequences that may be experienced by rural agrarian communities in the context of rapid global economic growth. Specifically, there is evidence that the problems faced by Indian farmers are the result of being forced into a global system that has brought economic hardship to many producers in the form of rising costs, crop loss, market constraints and debt (Mohanty, 2005; Gururaj, et al., 2004). However, while the global economy may have a negative impact on suicide rates in some nations, other nations may experience beneficial impacts owing to economic growth (Andrés, 2005).

Just as fluctuations in suicide rates may mirror social changes, they have also been shown to correlate with the introduction of a new economic order. For example, Udrasa and Logins (2004) examined fluctuations in rates of suicide and attempted suicide in Latvia over a thirty-year period and found that suicide rates increased with the decline of the Soviet-style central planning and the introduction of a free-market economy accompanied by privatization of property and merciless competition. The authors suggest that rates of suicide and attempted suicide are important indicators of changing psychological and social and economic realities of a society in transition.

Many studies have found evidence of a relationship among socioeconomic position, unemployment, and suicide rates. In an exploration of the relationship between suicide rates, unemployment, and labor force participation in men in twenty countries since 1975, Taylor (2003) found that, overall, higher rates of unemployment are positively correlated with a higher incidence of suicide, although important national differences persisted between and within countries. Similar evidence of a positive correlation between high unemployment and socioeconomic deprivation and increased suicide rates has been found in studies from Sweden (Johansson & Sundquist, 1997), Taiwan (Lin, 2006; Chuang & Huang, 1997), the USA (Ruhm, 2000), and the United Kingdom (Hawton, et al., 2001), as well as for men in Japan (Yamasaki, et al., 2005) and in Trinidad and Tobago (Hutchinson & Simeon, 1997). In contrast, several studies have found evidence that mortality from suicide behaves pro-cyclically in relation to unemployment and economic growth, that is, as unemployment levels rise, suicide rates decrease. This effect was found in Germany from 1980 to 2000 (Neumayer, 2004), among women in Italy (Preti & Miotto, 1999), and among youths in Sweden following the 1990s recession (Hagquist, et al., 2000).

In some cases, suicide rates may be more closely related to a change in employment or economic circumstances than to economic conditions in general (Inoue, et al., 2006). Even when individuals are not in the work-force, social factors related to the labor market can influence suicide rates. An ecological study of late-life suicides in British Columbia (Canada) found that higher male unemployment and greater female labor force participation were associated with increased rates of suicide in elderly men, even though the latter are not involved in the labor force (Agbayewa, 1998). For elderly women in Japan, unemployment was found to be inversely associated with suicide mortality rates (Yamasaki, et al., 2005).

There is also evidence that the nature of the relationship between one's identity and one's economic status can lead to differential influences on suicide rates during times of economic transition. For example, in post-Soviet Kazakhstan and the former Soviet Union, where masculine identity is strongly linked to the economic arena and feminine identity less so, men have experienced substantial increases in suicide rates due to rising unemployment and economic instability, while the rates for women have remained relatively stable, reflecting an identity undefined by economic conditions (Buckley, 1997; Brainerd, 2001).

## THE SOCIAL ENVIRONMENT AND SUICIDE

Cultural and political contexts, as well as social and ecological environments, also emerge as themes in an examination of current research on the social determinants of suicide, although the evidence for these themes is not as widespread. Some examples include the protective effects of efforts to maintain cultural continuity on suicide in Aboriginal youth in Canada (Chandler & Proulx, 2006), an association between the type of government and suicide rates (Labor voters having the lowest and Conservative voters having the highest) in an extensive study conducted in New South Wales, Australia, for the period 1901-1998 (Page, et al., 2002), as well as geographic variations in suicide rates in European Russia, in a pattern supporting a correlation with historical processes of migration (Kandrychyn, 2004).

## CONCLUSION

Although research on the social determinants of suicide continues to provide convincing evidence that suicide is a result of more than individual-level factors, treatment models have lagged behind. Returning to Kleinman and Kleinman's (1997) hypothesis in light of this foray into the literature, we can see evidence for their assertion that globalization and social change have had marked effects on suicide mortality. It is clear that the focus on individually-based prevention efforts in contemporary suicidology is outmoded. While individual factors are important to the study and prevention of suicide, they cannot be separated from the social conditions from which individuals derive (and in which they subsequently act out) their suicidal behaviors. Environment and social ecology are vitally important to the study and treatment of suicide because they provide macro-level risk factors that can combine with individual-level factors to increase or decrease the likelihood of suicide. It is recommended that current prevention efforts make use of the population-based approach to suicide to account for the interdependence between individuals and their environments.

## REFERENCES

Agbayewa, M. O. (1998). Socioeconomic factors associated with suicide in elderly populations in British Columbia: an 11-year review. *Canadian Journal of Psychiatry,* 43, 829-836.

Andrés, A. R. (2005). Income inequality, unemployment, and suicide: a panel data analysis of 15 European countries. *Applied Economics,* 37, 439-451.

Bertolote, J. M., & Fleischmann, A. (2002). A global perspective in the epidemiology of suicide. *Suicidologi,* 7, 6-8.

Brainerd, E. (2001). Economic reform and mortality in the former Soviet Union: a study of the suicide epidemic in the 1990s. *European Economic Review,* 45, 1007-1019.

Buckley, C. (1997). Suicide in post-Soviet Kazakhstan: role stress, age and gender. *Central Asian Survey,* 16, 45-52.

Chan, K. P., Hung, S. F., & Yip, P. S. (2001). Suicide in response to changing societies. *Child & Adolescent Psychiatric Clinics of North America,* 10, 777-795.

Chandler, M., & Proulx, T. (2006). Changing selves in changing worlds: youth suicide on the fault-lines of colliding cultures. *Archives of Suicide Research,* 10, 125-140.

Chuang, H. & Huang, W. (1997). Economic and social correlates of regional suicide rates: a pooled cross-section and time-series analysis. *Journal of Socio-Economics,* 26, 277-289.

Cocoran, P., Burke, U., Byrne, S., et al. (2004). Suicidal behaviour in Ireland. In A. Schmidtke, U. Bille-Brahe, D. DeLeo, et al. (Eds.) *Suicidal behaviour in Europe: results from the WHO/EURO multicentre study on suicidal behaviour,* pp. 97-105. Ashland, OH: Hogrefe & Huber.

Desjarlais, R., Eisenberg, L., Good, B., et al. (1995). *World mental health: problems and priorities in low-income countries.* New York: Oxford University Press.

Durkheim, E. (1897/1951). *Suicide: A study in sociology.* New York: Free Press.

Gailiene, D. (2004) Suicidal behaviour in Lithuania. In A. Schmidtke, U. Bille-Brahe, D. DeLeo, et al. (Eds.) *Suicidal behaviour in Europe: results from the WHO/EURO multicentre study on suicidal behaviour,* pp. 167-170. Ashland, OH: Hogrefe & Huber.

Gururaj, G., Isaac, M. K., Subbakrishna, D. K., et al. (2004). Risk factors for completed suicides: a case-control study from Bangalore, India. *Injury Control & Safety Promotion,* 11, 183-191.

Hagquist, C., Silburn, S. R., Zubrick, S. R., et al. (2000). Suicide and mental health problems among Swedish youth in the wake of the 1990s recession. *International Journal of Social Welfare,* 9, 211-219.

Hawton, K., Harriss, L., Hodder, K., et al. (2001). The influence of the economic and social environment on deliberate self-harm and suicide: an ecological and person-based study. *Psychological Medicine,* 31, 827-836.

Hutchinson, G. A., & Simeon, D. T. (1997). Suicide in Trinidad and Tobago: associations with measures of social distress. *International Journal of Social Psychiatry,* 43, 269-275.

Inoue, K., Tanii, H., Fukunaga, T., et al. (2006). Significant correlation of yearly suicide rates with the rate of unemployment among men results in a rapid increase of suicide in Mie Prefecture, Japan. *Psychiatry & Clinical Neurosciences,* 60, 781-782.

Jakovljevic, M., Sedic, B., Martinac, M., et al. (2004). Update of suicide trends in Croatia 1966-2002. *Psychiatria Danubina,* 16, 299-308.

Jarosz, M. (1999). Suicide as an indicator of disintegration of the Polish society. *Polish Sociological Review,* 3, 427-444.

Johansson, S. E., & Sundquist, J. (1997). Unemployment is an important risk factor for suicide in contemporary Sweden: an 11-year follow-up study of a cross-sectional sample of 37 789 people. *Public Health,* 111, 41-45.

Kandrychyn, S. (2004). Geographic variation in suicide rates: relationships to social factors, migration, and ethnic history. *Archives of Suicide Research,* 8, 303-314.

Kleinman, A. & Kleinman, J. (1997). Moral transformations of health and suffering in Chinese society. In A. M. Brandt & P. Rozin (Eds.) *Morality and health,* pp. 101-118. New York: Routledge.

Leineweber, M., Bjerregaard, P., Baerveldt, C., et al. (2001) Suicide in a society in transition. *International Journal of Circumpolar Health,* 60, 280-287.

Lester, D. (1994). Applying Durkheim's typology to individual suicides. In D. Lester (Ed.) *Émile Durkheim le suicide: 100 years later,* pp.224-237. Philadelphia, PA: Charles Press.

Lester, D. (2005). Suicide and the Chinese cultural revolution. *Archives of Suicide Research,* 9, 99-104.

Lin, S. (2006). Unemployment and suicide: panel data analyses. *Social Science Journal*, 43, 727-732.

Makinen, I. H. (2000). Eastern European transition and suicide mortality. *Social Science & Medicine*, 51, 1405-1420.

Mohanty, B. B. (2005). 'We are like the living dead': farmer suicides in Maharashtra, Western India. *Journal of Peasant Studies*, 32, 243-276.

Mokhovikov, A., & Donets, O. (1996). Suicide in the Ukraine: epidemiology, knowledge, and attitudes of the population. *Crisis*, 17, 128-134.

Moller, D. W. (1996). *Confronting death: values, institutions, and human mortality*. New York: Oxford University Press.

Neumayer, E. (2004). Recessions lower (some) mortality rates: evidence from Germany. *Social Science & Medicine*, 58, 1037-1047.

Otsu, A., Araki, S., Sakai, R., et al. (2004). Effects of urbanization, economic development, and migration of workers on suicide mortality in Japan. *Social Science & Medicine*, 58, 1137-1146.

Page, A., Morrell, S., & Taylor, R. (2002). Suicide and political regime in New South Wales and Australia during the 20$^{th}$ century. *Journal of Epidemiology & Community Health*, 56, 766-772.

Phillips, M. R., Liu, H., & Zhang, Y. (1999). Suicide and social change in China. *Culture, Medicine & Psychiatry*, 23, 25-50.

Preti, A. & Miotto, P. (1999). Social and economic influence on suicide. *Archives of Suicide Research*, 5, 141-156.

Ruhm, C. J. (2000). Are recessions good for your health? *Quarterly Journal of Economics*, 115, 617-650.

Taylor, P. (2003). Age, labour market conditions and male suicide rates in selected countries. *Ageing & Society*, 23, 25-40.

Tester, F. J., & McNicoll, P. (2004). Isumagijaksaq: mindful of the state: social constructions of Inuit suicide. *Social Science & Medicine*, 58, 2625-2636.

Udrasa, S. & Logins, J. (2004). Suicidal behaviour in Latvia. In A. Schmidtke, U. Bille-Brahe, D. DeLeo, et al. (Eds.) *Suicidal behaviour in Europe: results from the WHO/EURO multicentre study on suicidal behaviour*, pp. 201- 201. Ashland, OH: Hogrefe & Huber.

Varnik, A., Kolves, K., & Wasserman, D. (2005). Suicide among Russians in Estonia: database study before and after independence. *British Medical Journal*, 330, 176-177.

World Health Organization (2002a). Self-directed violence. In E. G. Krug, L .L. Dahlberg, J. A. Mercy, et al. (Eds.) *World report on violence and health*, pp. 183-212. Geneva, Switzerland: World Health Organization.

World Health Organization (2002b). *Suicide prevention and special programmes*. Available at www.who.int/mental_health/prevention/suicide/charts/en/index.html. Accessed 8 February 2007.

Yamasaki, A., Sakai, R., & Shirakawa, T. (2005). Low-income, unemployment, and suicide mortality rates for middle-age persons in Japan. *Psychological Reports*, 96, 337-348.

Yip, P. S. F., Liu, K. Y, Hu, J., et al. (2005). Suicide rates in China during a decade of rapid social changes. *Social Psychiatry & Psychiatric Epidemiology*, 40, 792-798.

Zonda, T., Bozsonyi, K., & Veres, E. (2005). Seasonal fluctuation of suicide in Hungary between 1970-2000. *Archives of Suicide Research*, 9, 77-85.

Chapter 15

# IMMIGRATION AND RISK FOR SUICIDE

## *Megan E. Johnston*

In recent years, as the world has become more global with regard to trade, economies, and borders, people have also become increasingly free to move around the globe. In the last fifty years, immigration levels have doubled, resulting in an estimated 200 million immigrants worldwide (GCIM, 2005). Although migration between nations can have many positive consequences, including diverse multi-cultural communities, many immigrants face significant challenges in their new homes. In particular, research demonstrates a significant prevalence of mental health concerns in immigrants, including suicidal behavior (Stack, 1981). In studies across nations, research consistently shows an increased incidence of suicide in immigrants to a country as compared to natives of a country (e.g., Johansson, et al., 1997; Sundaram, et al., 2006).

What is striking about immigration as a risk factor for suicidal behavior is its universality. In any country where this association has been studied, a clear detrimental impact of migration to a new country has been found (but see below for some studies that suggest a possible variation in this relation in Canada and the USA). Johansson and colleagues (1997) found that, in comparison to persons native to Sweden, suicide levels are higher among foreign-born minorities. In some parts of the USA, immigrants have been shown to commit suicide at a rate twice that of non-immigrant citizens (Kposowa, et al., 2008). Pena and colleagues (2008) report that immigrant generation status predicts suicide attempts in Latino immigrants in the USA while, in another American study, Eshun (2006) followed a group of Ghanaian immigrants and found a significant association between length of residency in the U.S. and negative suicide attitudes. Immigrants in England and Wales also show elevated suicide rates as compared to the general population (Harding & Balarajan, 1996).

In addition to the consistent finding of increased suicide risk in immigrants, research has also demonstrated that some immigrant groups differ from one another in their risk for suicidal behavior, with the most vulnerable group dependent on the home nation. For example, Irish migrants living in Britain have suicide rates that are higher than both those in the general population and than in other minority groups living in Britain (Raleigh & Balarajan, 1992; Harding & Balarajan, 1996). In Denmark, Sundaram, et al. (2006) found that suicide risk was higher in foreign-born individuals than in the majority population. This research has also found that suicide risk was highest in Nordic-born foreigners and lowest in Asian-born individuals. Thus, the host country in which immigrants reside is an important determinant of the suicide rate in particular ethnic groups. The political climate of the country and the cultural similarities between the origin and host countries will also influence whether immigrants from a certain country or ethnic group have elevated levels of mental health issues and suicidal behavior.

## IMPORTANCE OF SUICIDE RATES IN THE COUNTRY OF ORIGIN

Although the link between immigration and risk for suicidal behavior seems clear, some Canadian and American studies have found a distinctly opposite pattern. Specifically, some research has found that the suicide rates of immigrants are lower than native-born citizens (Malenfant, 2004; Mullen & Smyth, 2004). For example, Singh and Siahpush (2002) analyzed national data-sets from the USA and reported that immigrants had lower suicide rates than native-born Americans. Particularly in American and Canadian youth, suicide rates are consistently reported as lower among immigrants as compared to non-immigrants (Greenfield, et al., 2006). Additional research from Britain has found that some immigrant groups have lower suicide rates than native-Britains (Crawford, et al., 2005). Specifically, this study found that, as compared to individuals born in England, suicide rates were lower in ethnic minority groups but higher among UK-born migrants to England. This research found that symptoms of mental distress were most important as a risk factor for suicidal ideation, which was common across the various ethnic groups (Crawford, et al., 2005).

Research demonstrating these inconsistencies in the association between immigration status and suicide rates has increasingly highlighted the importance of considering the suicide rates from an immigrant's country of origin in addition to the rates in his or her new country. This idea was originally explored by Kliewer and Ward (1988) who found a significant degree of convergence in Canadian immigrant suicide rates to the rate of suicide among native-born Canadians. Specifically, immigrant suicide rates converged by approximately 40% of the difference between rates for the origin country and the rate of Canadians. This research also found that immigrant females had higher rates of suicide and were also more likely to differ from the rates typical in their country of origin compared to immigrant males (Kliewer & Ward, 1988). More recent research has further recognized the importance of country of origin suicide rates (e.g., Mullen & Smyth, 2004).

Several studies indicate that immigrant suicide rates are highly correlated with suicide rates in countries of origin (Burvill, 1998; Lester, 1998). However, the suicide rate of immigrants is typically higher than the rates found in the country of origin and in the new host country (Burvill, 1998; Kramer, et al., 1972). Thus, even in countries where the suicide rates of particular ethnic immigrant groups are lower than that of native-born citizens, they are still likely to be inflated in comparison to rates in the country of origin (Kliewer & Ward, 1988). For many immigrants, suicide rates in Canada and the USA are higher than those of their countries of origin (e.g., India, Iran, Mexico, Puerto Rico and China [males]) (WHO, 2008). Thus, these immigrant groups may experience elevated suicide rates while still not reaching the level of native-born Americans and Canadians. It is imperative that analyses of immigrant suicide rates take into consideration the suicide rates in the country of origin.

## CAUSES OF INCREASED SUICIDE BEHAVIOR IN IMMIGRANTS

An examination of the common challenges faced by immigrants provides an indication of why increased levels of suicide behavior may occur in these individuals. For example, when moving to a new country, individuals are abruptly severed from their social environments (Stack, 2000). Social support networks of family and friends are often left behind, and unfamiliar geographic surroundings, combined with possible language barriers, create a challenging situation for many immigrants. Also, a main reason that many people emigrate to another country is for economic purposes. Thus, many people may emigrate with high economic expectations and, if these aspirations are not met, as is the case for a large number of immigrants, despair and social drift may result (Kposowa, et al., 2008). When not able to obtain gainful employment, immigrants may also feel a lack of social integration in their new country, leading to depression, anxiety and an increased risk of suicide.

Leavey (1999) argued that increased suicide rates in immigrant groups may be a consequence of a lack of social cohesion and integration. When first moving to a new country, individuals lack a social support network and may be submerged in a society with very different cultural norms from their own. This can lead to a sense of social isolation. Immigrants may also have issues integrating their cultural identity with an identity appropriate to their new environment, resulting in an inability to establish an authentic identity. In support of this idea, Canadian research by Kennedy and colleagues (2005) found that immigrants who identified closely with their cultural heritage were at an elevated risk of suicidal thoughts, and this did not vary by generation level. Thus, although maintaining aspects of one's cultural identity is important, an inability to adapt this identity to the new culture may have adverse effects on an individual's mental health. The risk of suicide behavior appears to increase when immigrants to a new society remain rigid in their identification with the identity associated with their culture of origin.

Kandrychyn (2004) similarly argued that suicide risk results from the combination of social organization and cultural traditions, plus biological and genetic factors. Importantly, Kposowa and colleagues (2008) argued that social integration makes immigrants resilient to suicide risk, highlighting the importance of this variable for decreasing immigrant suicide rates. Immigrant suicide rates may also be influenced by acculturative stress (Caplan, 2007). Acculturation refers to the process of adaptation to stressful changes that occurs in ongoing exchanges between individuals of different cultures (Redfield, et al., 1936). What causes acculturative stress may be different for different immigrants, but includes three dimensions: environmental (e.g., financial, language barriers and safety); interpersonal (e.g., family conflict, loss of social networks and social status); and societal (e.g., discrimination and political forces) (Caplan, 2007). Acculturative stress in Latino immigrants to the USA has been found to have a significant impact on physical and mental health, with a majority of these immigrants also negatively impacted by discrimination (Caplan, 2007). On the other hand, in research from the USA, immigrant length of residency was a stronger predictor of suicide attitudes than other measures of acculturation (Eshun, 2006). Thus, status as a recent immigrant seems to be an important predictor of suicide rates regardless of the level of acculturative stress experienced by an individual, although this stress clearly has a negative impact on the mental and physical health of immigrants.

Mullen and Smyth (2004) explored the role of hate speech toward ethnic immigrant groups in suicide rates among these groups. Their research demonstrated that ethnic immigrant groups who were subjected to higher levels of hate speech were more likely to commit suicide, even after controlling for origin suicide rates and the general impact of immigrant status on suicide rates. Thus, hate crimes and hate speech toward immigrants is an important contributor to the suicide rates among these groups and likely also contributes to the differences among different immigrant groups within the same country. Some ethnic groups face more discrimination than others in certain countries, resulting in higher suicide rates in these mistreated groups.

## ADOLESCENCE

As our world becomes more global and levels of immigration rise, an important consequence is an increase in immigrant children and adolescents. For example, in the USA, one in five children and adolescents live in an immigrant family (U.S. Census, 2000). Immigration during childhood and adolescence has many adverse effects on mental health which, left untreated, can lead to suicidal behavior (Garcia & Saewyc, 2007). In particular, this is a problem in light of the elevated suicide rate in the general adolescent population as compared to other age groups (Ryland & Kruesi, 1992). The added burden of acculturative stress during a time of life already characterized by stressful emotional, social, psychological and physical changes makes immigrant adolescents an especially vulnerable group. Consistent with this idea, a study by Borges and colleagues (2009) found that suicidal ideation was higher among Mexican-born immigrants who were 12 years of age or younger when they arrived in the USA, as compared to immigrants over the age of 12. An additional issue in adolescent immigrants is a lack of availability of mental health services, resulting from barriers to accessing care (Ku & Matani, 2001). In general, adolescents do not always receive the mental health treatment they need, and this lack of care is even more prevalent in adolescent immigrants (RAND, 2001). It is critical that mental health services be made accessible to all adolescents and, in particular, to adolescents who have immigrated to the country. Mental health services that are sensitive to multiple cultures should be integrated into the public school system and other institutional programs aimed at children and youth in order to prevent mental health problems that can lead to suicide.

## SUICIDE PREVENTION AND DIRECTIONS FOR THE FUTURE

As social integration is a primary consideration in immigrant suicide behavior, suicide prevention may best be served through increased attempts to integrate new residents to the society (Kposowa, et al., 2008). As outlined in this review of the literature, the specific links between immigration and suicide depend on the host country. Thus, it would be impractical to make widespread, omnibus recommendations. Rather, policies should be guided by suicide rates and risk factors on a national or even community basis. Those groups which are subjected to more hate crimes, social isolation and acculturative stress will differ between regions, but it is essential that these groups be identified and suicide prevention efforts implemented. One possibility is the initiation of suicide help-lines that are multi-lingual and culturally sensitive. Although suicide prevention will differ by region, research suggests higher suicide rates in recent immigrants (Kposowa, et al., 2008), and so it is important that policies are targeted at these individuals. Additionally, suicide in immigrant youth is an issue that requires special attention as this group may be particularly at risk.

A further issue is medical care for immigrants who attempt suicide or who have mental distress or suicidal ideation. Crawford, et al. (2005) found that White British and Irish individuals living in England are twice as likely to receive medical attention following suicide attempts than individuals from other ethnic groups. Thus, in addition to differential rates of suicidal behavior, an important consideration is differential access to medical treatment. In many countries, immigrant groups may have less access to medical care and may also be more reluctant to seek this care, based on factors such as language barriers (Garcia & Saewyc, 2007). It is important for suicide prevention efforts to pay special attention to minority group members and provide these individuals with opportunities to seek out and receive needed treatment. Multicultural awareness in particular appears to be a primary prevention tactic. Thus, mental health practitioners need to be educated about culturally appropriate resources for their clients, and policies need to be targeted at those individuals and groups most in need.

## REFERENCES

Borges, G., Breslau, J., Su, M., et al. (2009). Immigration and suicidal behavior among Mexicans and Mexican Americans. *American Journal of Public Health*, 99, 728-733.

Burvill, P. W. (1998). Migrant suicide rates in Australia and in country of birth. *Psychological Medicine*, 28, 201–8.

Caplan, S. (2007). Latinos, acculturation, and acculturative stress: a dimensional concept analysis. *Policy, Politics, & Nursing Practice*, 8, 93-106.

Crawford, M. J., Nur, U., McKenzie, K., et al. (2005). Suicidal ideation and suicide attempts among ethnic minority groups in England: results of a national household survey. *Psychological Medicine*, 35, 1369-1377.

Eshun, S. (2006). Acculturation and suicide attitudes: a study of perceptions about suicide among a sample of Ghanaian immigrants in the United States. *Psychological Reports*, 99, 295-304.

Garcia, C. M., & Saewyc, E. M. (2007). Perceptions of mental health among recently immigrated Mexican adolescents. *Issues in Mental Health Nursing*, 28, 37-54.

GCIM (Global Commission on International Migration). (2005). *Migration in an interconnected world: new directions for action*. New York: The Global Commission on International Migration, United Nations.

Greenfield, B., Rousseau, C., Slatkoff, J., et al. (2006). Profile of a metropolitan North American immigrant suicidal adolescent population. *Canadian Journal of Psychiatry*, 51, 155-159.

Harding, S., & Balarajan, R. (1996). Patterns of mortality in second generation Irish living in England and Wales: longitudinal study. *British Medical Journal,* 312, 1389-1392.

Johansson, L. M, Sundquist, J., Johansson, S., et al. (1997). Suicide among foreign-born minorities and native Swedes: an epidemiological follow-up study of a define population. *Social Science & Medicine,* 44, 181-187.

Kandrychyn, S. (2004). Geographic variation in suicide rates: relationships to social factors, migration, and ethnic history. *Archives of Suicide Research,* 8, 303-314.

Kennedy, M. A., Parhar, K. K., Samra, J., et al. (2005). Suicide ideation in different generations of immigrants. *Canadian Journal of Psychiatry,* 50, 353-356.

Kliewer, E.V., & Ward, R.H. (1988). Convergence of immigrant suicide rates to those in the destination country. *American Journal of Epidemiology,* 127, 640-653.

Kramer, M., Pollack, E. S., Redick, R. W., et al. (1972). *Mental disorders: suicide.* Cambridge, MA: Harvard University Press.

Ku, L., & Matani, S. (2001). Left out: immigrants' access to health care and insurance. *Health Affairs,* 20, 247–256.

Leavey, G. (1999). Suicide and Irish migrants in Britain: identity and integration. *International Review of Psychiatry,* 11, 168-172.

Lester, D. (1998). Suicide rates in immigrants. *Psychological Reports,* 82, 50.

Malenfant, E. C. (2004). Suicide in Canada's immigrant population. *Health Reports,* 15, 9–17.

Mullen, B., & Smyth, J. M. (2004). Immigrant suicide rates as a function of ethnophaulisms: hate speech predicts death. *Psychosomatic Medicine,* 66, 343–348.

Pena, J. B., Wyman, P. A., Brown, C. H., et al. (2008). Immigration generation status and its association with suicide attempts, substance use, and depressive symptoms among Latino adolescents in the USA. *Prevention Science,* 9, 299-310.

Raleigh, V. S., & Balarajan, R. (1992). Suicide levels and trends among immigrants in England and Wales. *Health Trends,* 24, 91-94.

RAND. (2001). *Research highlights: mental health care for youth.* Retrieved from: http://www.rand.org/health.

Redfield, R., Linton, R., & Herskovits, M. J. (1936). Memorandum for the study of acculturation. *American Anthropologist,* 38, 149-152.

Ryland, D. H., & Kruesi, M. J. P. (1992). Suicide among adolescents. *International Review of Psychiatry,* 4, 185-195.

Singh, G. K., & Siahpush, M. (2002). Ethnic-immigrant differentials in health behaviors, morbidity, and cause-specific mortality in the United States: an analysis of two national data bases. *Human Biology,* 74, 83–109.

Stack, S. (1981). The effect of immigration on suicide: a cross-national analysis. *Basic & Applied Social psychology,* 2, 205-218.

Stack, S. (2000). Suicide: a 15-year review of the sociological literature. Part II: modernization and social integration perspectives. *Suicide & Life-Threatening Behavior,* 30, 163–176.

Sundaram, V., Qin, P., & Zollner, L. (2006). Suicide risk among persons with foreign background in Denmark. *Suicide & Life-Threatening Behavior,* 36, 481-489.

U.S. Census Bureau. (2000). *U.S. Census 2000.* Retrieved from www.census.gov

WHO. (2008). *Mental health.* World Health Organization. Retrieved from: http://www.who.int/mental_health/prevention/suicide/country_reports/en/index.html.

Chapter 16

# THE IMPACT OF THE MEDIA ON SUICIDE

## *Steven Stack*

The notion that widespread media coverage of a suicide can result in an increase in suicide within society dates back at least to 1774. The main character in Goethe's popular novel, *The Sorrows of Young Man Werther*, commits suicide as a result of his enduring problems in love. The novel was reportedly linked to a wave of suicides among young people in the urban centers of Europe in the year of its publication. There was little scientific work on imitative suicide until two centuries later. Phillips (1974) assessed the impacts of 34 widely publicized suicide stories in the newspapers between 1948 and 1967, and determined that, on average, highly publicized suicide stories were associated with a 2.5% increase in the national suicide count during the two weeks after the story. During the month of the starlet Marilyn Monroe's suicide the suicide count increased 12%, amounting to an excess of 313 suicides.

Since Phillips' (1974) pioneering work, at least 108 scientific papers and theses have been published on the impact of suicide stories on suicidal behavior (Stack, 2005). While most of the research is based in the USA, studies have been published based on other nations including Australia, Austria, Canada, Germany, Hungary, Japan, Switzerland and the UK. However, there have been inconsistencies in the findings of this research. For example, in the first quantitative review, a review covering 293 research findings, two thirds of the findings reported no copycat effect (Stack, 2000). In addition, research investigations have demonstrated no copycat effects for stories appearing during wartime, stories appearing during the Great Depression, and stories about villains such as spies and corrupt government officials (Stack, 2000).

## ILLUSTRATIONS OF A MEDIA IMPACT

While most findings do not document a copycat effect, there are studies that demonstrate imitation of the method of suicide, copycat effects of a well-known celebrity suicide and copycat effects restricted to suicide attempts (not completions). For example, in the book,

*Final Exit*, a guide to suicide for terminally-ill persons, asphyxiation is the recommended means of suicide. In the year that *Final Exit* was published, suicides by asphyxiation in New York City rose by 313% from eight to thirty-three. Furthermore, a copy of *Final Exit* was found at the scene of 27% of these suicides. However, the general suicide rate in New York City did not increase (Marzuk, et al., 1994). In Germany, suicides by subway increased after a series of stories about the subway suicide of a student. Sometimes suicide in the media may affect only the choice of suicide method, not the suicide risk per se.

The suicides of well-known celebrities often spark imitative suicides. A study in Quebec by Tousignant and his colleagues (2005) determined that at least 14% of the suicides in the month following a widely-publicized suicide of a popular Quebec journalist were at least partially linked to the story. For example, a number of the suicides were found with a copy of the suicide story nearby. Ninety percent of the suicides used the same method (hanging) as the story. However, few media stories actually concern celebrities.

Hawton and his colleagues (1999) studied impact of a fictional suicide on a television drama series (*Casualty*) in the UK. The fictional suicide used paracetamol (acetominophen). Data were collected on self-poisoning attempters at 52 hospitals three weeks before and after the suicide. Of the 16% of the suicide attempters who reported having seen the episode (which was viewed by 22% of the UK population), 15% reported that it had influenced their decision to attempt suicide. However, the episode had no impact on completed suicide using paracetamol.

## EXPLANATIONS OF THE MEDIA IMPACT ON SUICIDE

Explanations of media impact on suicide have generally been framed in terms of social learning theory. The simplest rendition is the imitation explanation. Basically one learns that there are troubled people who solve their life's problems (e.g., divorce, terminal illness or dishonor) through suicide. Mentally-troubled persons in a society may simply copy the behavior of troubled people in the suicide stories. Herein the content and presentation of the suicide stories may be secondary to the basic message conveyed about problem-solving.

A more complex set of explanations revolves around the learning process of differential identification. If people tend to identify more with celebrities than ordinary people, the suicides of celebrities would be expected to have greater odds of triggering copycat suicides. Likewise, Americans may identify more with the stories about American suicides than about foreign suicides.

A third explanation focuses, not on the story characteristics, but on audience mood. The central thesis is that stories that appear when suicidogenic conditions are high in society (e.g., high unemployment and high divorce rates, which promote depressed mood) will elicit more of a copycat effect than others. This is the most understudied explanation.

### Confirmed Generalizations about the Media Impact on Suicidal Behavior

Stack (2000) performed the first meta-analysis of 293 findings from 42 studies on copycat suicide. A central distinction shaping suicide risk was whether the story was about a real suicide, as in the news media, or if it was based on a fictional account, such as those in movies or television soap operas. The analysis found that studies based on real suicide stories are 4.03 times more likely to report copycat effects than studies based on fictional suicides. For example, several investigations on television movies about teenage suicide which aired in the USA in 1984 generally found no imitative effect. People may tend to identify more with true-to-life suicides than with make-believe suicides in movies or soap operas.

A second meta-analysis was restricted to 55 studies containing 419 findings involving nonfictional suicides, the type of media suicides that place the audience at the greatest risk (Stack, 2005). For this group of studies, the single most important predictor of a study reporting a copycat effect involved celebrity status. Studies that measured the impact of either an entertainment or a political celebrity suicide were 5.27 times more likely to uncover a copycat effect. According to a reference group approach, if a Marilyn Monroe with all her fame and fortune cannot endure life, the suicidal person may say "Why should I?" Along these same lines, a recent study found that the assisted suicide of a well-known celebrity couple was associated with an increase in assisted suicides in Switzerland.

Unlike televised suicide stories, newspaper suicide stories can be saved, reread, displayed on one's wall or mirror, and studied. Television-based stories on suicide typically last less than twenty seconds and can be quickly forgotten or even missed. Studies have often found copies of suicide news stories near the body of individuals committing suicide. A meta-analysis determined that research based on television stories were 79% less apt to uncover a copycat effect than research based on newspapers (Stack, 2005).

A recurrent finding in the research is that the more coverage a suicide story receives, the greater the likelihood of a copycat effect and the greater the size of the effect (Stack, 2000).

## SUICIDE PREVENTION: MEDIA GUIDELINES

Professional organizations have often prepared guidelines for the media to follow in presenting suicide story content (e.g., Etzerdorfer & Sonneck, 1998; Maris, et al., 2000). For example, they often advise the media not to mention the method of suicide and to avoid presenting photos of the suicide. However, the effectiveness of such strategies for suicide prevention remains unclear. To date, only one of 108 studies systematically tested elements of suicide guidelines beyond recommendations concerning the amount of coverage.

Phillips and his colleagues (1989) studied characteristics of 32 televised suicide stories and their impact on teenage suicide in the USA. Aspects of story content were measured and included six that are often mentioned in suicide media guidelines: (1) mention of the method of suicide, (2) photo of the suicide in normal life, (3) photo of the suicide's body or coffin, (4) whether or not the motive was specified, (5) suicide reported as definite versus "apparent," and (6) if family and friends were interviewed.

None of these characteristics of the stories were associated with significant increases or decreases in suicide risk. For example, stories that mentioned the method of suicide were no more likely to be associated with increases in teenage suicide than ones that did not mention the method. This study needs to be replicated for adults. Further, it may have underestimated the effectiveness of media guidelines since it controlled out the amount of television coverage of the suicide, a possible correlate of variables in the guidelines (i.e., the longer the story, the more time there is to discuss motives, methods, etc.).

## POLICY IMPLICATIONS

Media guidelines might be expanded to include an empirically-verified aspect of coverage: negative definitions. A major finding from a meta-analytic review was that studies that focus on stories that stressed negative definitions of suicide were 99% less likely than other studies to report copycat effects (Stack, 2005). The mention of the negative consequences of suicide (e.g., pain and disfigurement) in suicide stories might reduce the imitative effect. These features of suicide are typically not included in suicide stories. One exception is the case of the mass suicide at Jonestown where bloated and rotting bodies (disfigurement) were shown in the stories. During this coverage American suicides declined. In a similar vein, the negative coverage of the suicide of the lead singer of the rock group Nirvana (Kurt Cobain) was not found to elicit a copycat effect.

The media might also control suicide by having fewer and shorter stories on the subject. For example, subway suicides in Vienna declined when reporting on subway suicides was decreased (Etzersdorfer & Sonneck, 1998). Since the suicides of celebrities are by far the most likely to trigger copycat effects, less attention should be paid to these "newsworthy" suicides. Coverage in the print media should be reduced since it triggers more copycat suicides than electronic media.

## REFERENCES

Etzersdorfer, E., & Sonneck, G., (1998). Preventing suicides by influencing mass-media reporting, the Viennese experience, 1980-1996. *Archives of Suicide Research*, 4, 67-74.

Hawton, K., Simkin, S., Deeks, J., et al. (1999). Effects of a drug overdose in a television drama on presentations to hospital for self poisoning: Time series and questionnaire study. *British Medical Journal*, 318, 972-977.

Maris, R., Berman, A., & Silverman, M. (2000). *Comprehensive textbook of suicidology*. New York: Guilford.

Marzuk, P., Tardiff, K., Hirsch, C., et al., (1994). Increase by suicide by asphyxiation in New York City after the publication of Final Exit. *Publishing Research Quarterly*, 10, 62- 68.

Phillips, D. P., Carstensen, L., & Paight, D. (1989). Effects of mass media news stories on suicide, with new evidence on story content. In C. Pfeiffer (Ed.) *Suicide among youth: perspectives on risk and prevention,* pp. 101-116. Washington, DC: American Psychiatric Press.

Stack, S. (2000). Media impacts on suicide: a quantitative review of 293 findings. *Social Science Quarterly*, 81, 957-971.

Stack, S. (2005). Suicide in the media: a quantitative review of studies based on nonfictional stories. *Suicide & Life-Threatening Behavior*, 35,121-133.

Tousignant, M., Mishara, B., Caillaud, A., et al. (2005). The impact of media coverage of the suicide of a well-known Quebec reporter: the case of Gaetan Girouard. *Social Science & Medicine*, 60, 1919-1926.

Chapter 17

# A STRAIN THEORY OF SUICIDE

## *Jie Zhang*

While suicidologists have interpreted the motives and risk factors of suicide in numerous ways, the ultimate objective is to find a theory that explains the majority of the variance in suicidal behaviors. Durkheim's (1951 [1897]) classical theory of social integration and regulation, explaining egoistic, altruistic, anomic and fatalistic suicide, is in theoretical and practical conflict with the psychopathological theories prevalent in today's world. However, substantial numbers of suicides, East and West, are carried out by individuals who appear to be socially integrated (Zhang, 2000; Zhang & Jin, 1998), and only a very small percentage of mentally ill people kill themselves (Mann, et al., 1999), although over 90% of suicides in the West have been diagnosed with mental disorders including major depression and alcohol or substance use disorders (NIMH, 2003). Also, in the Western world, individuals who are male, white or older are more likely to kill themselves than individuals who are female, black or younger. If the psychiatric model were valid, men, whites and older persons should be more abnormal psychologically than women, blacks and younger persons which is, of course, far from the truth (Thio, 2004). A psychiatric disorder may be a necessary condition for suicide, but it is definitely not sufficient, and in order to identify suicide risk factors, it is necessary to look beyond the presence of a major psychiatric syndrome (Mann, et al., 1999).

Furthermore, most previous studies of suicide have been restricted to one domain of possible risk factors such as the social (Brent, et al., 1993; Chiles, et al., 1989; Daly, et al., 1986; Maris, 1997; Roy, 1985; Roy & Segal, 1995; Schulsinger & Kety, 1979; Zhang & Thomas, 1991), psychiatric (Kaplan & Harrow, 1996; Rich & Runeson, 1995; Strakowski, et al., 1996), or psychological (Beck, et al, 1985; Nordstrom, et al., 1995; Pokorny, 1983; Zhang & Jin, 1998). Most of those studies are generally from medical perspectives and are exploratory in nature. Mann and colleagues (1999) developed and tested a stress-diathesis theory of suicide, but it is only a clinical model based on and for psychiatric patients. Heeringen's (2003) psychobiological model of suicidal behavior that focuses on a state-trait interaction seems more generalizable, but again is neurobiological in nature. In order to overcoming these deficiencies, this chapter proposes a basic paradigm that incorporates the available theories, hypotheses and findings explaining suicide in the world today. The new paradigm is built on previous notions of anomie and strain (Durkheim 1951 [1897]), although

Merton's (1957) strain theory of deviance and crime and Agnew's (1992) general strain theory have not in the past included suicide as a target for explanation.

## THE STRAIN THEORY OF SUICIDE

In daily life, we sometimes experience cognitive dissonance which is caused by holding two or more inconsistent notions or ideas or by the discrepancy between our own behaviors and our values (Festinger, 1957). It was discovered that dissonance is most powerful and most upsetting when people behave in ways that threaten their self-image. This is upsetting precisely because it forces us to confront the discrepancy between who we think we are and how we have in fact behaved (Aronson, 1998). Festinger and Aronson (1960) suggested three options to reduce this dissonance: (1) change our behavior to bring it in line with the dissonant cognition, (2) attempt to justify our behavior through changing one of the dissonant cognitions, or (3) attempt to justify our behavior by adding new cognitions. Strain, with regard to its psychological impact, could be even more powerful than the cognitive dissonance. The reduction of strain then may require something beyond the above three options for cognitive dissonance.

Strain is not equivalent to stress. People may frequently have the latter but not necessarily the former during their life. A pressure or stress in daily life is a single variable. When we say we have pressure at work, we mean that we have a lot of work to do, we have a deadline to meet or we have stressful relations with co-workers or bosses. A strain is made up by at least two pressures or two variables, similar to the formation of cognitive dissonance. Examples include two differential cultural values, aspiration and reality, one's own status and that of others, or a crisis and our coping ability. Like cognitive dissonance, strain is a psychological frustration (suffering) that one has to find a solution for reducing or doing away with but, in truth, it is more serious, frustrating and threatening than cognitive dissonance. The extreme solution for a strain is suicide. Figure 17-1 illustrates strain theory.

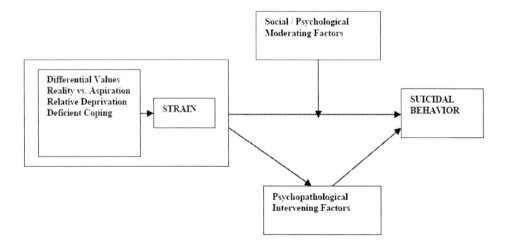

Figure 17-1. Diagram of the Strain Theory of Suicide.

Strain may lead to mental disorders, including substance abuse and alcohol abuse, and may precede other deviant behaviors, such as property crimes and personal assaults (Merton, 1957). In the relationship between strain and suicide, mental disorder may be an intervening variable, strengthening the association between strain and suicide. On the other hand, the relationship between strain and suicide may be moderated by social integration, social regulation and psychological factors such as personality. An individual well-integrated into a social institution, such as family, religion, school or employment, may be at lower risk of suicide, even when confronting a major strain (Durkheim, 1951 [1897]).

## THE FOUR SOURCES OF STRAIN FOR SUICIDE

I propose four types of strain that precede a suicide. Each of the four types of strain is derived from specific sources. A source of strain must consist of two, and at least two, conflicting social facts. If the two social facts are non-contradictory, there should be no strain.

### Source 1: Differential Values

When two conflicting social values or beliefs are competing in an individual's daily life, the person experiences *value strain*. The two conflicting social facts are the two competing personal beliefs internalized in the person's value system. A cult member may experience strain if the mainstream culture and the cult religion are both considered important in the cult member's daily life. Other examples include the second generation of immigrants in the United States who have to abide by the ethnic rules enforced in the family while simultaneously adapting to American culture with peers and at school. In China, rural young women appreciate gender egalitarianism advocated by the communist government but, at the same time, they are trapped in the sex discrimination traditionally cultivated by Confucianism. Another example found in developing countries is the differential values of traditional collectivism and modern individualism. When the two conflicting values are taken as equally important in a person's daily life, the person experiences great strain. When one value is more important than the other, then there is no strain.

### Source 2: Reality vs. Aspiration

If there is a discrepancy between an individual's aspiration or high goals and the reality the person has to live with, the person experiences *aspiration strain*. The two conflicting social facts are one's ideal or goal and the reality that may prevent one from achieving it. An individual living in the USA expects to be very rich or at least moderately successful like other Americans but, in reality, the means to achieve this goal is not equally available to the person because of his/her social status. Aspirations or goals can be the university a person aims to get in to, an ideal girl a boy wants to marry or a political cause a person strives for. If the reality is far from the aspiration, the person experiences strain. Another example might be from rural China. A young woman aspiring to equal opportunity and equal treatment may have to live within the traditional and Confucian reality, exemplified by her family and village, which does not allow her to try to get close to that goal. Ultimately, the larger the discrepancy between aspiration and reality, the greater will be the strain.

## Source 3: Relative Deprivation

In the situation where an extremely poor individual realizes that other people of the same or similar background are leading a much better life, the person experiences *deprivation strain*. The two conflicting social facts are one's own miserable life and the perceived richness of others. A person living in absolute poverty, where there is no comparison with others, does not necessarily feel bad, miserable or deprived. On the other hand, if the same poor person understands that other people like him/her live a better life, he or she may feel deprived and become upset about the situation. In an economically polarized society where the rich and poor live geographically close to each other, people are more likely to feel this discrepancy. In today's rural China, television, newspaper, magazines and the radio have brought home to rural youth how relatively affluent urban life is. Additionally, those young people who went to work in the cities (*dagong*) and returned to the village during holidays with luxury materials and exciting stories make the relative deprivation even more realistically perceived. Increased perception of deprivation results in relatively greater strain for individuals.

## Source 4: Deficient Coping

In facing a life crisis, some individuals are not able to cope with it and, thus, they experience *coping strain*. The two conflicting social facts are life crisis and the appropriate coping method. All people who have experienced crises do not experience strain. A crisis may be only a pressure or stressor in daily life, but those individuals who are not able to cope with the crisis have strain. Crises, such as loss of money, loss of status, loss of face, divorce or death of a loved one, may lead to serious strain in the person who does not know how to cope with these negative life events. A high school boy who is constantly bullied and ridiculed by peers may experience great strain if he does not know how to deal with the situation. Likewise, a Chinese rural young woman who is frequently wronged by her mother-in-law may have strain if she is not psychologically able to cope with the bad situation without support from other family members and the village. The less experienced one is in coping, the stronger the strain will be when a crisis takes place.

## CONCLUSION

A strain may be found preceding every suicide. Strain is frustration so unbearable that some solution must be taken to reduce the psychological pressure. For some people experiencing a strain, this solution may be through violence. Strain can lead to criminal behaviors towards others (Agnew, 2001; Merton, 1957) and, when the aggression is directed inwards, suicide occurs (Henry & Short, 1954).

For an individual experiencing great strain, social integration and regulation (Durkheim 1951 [1897]) may moderate (increase or decrease) the chance of suicide. While integration and regulation is pre-existent in the social context of all individuals, strain may be experienced and perceived only by certain individuals. Therefore, those who experience great strain and lack of social integration are at a higher risk of suicide than others who do not have both experiences at the same time.

Psychiatric illness, especially mood disorders and substance abuse, could be a function of severe strain and a lack of social integration. Strain as a consequence of certain life events or perceived social relations, coupled with lack of social integration, might have existed prior to the mental disorders that are present for the majority of suicides. Therefore, suicide prevention may have to begin by monitoring and curbing the strains in society.

Theory is crucial for advancing the understanding of a phenomenon, but it is striking to realize that very little has appeared in the past one hundred years since Durkheim's elegant theory of suicide. Suicidologists have remained content to propose and test a long list of psychopathological and social factors that increase the risk of suicide, combining the factors in a simple additive-regression model. However, empirical research without a theoretical basis is not very useful, and our understanding of suicide will not advance until better theories are proposed and tested (Lester, 2000). The strain theory of suicide is a reflection of such an effort.

In the near future, conceptual instruments may have to be established for each of the four strains. Another challenge for researchers will be to determine which types of strain lead to suicide within a certain subpopulation and why the relationship exists. These future research areas have the potential to provide significant support to the strain theory of suicide.

## REFERENCES

Agnew, R. (2001). Building on the foundation of general strain theory: specifying the types of strain most likely to lead to crime and delinquency. *Journal of Research in Crime & Delinquency,* 38, 319-361.

Agnew, R. (1992). Foundation for a general strain theory of crime and delinquency. *Criminology,* 30, 47-87.

Aronson, E. (1998). Dissonance, hypocrisy, and the self-concept. In E. Harmon-Jones & J. S. Mills (Eds.) *Cognitive dissonance theory: revival with revisions and controversies,* pp. 21-36. Washington, DC: American Psychological Association.

Beck, A. T., Steer, R. A., Kovacs, M., et al. (1985). Hopelessness and eventual suicide: a 10-year prospective study of patients hospitalized with suicidal ideation. *American Journal of Psychiatry,* 142, 559-563.

Brent, D. A., Perper, J. A., Moritz, G.., et al. (1993). Stressful life events, psychopathology, and adolescent suicide: a case control study. *Suicide & Life-Threatening Behavior,* 23, 179-187.

Chiles, J. A., Strosahl, K. D., Ping, Z.Y., et al. (1989). Depression, hopelessness, and suicidal behavior in Chinese and American psychiatric patients. *American Journal of Psychiatry,* 146, 339-344.

Daly, M., Conway, M., & Kelleher, M. J. (1986). Social determinants of self-poisoning. *British Journal of Psychiatry,* 148, 406-413.

Durkheim, E. (1897/1951). *Suicide: A study in sociology.* New York: Free Press.

Festinger, L. (1957). *A theory of cognitive dissonance.* Stanford, CA: Stanford University Press.

Festinger, L., & Aronson, E. (1960). The arousal and reduction of dissonance in social contexts. In D. Cartwright & A. Zander (Eds.) *Group dynamics,* pp. 214-231. Evanston, IL: Row & Peterson.

Freud, S. (1917/1957). Mourning and melancholia. In J. Strachey (Ed. and Trans.) *The standard edition of the complete psychological works of Sigmund Freud* (Vol. 14). London, UK: Hogarth Press.

Heeringen, K. V. (2003). The neurobiology of suicide and suicidality. *Canadian Journal of Psychiatry,* 48, 292-300.

Henry, A., & Short, J. (1954). *Suicide and homicide.* New York: Free Press.

Kaplan, K. J., & Harrow, M. (1996). Positive and negative symptoms as risk factors for later suicidal activity in schizophrenics versus depressives. *Suicide & Life-Threatening behavior,* 26, 105-121.

Lester, D. (2000). *Why people kill themselves.* Springfield, IL: Charles Thomas.

Mann, J. J., Waternaux, C., Haas, G. L., et al. (1999). Toward a clinical model of suicidal behavior in psychiatric patients. *American Journal of Psychiatry,* 156, 181-189.

Maris, R. W. (1997). Social and familial risk factors in suicidal behavior. *Psychiatric Clinics of North America,* 20, 519-550.

Merton, R. (1957). *Social theory and social structure.* New York: Free Press.

Nordstrom, P., Schalling, D., & Asberg, M. (1995). Temperamental vulnerability in attempted suicide. *Acta Psychiatrica Scandinavica,* 92, 155-160.

Pokorny, A.D. (1983). Prediction of suicide in psychiatric patients: report of a prospective study. *Archives of General Psychiatry,* 40, 249-257.

Roy, A. (1985). Family history of suicide in manic-depressive patients. *Journal of Affective Disorders,* 8, 187-189.

Roy, A., Segal, N.L., & Sarchiapone, M. (1995) Attempted suicide among living co-twins of twin suicide victims. *American Journal of Psychiatry,* 152, 1075-1076.

Schulsinger, F., Kety, S. S., Rosenthal, D., et al. (1979). A family study of suicide. In M. Schou & E. Stromgren (Eds.) *Origin, prevention and treatment of affective disorders,* pp. 277-287. New York: Academic Press.

Stack, S. (1979). Durkheim's theory of fatalistic suicide: a cross-national analysis. *Journal of Social Psychology,* 107, 161-168.

Strakowski S. M., McElroy, S. L., Keck, P. E.. Jr, et al. (1996). Suicidality among patients with mixed and manic bipolar disorder. *American Journal of Psychiatry,* 153, 674-676.

Thio, A. (2004). Deviant Behavior. 7th Ed. Boston, MA: Pearson Education.

Zhang, J. (2000). Collectivism or individualism: an analysis of Chinese interactive culture. *American Review of China Studies,* 1, 57-65.

Zhang, J., & Jin, S. (1998). Interpersonal relations and suicide ideation in China. *Genetic, Social, & General Psychology Monographs, 124(1),* 79-94.

Zhang, J., & Thomas, D. (1991). Familial and religious influences on suicidal ideation. *Family Perspectives,* 25, 301-321.

Chapter 18

# SUICIDE AND DISASTERS

*Dusica Lecic-Tosevski, Milica Pejovic Milovancevic and Smiljka Popovic Deusic*

Disasters of all kind are unfortunately frequent occurrences in contemporary world and, as such, cause immense human suffering. The most common natural disasters are hurricanes, floods and earthquakes, supplemented by industrial, nuclear and transportation accidents. Disasters can be analyzed in a physical context as a consequence of natural catastrophe or in a social context as a consequence of human behavior (e.g., terrorism or suicide bombers) (Lopez-Ibor, 2005). Common to all disasters is the enormous capacity to affect a huge number of people at the same time. This can lead to all sorts of stress reactions that can, subsequently, have a profound impact on personal mental health. Intense stressors such as exposure to the dead and dying, bereavement and social and community disruption frequently lead to mental health problems (Norris, et al., 2002).

Man-made disasters are caused by human behavior and, thus, cause more frequent and persistent psychological distress than natural disasters (Fullerton & Ursano, 2005). Mass violence is, unfortunately, also common in the contemporary world in spite of a growing trend toward globalization and unification. Violence has many faces and is manifest in wars, ethnic conflicts, terrorist acts and urban aggression.

The experiences of many countries and populations in the recent past have shown that wars are often justified with "higher" causes and a "wish to initiate peace." The question "why war," which Freud and Einstein (Freud, 1933) tried to answer years ago, is still an issue of the utmost importance. Wars and terrorism in many parts of the world (e.g., September 11th, terrorist acts in Madrid, London, Turkey and Thailand, wars and conflicts in Afghanistan, the Balkans, Cambodia, Chechnya, Iraq, Israel, Lebanon, Palestine, Russia, Rwanda, Sri Lanka, Somalia and Uganda) reveal that the "malady of death" and the power of destructive forces, both outside and within the individual and society, have never appeared as frequently as they do today.

Disasters may cause posttraumatic stress responses which can lead to additional severe secondary problems such as affective disorders, substance abuse or social and relational problems. All of these conditions lead to an increased risk of suicidal behavior (Mehlum, 2006).

## EMERGING CHALLENGES

No single factor has gained acceptance as a universal cause of suicide. However, depression is a common condition among those who commit suicide. Other factors are pain, stress, grief after loss, trauma, catastrophic injury, financial loss, terrorism especially related to religion (suicide bombing) and extreme nationalism. Taking into account the link between disasters and depression (Person, 2006; Aksaray, et al., 2006; Ahern, 2006) and between depression and suicide, it is reasonable to expect a link between disasters and increased suicide rates.

At least two possibilities can be discussed regarding the relationship between suicide and disaster. Suicide can be a consequence of a disaster, a result of personal breakdown after exposure to catastrophe and an incapacity to cope with such a catastrophe. On the other hand, individual suicide can be a trigger of disaster for many other persons - suicide bombers are an example of this. A suicide attack (such as a suicide bombing) is an attack carried out toward an enemy at the cost of the attacker's life and causes additional human suffering (Shalev, 2005). Suicide can also be a consequence of disasters among rescuers, solders or peacekeepers who are involved in disaster areas as part of their duties (Hansen-Schwartz, 2002).

Suicide can also result from socio-demographic factors since disasters provoke mass migration, problems of poverty, poor housing, lack of social support and unmet expectations. In addition, social factors and stressful life events play a significant role in increasing suicidal risk. Mass violence and civil conflicts also cause large movements of people and, because of them, the international community faces a global refugee problem of unprecedented proportions. It is estimated that there are close to twenty million international refugees in the world today. In addition to this, there are another twenty million displaced persons. For a large proportion of those forced to migrate, the relocation process itself is often associated with degradation, poverty, violence, dehumanization, torture, suicide or death (Marsella, et al., 1998).

## MENTAL MORBIDITY

The relationship between mental health problems and disasters is ambiguous. Some studies show only a minimal impact of disasters on mental health (Bravo, et al., 1990), but most studies show clear evidence of psychological sequelae after disasters. Posttraumatic stress disorder (PTSD), depression, insomnia, anxiety and problems such as substance abuse and domestic violence have been reported (Krug, et al., 1998). Suicide can also occur as a consequence.

The most often assessed and observed condition among people affected by disaster is PTSD (Norris, et al., 2002, Lecic-Tosevski & Draganic-Gajic, 2005; Lecic-Tosevski, et al., 2003), followed by depression and anxiety. Many disaster victims manifest nonspecific distress because of the elevation of various stress-related psychological and psychosomatic symptoms, including demoralization, perceived stress and negative affect.

## NATURAL DISASTERS

Natural disasters cause long lasting changes in everyday life. Victims of disasters may be injured or may lose family members, friends, property or jobs. After natural disasters, factors such as bereavement, property loss and the disruption of social networks are often associated with mental health problems including depression and hopelessness, known to be risk factors for suicide (Pearson, et al., 2006; Aksaray, et al., 2006; Vehid, et al., 2006).

Suicide rates increase after severe natural disasters such as floods, hurricanes and earthquakes. It was shown that suicide rates increased by 13.8% during the four years after one severe natural disaster (Krug, et al., 1998). Psychological problems can persist for three to five years after a disaster, although temporary symptoms are more common than severe long-term reactions (Freedy, et al., 1994). There are several possible reasons why people may commit suicide after a natural disaster, even months or years later. Psychological reactions may result from the stress directly caused by a disaster, as well as from disruption of community life (Warheit, et al., 1996).

Krug, et al. (1998) found increased suicide rates after severe floods, hurricanes, and earthquakes. Another study found that suicide rates for earthquake victims were higher than a low-exposure group who remained stable and consistent throughout the observational period (Yang, et al., 2005). Other studies, however, have demonstrated that disasters do not result in an increase in suicide rates (Shoaf, et al., 2004).

## MAN-MADE DISASTERS

Man-made disasters are caused by direct influence of humans on nature (change in climate, environmental disasters, pollution, etc) or are the result of wars, civil conflicts and terrorist attacks. Mass violence is, unfortunately, the most common disaster. It causes civil casualties, migration and displacement of people, and destroys the economy and infrastructure, resulting in a culture of poverty and insecurity. This affects the mental health of the survivors and of the population at large.

Many studies have documented that mass violence can have a devastating effect on the mental health of the affected population as a whole, especially in vulnerable groups such as children, adolescents, single mothers, the elderly, refugees and detained people. Psychosocial consequences are frequent and manifest as stress disorders (including PTSD), depression, psychosomatic disorders, aggression and violence among the young, somatization, and burnout syndrome in the medical staff dealing with traumatized persons and in those giving psychological aid (Lecic-Tosevski & Draganic-Gajic, 2005; Lecic-Tosevski, et al., 2006). These consequences may be further complicated by substance abuse, domestic and criminal violence, suicides, homicides and chronic medical illness (Jensen, 1996).

Mass violence prevents the normal development of children as it threatens their childhood and causes the development of personality disorders as well as a predisposition for adult mental disorders. Moreover, accumulated trauma, or severe and prolonged stress, if unresolved, might lead to lasting scars of the psyche in the form of personality changes, somatic disorders, brain changes and malignant, pernicious memories. In addition, unresolved hostilities lead to a spiral of violence which might be repeated in future generations through the transgenerational transmission of trauma and a compulsive repetition of violence and aggression. Prevention of mass violence might prevent this spiral which ultimately endangers mankind as a whole.

Wars and mass violence are connected with increased suicide rates, especially of those persons suffering from mental health problems prior to the war period (Loncar, et al., 2004). However, some studies have shown a decreased incidence of suicide during periods of war, pointing out that wars diminish the likelihood of suicide by strengthening the social bonds among people (Henderson, et al., 2006; Petrovich, et al., 2001; Somasundram & Rajadurai, 1995; Lester, 1993). Indeed, during the period of bombardment of Serbia in the Spring of 1999, the number of registered patients in psychiatric services significantly decreased.

Suicide bombing is one of the most deadly weapons, causing approximately 60% of all civilians' deaths in the years 2000-2004 and giving rise to a larger number of psychological consequences (Shalev, 2005). Suicide bombers intend to kill others and to die in the process. Ninety-five percent of such attacks in recent times have some specific strategic goal - to cause the occupying army to withdraw forces from a disputed territory (Pape, 2005). Suicide bombing is a complex phenomenon, a result of despair on one hand and desire for revenge and defiance on the other (Sarraj & Qouta, 2005). In some cultures suicide bombing is seen as a holy battle against the aggressor and as an honest fight with justified causes. The tangible and intangible incentives and rewards mostly motivate very young people to become suicide bombers (Berko & Erez, 2005). A martyr is glorified and respected, and new bombers are likely to continue actions until their enemy publicly acknowledges guilt and responsibility (Nixon & Stewart 2005).

## OUR EXPERIENCES

Since 1991, Serbia and Montenegro underwent a period of war, economic sanctions, NATO bombing, social transition and political upheaval. Most of the population was exposed to prolonged stress which became a part of everyday life. During the war years the rate of suicides increased, reaching its peak in 1993. Male suicides outnumbered female suicides by a ratio of 2:1 (Selakovic-Bursic, et al., 2006). However, the suicide rate of both sexes declined in the period of 1997-2004. The second highest suicide rate, for both sexes, was in 2000 (female suicide rate 9.7, male suicide rate 19.7), which is not surprising bearing in mind the NATO intervention of the preceding year (Nikolic-Balkoski, et al., 2006). The highest suicide rate for both sexes was in the lowest educational category (less than eight years of education). In Belgrade unemployed males committed suicide more frequently than unemployed females (2.8:1), probably due to an interaction of socioeconomic circumstances and stressful life events. The number of adolescent suicides increased and reached its peak in 1997 compared with the numbers in 1990 and 2003. Suicide rates appeared to correspond with the social crisis (economic sanctions, the political upheaval, social transitions and turmoil) (Curcic, 2005).

## INTERVENTION STRATEGIES

According to Raphael (1986), in the first hours after a disaster, at least 25% of the population may be stunned and dazed, apathetic and wandering, suffering from the disaster syndrome. This is especially true if the impact has been sudden and totally devastating. At this point, psychological first aid is necessary.

It is imperative to develop and evaluate interventions that will address the psychological reactions of people who have been exposed, directly or indirectly, to disasters of any kind. Some interventions should target the entire population, and some should target individuals with mental health problems resulting from traumatic events. Several recommendations can be given: acute psychological assessment and triage, crisis intervention for individuals, psychological first aid and facilitating access to appropriate levels of care when needed. Formal crisis intervention should always be based upon individual's natural coping mechanisms and resources as long as they are functioning effectively (Foa, et al., 2005; Everly & Flynn, 2006; Parker, et al., 2006). Different coping strategies seem to be protective for males and females, and social and cultural variables may be influential as well (Gavrilovic, et al., 2003; Lecic-Tosevski, et al., 2003).

Psychological help should be provided by trained professionals, especially health workers and helpers who should be able to perform the following: active listening skills, prioritizing and responding to human needs, recognizing and providing information on psychological and behavioral reactions, teaching acute stress management techniques and recognizing and reducing risk factors for adverse outcomes associated with interventions (Parker, et al., 2006).

## PREVENTION

Mental health support is needed after severe disasters. It should be available for varying periods, and should take into account the needs of various age groups. The psychological support should be adapted to each individual's needs (Lecic-Tosevski & Draganic-Gajic, 2005). Medicalization of problems should be avoided, and the traumatized person empowered so that personal autonomy can be maintained. Prevention should include providing social support and facilitating aid to victims. Mental health programs or other preventive strategies might be more effective by specifically targeting victims rather than simply targeting individuals living in disaster affected areas (Chou, et al., 2003).

Unfortunately, there is no evidence that screening for suicide risk is effective in reducing suicide rates, and a routine medical history is often not sufficient to recognize suicide risk or suicidal intent. This is especially true in time of disasters when the whole population is preoccupied with essential existential issues. In time of disasters, professionals should be aware of a variety of stress reactions that people can experience. Training primary care physicians to recognize and appropriately treat underlying mental health problems such as depression and substance abuse, and to become aware of their connection to potential suicidal behavior may be effective. Physicians should be alert to potential suicidal ideation when the history reveals risk factors for suicide, such as depression, alcohol or other drug abuse, other psychiatric disorder, prior attempted suicide, recent divorce, separation, unemployment and recent bereavement (US Preventive Task Forces, 1996).

In 1999, WHO started a worldwide initiative for suicide prevention and published a series of booklets to address various professionals (primary care workers, prison officers, school teachers, those working in media, survivors' groups, etc) (WHO, 2000).

Freud (1933) claimed that disasters of all kinds, including wars unfortunately, are inevitable, even in the so-called civilized and developed world, since man is much better in destroying than in creating, for the greatest part of him, like an iceberg, is submerged in a destructive element. Given this perspective, man-made disasters are likely to continue in the foreseeable future. Indeed, every day, civilians are dying as a result of hostilities or facing consequences such as extreme poverty. This being said, mental health professionals must be prepared to deal with the psychosocial consequences of disasters at any time, as well as be willing to devote their energy and time to alleviating the suffering of survivors, while also trying to decrease the spiral of stress and violence.

# REFERENCES

Ahern, J., & Galea, S. (2006). Social context and depression after a disaster: the role of income inequality. *Journal of Epidemiology & Community Health*, 60, 766-770.

Aksaray, G., Kortan, G., Erkaya, H., et al. (2006). Gender differences in psychological effect of the August 1999 earthquake in Turkey. *Nordic Journal of Psychiatry*, 60, 387-391.

Berko, A., & Erez, E. (2005). "Ordinary people" and "death work": Palestinian suicide bombers as victimizers and victims. *Violence & Victims*, 20, 603-623.

Bravo, M., Rubio-Stipec, M., Canino, G. J., et al. (1990). The psychological sequelae of disaster stress prospectively and retrospectively evaluated. *American Journal of Community Psychology*, 18, 661-680.

Chou, Y. J., Huang, N., Lee, C. H., et al. (2003). Suicides after 1999 Taiwan earthquake. *International Journal of Epidemiology*, 32, 1007-1014.

Curcic, V. (2005). Mental health of adolescents: risk and chance. *Psychiatry Today*, 37, 97-107.

Everly, G. S., & Flynn, B. W. (2006). Principles and practical procedures for acute psychological first aid training for personnel without mental health experience. *International Journal of Emergency Mental Health*, 2, 93-100.

Foa, E. B., Cahill, S. P., Boscarino, J. A., et al. (2005). Social, psychological, and psychiatric interventions following terrorist attacks: recommendations for practice and research. *Neuropsychopharmacology*, 30, 1806-1817.

Freedy, J. R., Saladin, M. E., Kilpatrick, D. G., et al. (1994). Understanding acute psychological distress following natural disaster. *Journal of Traumatic Stress*, 7, 257-273.

Freud, S. (1933/1963). *Civilisation and its discontents*. London, UK: Norton.

Fullerton, C. S., & Ursano, R. J. (2005). Psychological and psychopathological consequences of disaster. In J. J. Lopez-Ibor, G. Christodoulou, M. Maj, et al. (Eds.) *Disaster and mental health*, pp. 13-37. Chichester, UK: Wiley

Gavrilovic, J., Lecic-Tosevski, D., Dimic, S., et al. (2003). Coping strategies in civilians during air attacks. *Social Psychiatry & Psychiatric Epidemiology*, 38, 128-133.

Hansen-Schwartz, J., Jessen, G., Andersen, K., et al. (2002). Suicide after deployment in UN peacekeeping missions: a Danish pilot study. *Crisis, 23*, 55-58.

Henderson, R., Stark C., Humphry, R. W., et al. (2006). Changes in Scottish suicide rates during the Second World War. *BMC Public Health, 23*, 167.

Jensen, S. B. (1996). Mental health under war conditions during the 1991-1995 war in the former Yugoslavia. *World Health Statistics Quarterly, 49*, 213-217.

Krug, E. G., Kresnow, M., Peddicord, J. P., et al. (1998). Suicide after natural disaster. *New England Journal of Medicine, 338*, 373-378.

Lecic-Tosevski, D., & Draganic-Gajic, S. (2005). The Serbian experience. In J. J. Lopez-Ibor, G. Christodoulou, M. Maj, et al. (Eds.) *Disaster and mental health*, pp. 247-257. Chichester, UK: Wiley

Lecic-Tosevski, D., Gavrilovic, J., Knezevic, G., et al. (2003). Personality factors and posttraumatic stress: associations in civilians one year after air attacks. *Journal of Personality Disorders, 17*, 537-549.

Lecic-Tosevski D., Pejovic Milovancevic, M., Pejuskovic, B., et al. (2006). Burnout syndrome of general practitioners in postwar period. *Epidemiologia e Psychiatria Sociale, 15*, 319-322.

Lester, D. (1993). Suicide rates in Army personnel in times of peace and war. *Military Medicine, 158*, A7.

Loncar C., Definis-Gojanovic M., Dodig G., et al. (2004). War, mental disorder and suicide. *Collegium Anthropologicum, 28*, 377-384.

Lopez Ibor, J. J. (2005). What is disaster? In J. J. Lopez-Ibor, G. Christodoulou, M. Maj, et al. (Eds.) *Disaster and mental health*, pp. 1-13. Chichester, UK: Wiley

Marsella, A.J., Bornemann, T., Ekblad, S., et al. (1998). *Amidst peril and pain: the mental health and well-being of the world's refugees.* Washington, DC: American Psychology Association.

Mehlum, L. (2006). Trauma as a life event and its impact on suicidal behavior. *Psychiatria Danubina, 18*, 76.

Nikolic-Balkoski, G., Pavlicevic, V., Jasovic-Gasic, M., et al. (2006). Suicide in the capital of Serbia and Montenegro in the period 1997-2004 - sex differences. *Psychiatria Danubina*, 18, 1–2, 48-54.

Nixon, R. G., & Stewart, C. E. (2005). Recognizing imminent danger: characteristics of a suicide bomber. *Emergency Medical Services, 34*, 74-75.

Norris, F. H., Friedman, M. J., Watson P. J., et al. (2002). 60.000 disaster victims speak: Part I. An empirical review of the empirical literature, 1981-2001. *Psychiatry, 65*, 207-239.

Norris, F. H., Friedman, M. J., & Watson, P. J. (2002). 60.000 disaster victims speak: Part II. Summary and implications of the disaster mental health research. *Psychiatry, 65*, 240-260.

Parker, C. L., Everly, G. S., Barnett, D. J., et al. (2006). Establishing evidence-informed core intervention competencies in psychological first aid for public health personnel. *International Journal of Emergency Mental Health, 8*, 83-92.

Person, C., Tracy, M., & Galea, S. (2006). Risk factors for depression after a disaster. *Journal of Nervous & Mental Disease, 194*, 659-666.

Petrovich, B., Todorovich, B., & Kocich, B., et al. (2001). Influence of socio-economic crisis on epidemiological characteristic of suicide in the region of Nis (Southeastern part of Serbia, Yugoslavia). *European Journal of Epidemiology, 17*, 183-187.

Raphael, B. (1986). *When disaster strikes*. New York: Basic Books.

Sarraj, E. E., & Qouta, S. (2005). The Palestinian experience. In J. J. Lopez-Ibor, G. Christodoulou, M. Maj, et al. (Eds.) *Disaster and Mental Health*, pp. 229-239. Chichester, UK: Wiley.

Selakovic-Bursic, S., Haramic, E., & Leenaars, A. A. (2006). The Balkan piedmont: male suicide rates pre-war, wartime, and post-war in Serbia and Montenegro. *Archives of Suicide Research,* 10, 225-238.

Shalev, A.Y. (2005). The Israeli Experience. In J. J. Lopez-Ibor, G. Christodoulou, M. Maj, et al. (Eds.) *Disaster and mental health*, pp. 217-229. Chichester, UK: Wiley.

Shoaf, K., Sauter, C., Bourque, L.B., et al. (2004). Suicides in Los Angeles County in relation to the Northridge earthquake. *Prehospital & Disaster Medicine,* 19, 307-310.

Somasundaram, D. J., & Rajadurai, S. (1995). War and suicide in northern Sri Lanka. *Acta Psychiatrica Scandinavica,* 91, 1-4.

Vehid, H. E., Alyanak, B., & Eksi, A. (2006). Suicide ideation after 1999 earthquake in Marmara, Turkey. *Tohoku Journal of Experimental Medicine,* 208, 19-24.

U.S. Preventive Services Task Force. (1996). *Guide to clinical preventive services*, 2nd Ed. Washington, DC: U.S. Department of Health and Human Services, Office of Disease Prevention and Health Promotion.

Warheit, G. J., Zimmerman, R. S., & Khoury, E. L., et al. (1996). Disaster related stresses, depressive signs and symptoms, and suicidal ideation among a multi-racial/ethnic sample of adolescents: a longitudinal analysis. *Journal of Child Psychology & Psychiatry & Allied Disciplines,* 37, 435-444.

World Health Organization. (2000). *Preventing suicide series.* Geneva, Switzerland: Mental and Behavioural Disorders Department of Mental Health World Health Organization.

Yang, C. H., Xirasagar, S., Chung, H. C., et al. (2005). Suicide trends following the Taiwan earthquake of 1999: empirical evidence and policy implications. *Acta Psychiatrica Scandinavica,* 112, 442-448.

# Part 3: Suicide Across Cultures

**Chapter 19**

# CULTURAL PSYCHODYNAMICS AND SUICIDAL BEHAVIOR

## *Vijoy K. Varma*

Just as mental health and illness are dependent upon individual biological and psychological variables, they are also correlated with socio-cultural factors. Differences across individuals may relate to individual factors, but also to differences in social organization and cultural norms and mores. In so far as differences *across* cultures exceed those *within* a cultural group, culture can be said to play a significant role in mental health and illness. Separating cross-cultural differences from those within individuals in a social group would thus indicate their differential contribution. This may also help in understanding the core nature of mental illness better.

It has been increasingly recognized that simply looking at the individual variables in the etiology and manifestations of psychopathology is not enough. If a certain psychopathology is largely distributed in the society, it would be more worthwhile to look for the factors in the society and culture which may be responsible, partly or wholly, in the causation of the malady and in modifying its nature and course (Varma, 1999).

In this chapter, I have attempted to correlate suicidal behavior with certain socio-cultural variables. If we were to simply look at individual variables, there may be as many explanations as the number of subjects. To illustrate, if we study divorce, each case may have its own unique grounds. However, to formulate theories, we have to make generalizations.

Psychological factors can operate at an individual level or at a social level, applicable to all or most of members of the group or society. A psychodynamic explanation of a pathology could apply to and explain individual differences, or it could apply to the society and culture as a whole.

Many people have a built in resistance to viewing cultures as a whole. Their argument is that within a society or a culture people may differ greatly. For example, in comparing Americans with Indians, are we talking about the poor rural Indian or the upward mobile urbanite?

Many terms to describe cultures are overgeneralizations, using simple catchall phrases. For example, we talk of the divides of Eastern-Western, developing-developed, traditional-technologically advanced, etc, but there are wide variations within each rubric. However, each divide carries some meaning. Ultimately, no research or theory is possible unless we gloss over some individual differences. The differences across categories can be significantly greater than those within the categories. Statistics can provide this. For example, when we do an analysis of variance, a significant 'F' ratio means that differences across groups are greater than those within.

## CULTURE AND SUICIDE

According to the World Health Organization, nearly a million people commit suicide every year. The fatalities are likely to rise to 1.5 million by 2020. In almost every country, the incidence of suicide is higher than that of intentional homicide. The incidence of suicide varies across countries although it remains within certain limits. The rate is said to be about 7 per 100,000 in my country, India. The incidence is the highest in Europe's Baltic countries, about 40 per 100,000 per year. Malta is said to have the lowest rates - zero in some years. The USA rate is roughly 20 for males and 5 for females. There are a number of possible explanations for the variation in the incidence of suicide across cultures and countries. For example, Malta's low rates are ascribed to it being a devout Catholic country.

Women are more likely to attempt suicide. It is possible that, in their case, attempted suicide is just a cry for help. On the other hand, men may see a non-fatal suicidal act as a failure and a reason for shame. Suicide rates are highest among the unemployed, retired, divorced, childless, urbanites, empty nesters and those who live alone. It is also related to socio-economic disadvantage, such as limited education, homelessness, unemployment, economic dependence and contact with the judicial or penal system. Suicide rates are higher among the mentally ill. Schizophrenia, depression, bipolar disorders, alcoholism and drug dependence are recognized as likely risk factors. However, suicidal behavior often contributes to someone being labeled as mentally ill and, as such, there may be the 'chicken-and-the-egg' problem here.

## SOCIO-CULTURAL VARIABLES RELEVANT TO DEPRESSION AND SUICIDAL BEHAVIOR

Two key socio-cultural variables that may be related to suicidal behavior are autonomy and guilt-proneness.

### Dependence Versus Autonomy

Our relationship with society leads to the development of "me/not-me" differentiation, to *autonomy* versus *dependence*. Different cultures tend to differ on this variable, with autonomy-based societies developing increasingly judgmental and litigious traits.

Dependence can be said to be an integral part of human existence. It has been pointed out that, on account of the disparity between the dimensions of the birth canal and the projected head size, the human infant must be born incomplete and much of the development completed after birth. This gives rise in the human infant to a protracted period of dependence which influences all interpersonal relationships throughout life.

Cultures differ from each other in the quantity of dependence and autonomy. Traditional, developing, Eastern cultures can be said to exemplify dependence, and developed, industrialized societies of the West autonomy. In dependence-prone societies there is greater dependence, in chronological order, on parents, peer groups, spouse and, finally, on one's children. This leads to a system of inter-relationships, with everybody leaning on everybody else. In contrast, increasing autonomy has characterized the industrialized, technologically developed countries of the West (Varma, 1985a, 1985b, 1986, 1988, 1995, 1999; Neki, 1976).

The autonomous individual develops a heightened sense of self-reliance and is more cognizant of his responsibilities, rights and prerogatives. Since he is self-reliant, he expects everybody else also to be so. The relentless pursuit of autonomy in Western countries has had undesirable consequences which are now being increasingly recognized. The heightened need for self-reliance does not permit dependence even in situations where it is a biological imperative in children, the aged, the infirm and the disabled. It has given rise to what can be termed as the "death of childhood" and the "death of old age," negating the dependency needs at these life-stages. The pursuit of autonomy has led to an intense righteous indignation, assigning responsibility to specific individuals for every lapse and mishap. Nothing happens by chance, everything is caused by individuals, and hence responsibility must be fixed. It leads to finger-pointing, a particularly American trait, and litigiousness. It ignores the fact that the cause-and-effect relationships between events are neither straightforward nor linear. Many mishaps such as traffic accidents are just that – accidents - in which chance plays a large role and imponderables determine its occurrence. In comparison, the dependence perspective admits that we all live in a social system, in an ongoing relationship with our environment, and the variables are multiple and often intangible. It teaches us greater understanding in judging our fellow human beings.

Neither total dependence nor total autonomy is possible in any functioning society (Hsu, 1972). The problems of the relentless pursuit of autonomy in the West are becoming increasingly apparent - an exalted sense of responsibility (of self and of others), litigiousness, and denial of needed support and social isolation. Without resorting to total abrogation of responsibility leading to social nihilism, there is every need for moderation and humility in judging others. The functional social matrix of the third world has a message which could help the West.

The socio-cultural variable of autonomy-dependence is intimately linked also with mental illness. It has been pointed out by others (e.g., Arieti, in his conceptualization of schizophrenic breakdown) that manifest psychopathology is the culmination of the organism's coping mechanism. In other words, when coping fails, the underlying anxiety may be manifest in psychotic and neurotic symptoms. In the context of schizophrenia, Manfred Bleuler, alluding to his illustrious father, mentioned that there reaches a point in human misery when the person decompensates into a psychotic state. The decompensation can take a number of forms. However, there are clear-cut limitations in the forms of coping mechanisms that can be used.

I conceptualize the relationship of autonomy-dependence to the psychogenesis of illness in the following way. As we have seen, the autonomous individual likes to retain full control and assume all responsibility for his actions and emotions. Faced with stress, he will, accordingly, try to retain control over himself as much and as long as possible. Hence, he may fight off the illness, have only a neurotic illness or delay the genesis of a psychotic illness. There is some evidence now, coming from transcultural research, that the duration of illness at the index therapeutic contact is longer in developed Western countries than in the traditional societies of the developing world. However, in the autonomous individual, once decompensation starts, it is more rapid and precipitous. It may be that, in Western countries, a psychotic illness may indicate a "greater" psychopathology than in the third world. This may explain the reported less favorable outcome of the illness there. There is also evidence from the geriatric research that in Western countries, age-related decompensation starts later, but is more precipitous. Also, in traditional societies and developing countries, it has been shown that there is a significant amount of psychotic disorder with good prognosis, particularly those psychoses of acute onset. It appears that the dependence-prone personality is more open to break down which may be facilitated by the realization that one lives in a society where he can rely on the social milieu in which he lives. Lack of social support and of nurturing, abiding relationships within the society may further explain the less favorable outcome. The sick may resist seeking support even when it may be forthcoming on account of its aversion to such sustenance and the social value of extolling independence.

## Recent Research into Autonomy-Dependence

Sato and McCann (2007) reported that Beck and associates, by meticulously compiling clinical observations of depressed individuals in cognitive therapy, suggested two dimensions of personality, sociotropy and autonomy, that influence vulnerability to depression. Sociotropy includes beliefs, behavioral dispositions and attitudes that draw an individual to attend to and depend on others for personal satisfaction. Sociotropic individuals emphasize interpersonal interactions involving relatedness, intimacy, empathy, approval, affection, protection, guidance and help (Beck, 1987). On the other hand, autonomy is considered to be a combination of beliefs, behavioral dispositions and attitudes that draw an individual to invest in one's self for one's own uniqueness, mastery over one's bodily functioning, and control over one's environment. Autonomous individuals emphasize individuality, self-reliance, personal achievements and a sense of power to do what they want (Beck, 1987).

The concepts of sociotropy and autonomy are virtually identical to my concepts of dependence and autonomy, respectively. According to Beck (1983), both highly sociotropic and autonomous individuals are vulnerable to depression when faced with a threat or a loss in a domain corresponding to their specific type of individual investment. Loss of a significant person in one's life is likely to cause depression in a highly sociotropic individual. On the other hand, repeated failure in performing a personal task may lead to depression in a highly autonomous individual.

## AUTONOMY-DEPENDENCE AND SUICIDAL BEHAVIOR

An autonomous individual, with his exalted sense of control and mastery over his body, not only assumes greater responsibility over his or her failings, but also assumes the prerogative to do whatever he wants to his body. One of the things that he can do is to kill it. Although contrary to the philosophy of most religions that only God gives (and thus can take away) life, an autonomous individual assumes the right to terminate his physical existence. With his or her sense of self-reliance, responsibilities for actions, rights and prerogatives, he has only himself to blame.

On the other hand, the dependence-prone individual sees cause and effect in a larger context, with the entire social milieu participating in it. His failings are not only his, but perhaps reflect what is wrong with the society. Also, he is more likely to seek support from his family and friends.

Kaslow and co-workers have identified four key psychodynamic concepts of suicidal behavior, namely, self-directed aggression, object loss, ego functioning disturbance and pathological object relations (Kaslow, et al., 1998). Modestin (1992) related the psychodynamic basis of suicidal behavior to the psychology of drive, ego, object relations and self. Modestin (1997) further pointed out that suicidal behavior always occurs in the context of interpersonal relationships.

According to Hendin (1991), the psychodynamic meaning of suicide derives from both affective and cognitive components. Rage, hopelessness, despair and guilt are important affective states. The meanings of suicide can be conscious and unconscious: death as a reunion, death as rebirth, death as retaliatory abandonment, death as revenge, and death as self-punishment or atonement.

According to Poldinger (1989), there are two main reasons for self-destructive behavior, one of which is self-destruction as a result of inhibited aggression. This is one of the main theories on self-aggression based on theories of Sigmund Freud. The second reason, seen especially in attempted suicide, is the so-called "cry for help" described by Farberow and Shneidman. Psychodynamics show that suicidal behavior is akin to self-aggression (Poldinger & Holsboer-Trachsler, 1989). The wish to die generally goes along with the wish to stay alive.

## Shame-Cultures and Guilt-Cultures

Different cultures are said to differ on the variable of guilt and shame. It has been said by many workers that so-called primitive cultures are relatively free of guilt. Lack of guilt-proneness is said to be responsible for a lower incidence of depression in non-Western societies. Although, workers are becoming increasingly aware that this may be a relative oversimplification, and that people in primitive cultures also display guilt, there is a valid point here. Many studies from India have demonstrated a significant amount of guilt in depressed patients (Venkoba Rao, 1973, Teja, et al., 1971). It may be perhaps true that, in the case of the Indian patient, the guilt feeling may be related to certain values other than those important in the Western culture and may be thought to be based sometimes on misdeeds of an earlier birth (Varma, 1982).

Guilt-proneness is said to be greater in the Western cultures. It could be related to the religious ethos. It is possible that, whereas societies following the Judeo-Christian religions are guilt-prone because of subscribing to the view that man was created in sin and attempt, therefore, to absolve him from such sin (Christ died for our sins, saving one's soul, the concept of damnation, etc.), Eastern religions do not subscribe to guilt as a prerequisite of human existence (Varma, 1985a).

Guilt refers to seeing or projecting one's mistakes. Guilt has a prominent place in the Western mind because of the Judeo-Christian background of the culture. The concept of being born with an "original sin" – for which we personally are not responsible – easily puts a feeling of guilt in the mind. The presentations in several Christian traditions can give the impression that one should feel guilty and ashamed for having fun.

Rules about responsibility and blame are not the same across cultures, or even across different sectors of the same culture. Dodds (1951) first articulated the differences between "shame" cultures and "guilt" cultures. In her landmark study, comparing the American and the Japanese cultures, Benedict (1967) spelled out the differences between the two cultures. She distinguished between the "guilt" culture, with which the West is familiar from its criminal justice system, and the "shame" culture of Japan. She concluded that the USA is a guilt culture while Japan is a shame culture. In guilt cultures, your actions reflect on you and that ethics and truth are universal whereas, in shame cultures, your actions reflect on others and ethics and truth are situational.

The European and North American cultures, claiming a Judeo-Christian heritage, are guilt cultures. Psychologically, guilt is proclaimed to be a more "advanced" emotion than shame. Erikson (1965) saw shame as a part of the second stage of growth of the ego, but guilt as the third.

Neither culture is perfect; neither is alien to our experience. Expression of "fault" and "fairness" can be found in both, but they operate according to very different rules.

In the guilt-prone cultures, there are always two parties to the process - myself and other people. If you did not do anything wrong, you have to protest your innocence and fight the accusation. In a guilt-prone culture, you feel guilty if you think that you did something wrong, even if others do not think so. On the other hand, in a shame-prone culture, "no one knows and, therefore, I am not ashamed." But, even if you did not do it, you feel ashamed and dishonored if others believe that you did it.

## GUILT AND SHAME-PRONENESS AND SUICIDAL BEHAVIOR

The other socio-cultural variable that can be said to be linked to suicidal behavior could be the differential proneness to guilt versus shame. Shame comes from the surveillance of other people, someone to point a finger at you, to point out that you have done something wrong. The process of guilt is more internalized. It comes from within; from a fully-assimilated superego. It does not require anyone pointing it out to you.

Guilt clearly plays a pivotal role both in depression and suicidality. Depressed patients often feel and verbalize guilt for real as well as presumed wrong-doings. Many of these relate to trivial lapses. Guilt leads to aggression turned inwards, and thus to depression and self-harm.

## CONCLUSION

Suicide is an unfortunate outcome of a large number of factors. Many of these emanate from the individual factors such as demographic, genetic and other variables relating to the unique experience and upbringing of the individual. However, socio-cultural dynamics also play a large part. To some extent, culture may explain the varying incidence of suicide across cultures and countries. The interaction between the two groups of variables may ultimately add to our understanding of suicide and, hopefully, help in a favorable intervention.

## REFERENCES

Beck, A. T. (1983). Cognitive therapy of depression: new perspectives. In P. J. Clayton & J. E. Barrett (Eds.) *Treatment of depression: old controversies and new approaches*, pp.265-290. New York: Raven Press.

Beck, A. T. (1987). Cognitive models of depression. *Journal of Cognitive Psychotherapy*, 1, 5-37.

Benedict, R (1967). *The chrysanthemum and the sword*. London, UK: Routledge and Kegan Paul.

Dodds, E. R. (1951). *The Greeks and the irrational*. Berkeley, CA: University of California Press

Erikson, E. (1965). *Childhood and society*. Harmondsworth, UK: Penguin

Hendin, H. (1991). Psychodynamics of suicide with particular reference to the young. *American Journal of Psychiatry*, 148, 1150-8.

Hsu, F. L. K. (1972). *Psychological anthropology*. Cambridge, MA: Schenkman.

Kaslow, N. J., Reviere, S. L., Chance, S. E., et al. (1998). An empirical study of the psychodynamics of suicide. *Journal of the American Psychoanalytic Association*, 46, 777-96.

Modestin, J. (1992). The psychodynamic aspects of suicidal behaviour. *Psychotherapie Psychosomatik Medizinische Psychologie*, 42, 430-35.

Modestin, J. (1997). Interpersonal aspects of suicidal psychodynamics. *Psychotherapie Psychosomatik Medizinische Psychologie*, 47, 413-18.

Neki, J. S. (1976). An examination of the cultural relativism of dependence as a dynamic of social and therapeutic relationship. I. Socio-developmental. *British Journal of Medical Psychology*, 49, 1-10.

Poldinger, W. J. (1989). The psychopathology and psychodynamics of self-destruction. *Crisis*, 10, 113-22.

Poldinger, W. J., & Holsboer-Trachsler, E. (1989). Psychopathology and psychodynamics of self-destruction. *Schweizerische Rundschau Medizin Praxis*, 78, 214-18.

Sato, T., & McCann, D. (2007). Sociotropy-autonomy and interpersonal problems. *Depression & Anxiety*, 24, 153-162.

Teja, J. S., Narang, R. L., & Aggarwal, A .K. (1971). Depression across cultures. *British Journal of Psychiatry*, 119, 253.

Varma, V. K. (1982). Present state of psychotherapy in India. *Indian Journal of Psychiatry*, 24, 209-226.

Varma, V. K. (1985a). Psychosocial and cultural variables relevant to psychotherapy in the developing countries. In P. Pichot, A. Brenner, R. Wolf, & K. Thau (Eds.) *Psychiatry: the state of the art, Vol. 4: psychotherapy, psychosomatic medicine,* pp. 159-165. New York: Plenum Press

Varma, V. K. (1985b). The Indian mind and psychopathology. *Integrative Psychiatry,* 3, 290-296.

Varma, V. K. (1986). Cultural psychodynamics in health and illness. *Indian Journal of Psychiatry,* 28, 13-34.

Varma, V. K. (1988). Culture, personality and psychotherapy. *International Journal of Social Psychiatry,* 34, 142-149.

Varma, V. K., & Chakrabarti, S. (1995). Social correlates and cultural dynamics of mental illness in traditional society: India. In I. Al-Issa (Ed.) *Handbook of culture and mental illness: an international perspective,* pp. 115-127. Madison, CT: International Universities Press.

Varma, V. K. (1999). Transcultural psychiatry. In J. N. Vyas & Niraj Ahuja (Eds.) *Textbook of postgraduate psychiatry. 2$^{nd}$ Ed,* pp. 945-968. New Delhi, India: Jaypee Brothers Medical Publishers.

Venkoba Rao, A. (1973). Depressive illness and guilt in Indian culture. *Indian Journal of Psychiatry,* 15, 231.

*Chapter 20*

# HIDDEN SUICIDE IN THE DEVELOPING WORLD

## Colin Pritchard

Ambivalence about suicide exists across most cultures, even in Japan despite its Samurai tradition (Leenaars, 2004) and, in many Western Developed Countries (WDC), the stigma continues. Indeed, in rural Greece, suicides may sometimes be refused burial in 'hallowed ground,' and it was only in 1962 that suicide was decriminalized in Great Britain (Pritchard & Hansen, 2005a, 2005b).

The stigma surrounding suicide led to some authorities to suggest that, in order to save families further distress, sometimes Open or Misadventure Verdicts be given rather than suicide (Stanistreet, et al., 2001; Linsley, et al., 2001, Salib, et al., 2005). Such verdicts are classified by the WHO as undetermined and appear as 'Other External Causes of Death' (OECD). It has been argued that OECD may be the depository of hidden suicides and should be included in studies of the incidence of suicide (Linsley, et al., 2001; Stanistreet, et al., 2001; Salib, et al., 2005). Moreover, OECD are often violent and are undetermined because "information is insufficient to enable the medical or legal authority to make a distinction between accident, self-harm and assault" (WHO, 1992). The types of lethality are often methods of suicide, such as hanging, drowning and falls, and so OECD may also contain hidden homicides as well as hidden suicides.

This leads us to consider the extent to which developing countries may also have possible hidden suicides as a result of cultural attitudes towards suicide. Such attitudes stem largely from a country's religious traditions. The four great faiths (Buddhism, Hinduism, Christianity and Islam) have different views, ranging from an acceptance in Buddhism to formal rejection in Islam, although it is recognized that, within these major faiths, there are different views even between countries of the same faith (Becker, 1990; Jayaram, 2007; Neeleman, et al., 1997; Pritchard & Amunalla, 2007).

Suicide is mentioned in the Christian Bible and the Jewish Talmud but without any moral comment (Barraclough, 1992). However, during Saint Augustine's time (354 AD-430 AD), the Christian church theologically reprimanded suicides. This still persists in the Roman Catholic and 'Orthodox' (Bulgarian, Greek, Macedonian and Russian) Churches and, traditionally, suicides are condemned to hell. In Islam suicide is expressly forbidden in the

Qur'an. Surah 4 verse 29 states, "Do not kill or destroy yourself" while verse 30 condemns offenders to the extreme penalty (Al-Hilali & Khan, 1420 AH). However, there are different emphases and interpretations of the Qur'an in the various Islamic regions (Hourani, 2002). In some countries, such as Kuwait or Pakistan, suicide is still a criminal offence (Suleiman, et al., 1989, Khan & Hyder, 2006). However, there is good historical evidence of an advanced, liberal and humane non-judgmental response to mental illness, with Islamic doctors such as the great Avicenna and Elrazi influencing positively their more primitive medieval European contemporaries (Hourani, 2002; Okash, 2005).

This chapter draws together new research of possible hidden suicides in the most traditional Catholic and Islamic countries, namely 17 predominately Islamic and 18 Latin American (LA) developing countries, although all such countries contain minorities of others faiths and denominations. Patterns of suicide and OECD are analyzed by gender to explore the possibility of hidden suicides amongst OECD rates. The suicide/OECD ratios of developing countries are compared with those of the ten WDC, with a focus upon Younger Aged [15-34] people because of the recent rise in suicide in WDC by Younger Aged males (Pritchard & Hansen, 2005a). A detailed exposition of the methodology and literature can be found elsewhere (Pritchard & Baldwin, 2000; Pritchard & Hansen, 2005a, 2005b; Pritchard & Amunalla, 2007; Pritchard & Hean, 2008).

## RESULTS

The WDC All Age suicide rates per million [pm] by gender and for Youth [15-24] and Young Adults [25-34] are listed in Table 20-1 along with their suicide to OECD ratios. The closest suicide to OECD ratio was in the UK, where All Age male ratios were 1 suicide to 0.44 OECD and 1: 0.66 OECD for females. Average WDC ratios were under 1: 0.18 for both genders and all age bands.

All the Islamic countries' data are listed in Table 20-2 ranked by bigger ratios, based on the latest 3-year average rates where possible. Some countries, including Qatar, Iran and Syria, have very restricted data but were included for comprehensiveness, while Pakistan and Syria report virtually no suicide or OECD, although a recent study from Pakistan did find more suicides in one province than were reported nationally (Khan & Hyder, 2006).

Five Islamic countries had higher male suicide rates than the UK, while the OECD rates of seven countries were higher than their suicide rates, and the OECD rates of eleven Islamic countries were higher than average WDC rates (20 pm). Some were extraordinarily high, including Qatar at 420, Bahrain at 180 and Egypt at 136, which reported virtually no suicides. The suicide to OECD ratios of twelve countries were statistically significantly higher than those of the WDC, indicated by a # in the tables, highlighting just how different they are from the WDC.

Table 20-3 lists the suicide to OECD ratios of 18 Latin American (LA) countries. Ten LA countries had more OECDs than suicides, and markedly so among Younger Aged [15-34] males, while Youth [15-24] females had higher rates of both compared to all females, indicating a particular vulnerability amongst Younger Aged [15-34] people. While only Cuba (214 pm) and Uruguay (290) male suicide rates exceeded the WDC average (186), only El Salvador and Uruguay OECD male rates were lower than WDC averages (20). The rest exceeded the WDC considerably, with the OECD rates of eight LA countries exceeding 100, including Argentina, Brazil and Colombia, which have three of the four biggest LA populations. When comparing WDC suicide to OECD ratios, with the exception of Chile, Cuba, El Salvador and Uruguay, all the other 14 LA countries had significantly different suicide to OECD ratios than the WDC, indicated by a # in the tables.

**Table 20.1. Suicide and Other External Cause Deaths(OECD) in the Western Developed Countries, 2000 [rates per million] and Ratios of Suicide to OECD**

| Country 2000 Suicide & OECD | All Age Male–Female | Youth Male–Female | Young Adult Male-Female |
|---|---|---|---|
| Australia | 198 – 52 | 237 - 58 | 358 -77 |
| OECD | 5 -3 | 15 -2 | 13- 6 |
| **Ratio** | **0.03 – 0.06** | **0.06 – 0.03** | **0.04 – 0.08** |
| Canada | 184 - 52 | 214 -51 | 245 -57 |
| OECD | 20 – 7 | 14 – 2 | 21 – 5 |
| **Ratio** | **0.11 – 0.13** | **0.07 – 0.04** | **0.09 – 0.09** |
| France | 274 - 95 | 125 - 35 | 260 -76 |
| OECD | 13 – 4 | 9 – 3 | 17 -3 |
| **Ratio** | **0.05 – 0.04** | **0.07-0.09** | **0.07 – 0.04** |
| Germany | 203 – 70 | 126 -31 | 178 -46 |
| OECD | 37 – 25 | 25 -8 | 34- 8 |
| **Ratio** | **0.18 -0.36** | **0.20 – 0.26** | **0.19- 0.17** |
| Italy | 109 - 35 | 71 - 17 | 107 -27 |
| OECD | 20 – 10 | 14 -3 | 12 -4 |
| **Ratio** | **0.18 – 0.29** | **0.20- 0.18** | **0.11- 0.15** |
| Japan | 352 – 134 | 150 -67 | 256 -110 |
| OECD | 22 – 10 | 12 – 5 | 15-10 |
| **Ratio** | **0.06 – 0.07** | **0.08- 0.07** | **0.06 – 0.09** |
| Netherlands | 127 - 62 | 90 -32 | 152-59 |
| OECD | 4 – 3 | 4 – 0 | 6 – 2 |
| **Ratio** | **0.031 – 0.05** | **0.04- n/a** | **0.04- 0.03** |
| Spain | 131 – 40 | 74 -17 | 123 -29 |
| OECD | 4 – 1 | 2 – 1 | 4 -2 |
| **Ratio** | **0.03 – 0.03** | **0.03- 0.06** | **0.03- 0.07** |
| UK | 113 – 32 | 87 - 24 | 166 -34 |
| OECD | 50 - 21 | 63 – 18 | 78 – 24 |
| **Ratio** | **0.44 – 0.66** | **0.72- 0.75** | **0.47 – 0.71** |
| USA | 171 – 40 | 179 -32 | 223 -46 |
| OECD | 23 – 9 | 19 – 5 | 31 – 10 |
| **Ratio** | **0.13 – 0.23** | **0.11 – 0.16** | **0.14 – 0.22** |
| Averages | 186 -61 | 135 -36 | 207 – 56 |
| OECD | 20 – 9 | 18 – 5 | 23 – 7 |
| Ratio 1: | 0.13 – 0.17 :1 | 0.13 – 0.14 | 0.11 -0.13 |

It is clear that suicide and OECD rates of the majority of Islamic and LA countries differ markedly from WDC. The results for Argentina, Azerbaijan, Bahrain, Brazil, Columbia, Costa Rica, Dominican Republic, Ecuador, Egypt. Guatemala, Guyana, Iran, Kuwait,

Malaysia, Mexico, Nicaragua, Panama, Peru, Qatar and Venezuela strongly suggest that they probably have substantial levels of hidden suicides in their OECD.

**Table 20.2. Islamic Suicide and OECD by Ratios and Rates per Million by Age and Significant Differences from WDC #**

| Country & 3Years OECD or OVD rates | All Age Male-Female | 15-24 Male-Female | 25-34 Male-Female |
|---|---|---|---|
| 1. Qatar 1995. | 0-0 | 0– 0 | 0- 0 |
| OVD 1 | 420 – 129 | 548- 188 | 489 – 54 |
| Ratio 1: | xx-xx #-# | Xx - xx # - # | xx - xx #-# |
| 2. Egypt - 2000 | 1 – 0 | 2 – 0 | 2 – 0 |
| OECD | 136 – 76 | 150 - 98 | 149 – 59 |
| Ratio 1: | 136 – xx #-# | 75.0 - xx #-# | 74.5 – xx #-# |
| 3. Malaysia 1997 | 12- 4 | 15 – 7 | 36 – 10 |
| OVD | 166-36 | 561 – 86 | 460 – 76 |
| Ratio 1: | 13.8 –9.0 #-# | 37.4 – 12.3 #-# | 11.1 – 7.6 #-# |
| 4. Iran [Cities] 1991 | 3- 2 | n/a | n/a |
| OVD | 22 - 2 | n/a | n/a |
| Ratio 1: | 7.3 – 1.0 #-n.s | n/a | n/a |
| 5. Bahrain 1998-2000 | 36 – 5 | 23 – 7 | 88 – 12 |
| OECD | 180-19 | 190- -47 | 153 – 68 |
| Ratio 1: | 5.0 – 3.8 # -# | 8.3 – 6.7 # - # | 1.7 – 5.7 # - # |
| 6. Azerbaijan 2000-02 | 30-10 | 31 - 6 | 34 – 14 |
| OECD | 88-19 | 92 - 12 | 126 – 11 |
| Ratio 1: | 2.93 – 1.90 #-# | 2.9 – 2.0 #-# | 3.7 – 0.79 #- # |
| 7. Kuwait 2000-02 –ICD 10 | 17 – 14 | 29 - 16 | 27 – 35 |
| OECD | 35 – 2 | 34 – 2 | 49 – 3 |
| Ratio 1: | 2.1 - 0.14 #-n.s | 1.17 – 0.13 #-n.s | 1.81 – 0.09 #-n.s |
| 8. Bosnia 1989-91 | 177-37 | 188 – 37 | 256 – 37 |
| OVD | 166-74 | 108 – 50 | 97 – 43 |
| Ratio 1: | 0.94- 2.0 # - # | 0.57 – 1.35 #-# | 0.38 – 1.71 #-# |
| 9. Kyrgyzstan 2000-02 | 187-37 | 134 – 47 | 252 – 28 |
| OECD | 134 –36 | 59 – 26 | 134 – 26 |
| Ratio | 0.72 –0.97 # - # | 0.44 – 0.55 #-# | 0.53 – 0.93 #-# |
| 10. Kazakhstan 2000-02 | 506-89 | 457 – 113 | 714 – 107 |
| OECD 11 | 253-66 | 162 – 38 | 309 – 65 |
| Ratio | 0.5 – 0.74 # -# | 0.35 – 0.34 # - # | 0.43 – 0.61 #-# |
| 11. Syria 1984-85 | 2 – 0.2 | 0 - 0 | 0-0 |
| OECD | 1 – 0.5 | 4 – 0 | 1 - 0 |
| Ratio 1: | 0.5 – 2.5 n.s | Xx - xx | xx- xx |
| 12. Uzbekistan1998-200 | 112 – 34 | 130 - 68 | 187 – 53 |
| OECD | 50 - 15 | 35 – 7 | 63 – 13 |
| Ratio | 0.45 - 0.44 # - # | 0.27 - 0.13 #-n.s | 0.34 – 0.24 #-n.s |
| 13. Tajikistan 2.8-2.8 1998-2000 | 42 – 16 | 39 – 24 | 81 - 31 |
| OECD | 11 – 3 | 4 - 1 | 14 - 1 |
| Ratio 12 | 0.26 – 0.19 # -n.s | 0.10 - 0.04 n.s | 0.17 – 0.03 n.s |
| 14. Albania 1999-2001 | 53 – 28 | 57 – 49 | 54 – 25 |
| OECD | 6 –5 | 16 - 7 | 34 – 9 |
| Ratio 1: | 0.11 – 0.18 n.s | 0.28 – 0.14 n.s | 0.63 – 0.36 #- # |
| 15. Turkmenistan 1998-2000 | 118 – 30 | 188 – 68 | 185 - 30 |

# Hidden Suicide in the Developing World

| OECD 13 | 13 – 5 | 9 - 9 | 19 - 5 |
|---|---|---|---|
| Ratio | 0.11- 0.17 n.s | 0.05 - 0.13 | 0.10 - 0.17 |
| Country & 3Years OECD or OVD rates | All Age Male Female | 15-24 M ale Female | 25-34 Male Female |
| 16. Turkey 1987 OVD Ratio 1: | 3- 1 0.2- 0.1 0.07 –0.1 n.s | n/a | n/a |
| 17. Pakistan 2001 OECD 1: | 0.1– 0.02 n/a n.s | n/a | n/a |
| Western Average 2000 OECD Ratio | 186 –61 20 – 9 0.13 – 0.17 | 135- 36 18 - 5 0.13 – 0.14 | 207 – 56 23 - 7 0.11 - 0.13 |

All chi square tests df=1; #=statistically significant, n.s = not significant, # = sig different from MDC

### Table 20.3. LA Suicide and OECD by Ratios and Rates and Significant Differences from WDC #

| Country, Year & Rank Order of Deaths | GPR Male - Female | Youth 15-24 Male - Female | Young Adult 25-34 Male - Female |
|---|---|---|---|
| 1. Guatemala 1999- 16 O. V.D * - 2 Ratio | 34 – 8 475 – 110 13.97-13.75 #-# | 50 - 16 486 – 120 9.72-7.50 #-# | 73 – 9 794 – 102 10.8-11.3 #-# |
| 2. Peru [No's] - 18 OECD - 9 Ratio # | 11 - 6 60 - 27 5.45- 4.50 #-# | [109] 41% –[66] 60% [155] 19% – [177]48% 3.60 –3.69 #-# | [40] 27%- [14] 18% [135] 17% –[47] 13% 3.38 – 3.36 #-# |
| 3 Dominican Rep 1998-17 OECD [No's] - 5 Ratio # | 27 – 10 128 - 37 4.74 – 3.70 #-# | [20]18% - [10] 24% [118]22% -[23] 15% 5.90 - 2.30 #-# | [29]26% -[5] 12% [94]17% -20] 13% 3.24 - 4.00 #-# |
| 4. Venezuela 2000 - 9 OECD. - 3 Ratio | 88 – 15 318 – 43 3.61 – 2.87 #-# | 110 – 26 655 – 37 5.95 – 1.42 #-# | 150 – 19 586 – 38 3.91- 2.00 #-# |
| 5. Guyana 1996 - 4 O. V.D * - 1 Ratio | – 23 506 – 167 3.47 – 7.26 #-# | 170 – 48 486 – 168 2.89 – 3.5 #-# | 295 – 15 787 – 134 2.67 – 8.93 #-# |
| 6. Ecuador 2000- 14 OECD - 6 Ratio | 60 – 26 129 –27 2.15- 1.04 #-# | 104 – 59 151 – 38 1.45-0.64 #- # | 85 – 46 202 –26 2.38-0.57 #-# |
| 7. Brazil 2000 – 12 OECD - 7 Ratio | 64 - 16 117 - 26 1.83 –1.63 #-# | 60 - 20 131 – 18 2.18 –0.90 #-# | 87 – 19 152 – 17 1.75-0.89 #-# |
| 8. Colombia 1999 - 11 OECD. - 8 Ratio | 81 – 24 109 – 28 1.35-1.17 #-# | 127 – 61 132 –23 1.04- 0.38 #- # | 123 – 28 148 – 18 1.20-0.64 #-# |
| 9. Argentina 2001 – 5 O.E.CD - 4 . Ratio | 134 - 35 156 - 33 1.16 – 0.94 #-# | 153 - 50 229 – 29 1.50 –0.58 #- # | 137 - 30 198 – 23 1.45 – 0.77 #-# |
| 10. Paraguay 2000 - 15 OECD. - 11 Ratio | 39 – 17 41 - 15 1.05- 0.88 #-# | 51 – 43 55 - 26 1.08-0.60 # - # | 82 – 5 50 - 20 0.61-4.00 #-# |
| 11. Mexico 2001 – 13 OECD. - 12= Ratio | 63 – 13 40 - 8 0.63- 0.62 #-# | 90 – 26 35 - 9 0.39- 0.35 # - n.s | 105 – 15 51 - 8 0.49- 0.53 #- # |

**Table 20.3. Continued**

| Country, Year & Rank Order of Deaths | GPR Male - Female | Youth 15-24 Male - Female | Young Adult 25-34 Male - Female |
|---|---|---|---|
| 12. Nicaragua [No's] - 8<br>OECD. – 10<br>Ratio # | 104 – 47<br>59 – 12<br>0.57 – 0.25 | [109] 44% –[66] 52%<br>[ 37 ] 26% -[ 6] 21%<br>0.34 – 0.10 | [68] 27% –[18] 16%<br>[21] 15% -[ 1] 4%<br>0.31- 0.06 |
| 13. Panama 2000- 10<br>OECD. - 12=<br>Ratio | 84 – 13<br>40 - 6<br>0.48 – 0.46 #- x | 90 – 30<br>43 - 15<br>0.48 – 0.50 #- # | 118 – 28<br>32 - 8<br>0.27-0.29 # -n.s |
| 14. Costa Rica 2002– 6=<br>0ECD. - 15<br>Ratio | 116 – 20<br>28 – 8 #-n.s<br>0.24 –0.40 | 142 – 46<br>12 – 10<br>0.08-0.22 n.s | 167 – 26<br>28 –3<br>0.17-0.12 n.s |
| 15. Chile 2001 - 3<br>OECD. - 14<br>Ratio | 182 - 30<br>32 – 5<br>0.18 –0.17 n.s- n.s | 199 - 49<br>42 – 6<br>0.21 – 0.12 | 244 - 44<br>35 – 3<br>0.14 – 0.07 |
| 16. Cuba 2001 - 2<br>OECD. - 16<br>Ratio | 214 – 80<br>29 – 11<br>0.14 – 0.14 n.s.- n.s | 100 – 60<br>13 – 3<br>0.13-0.05 | 197 – 71<br>20 – 8<br>0.10-0.11 |
| 17. Uruguay 2000 - 1<br>OECD. - 17<br>Ratio | 290 – 55<br>5 – 5<br>0.02- 0.09 #!-n.s | 110 – 26<br>0 - 8<br>xx- 0.31 #!- n.s | 252 – 55<br>8 - 0<br>0.03-xx #!- #! |
| 18. El Salvador 1999-6=<br>OECD. - 18<br>Ratio | 116 – 54<br>1 – 0<br>0.01-xx #-#! | 174 – 144<br>0 –0<br>Xx #-#! | 184 – 57<br>0 - 0<br>Xx-xx #-#! |
| Average MWC<br>OECD<br>Ratio 1: | 186-61<br>20-9<br>0.13 -0.17 | 135036<br>18<br>0.13 – 0.14 | 207 –56<br>23 – 7<br>0.11 – 0.13 |

All chi square test df=1; # indicates that the LA OECD rates significantly lower than WDC.

# DISCUSSION

It is recognized that these results are only as good as the reliability of the data reported to the WHO. However, these are the best data available. It is also recognized that OECD could hide homicides, although this is unlikely in many LA countries as their homicide rates far exceed both suicide and OECD rates. This chapter provides a number of new findings that should challenge stereotypes about the traditional response to suicide of Islamic and Latin American countries.

First, suicide is a major problem in more Islamic countries than would be expected. This is seen in the high suicide rate of many former USSR Islamic countries, with more suicides being reported in one Pakistani province than were reported nationally (Khan & Hyder, 2006). This strongly suggests that OECD in these Islamic countries probably do contain hidden suicides. Hence, our psychiatric colleagues in these countries need all the support they can have in order to deal with the underlying problems which may include the taboo surrounding suicidal behavior as well as inadequately treated mental disorders which lead to suicide. Second, OECDs in 20 of the 35 developing countries are highly likely to contain hidden suicides since their OECD rates exceeded their suicide rates.

Another important finding was the relative vulnerability of the Younger Aged [15-34] males, especially in Latin America, as well as the Youth [15-24] females. These may well mirror the psychosocial changes in the West where Younger Aged male suicide rates have increased over the past 20 years (Pritchard & Hansen, 2005a), although the reasons for the various patterns of suicide require country-specific research. Finally, the majority of Islamic and Latin American countries' patterns of suicide and OECD are significantly different from the dominant Western model. Consequently, in order to reduce the toll of possible hidden suicides, there needs to be a more open discussion of suicide in these developing countries.

## REFERENCES

Al-Hilali, M. T., & Khan, M. M. (1420 A.H.). *The noble Qur'an in the English language.* Madinah, Saudi Arabia: King Fahd Complex.

Barraclough, B. (1992). The Bible suicides. *Acta Psychiatrica Scandinavia,* 86, 64-69.

Becker, C. B. (1990). Buddhist views of suicide and euthanasia. *Philosophy East & West,* 40, 543-555.

Hourani, A. (2002). *A history of the Arab peoples.* London, UK: Faber & Faber.

Jayaram, Y. (2007). *Hinduism and suicide.* www.hinduwebsite.com.

Khan, M. M., & Hyder, A. A. (2006). Suicides in the developing world: a case study from Pakistan. *Suicide & Life-Threatening Behavior,* 36, 76-81.

Linsley, K. R., Schapira, K., & Kelly, T. P. (2001). Open verdict versus suicide: importance to research. *British Journal of Psychiatry,* 178, 465-468.

Leenaars, A. A. (2004). *Psychotherapy with suicidal people.* Chichester, UK: John Wiley & Sons.

Neeleman, J., Halpern, D., Leon, D., et al (1997). Tolerance of suicide, religion and suicide rates: an ecological and individual level study in 19 Western countries. *Psychological Medicine,* 27, 1165-1171.

Okash, A. (2005). Mental health in Egypt. International Journal of Psychiatry & Related Science, 42, 116-125.

Pritchard, C., & Amunalla, S. (2007). An analysis of suicide and undetermined deaths in 17 predominately Islamic countries contrasted with the UK. *Psychological Medicine,* 37, 421-430.

Pritchard, C., & Baldwin, D. S. (2000). Effects of age and gender on elderly suicides in Catholic and Orthodox countries: an inadvertent neglect? *International Journal of Geriatric Psychiatry,* 12, 271-275.

Pritchard, C., & Hansen, L. (2005a). Child, adolescent and youth suicide and undetermined deaths in England & Wales compared with Australia, Canada, France, Germany, Italy, Netherlands, Spain and the USA. *International Journal of Adolescent Medicine & Health,* 17, 239-53.

Pritchard, C., & Hansen, L. (2005b). Comparison of suicide in people aged 65-74 and 75+ by gender in England & Wales and the major Western countries. *International Journal of Geriatric Psychiatry,* 20, 17-25.

Pritchard, C., & Hean, S. (2008). Suicide and undetermined deaths among youths and young adults in Latin America: comparison with the 10 major developed countries: a source of hidden suicides? *Crisis*, 29, 145-153.

Salib, E. S., El-Nimar, G., & Habeeb, B. (2005). Elderly suicide: an analysis of coroner's inquests into two-hundred cases in Cheshire 1989-2001. *Medicine, Science & the Law*, 45, 71-80.

Suleiman, M. A., Moussa, M. A., & El-Islamic, M. F. (1989). The profile of parasuicide repeaters in Kuwait. *International Journal Social Psychiatry*, 35, 146-155.

Stanistreet, D., Taylor, S., Jeffrey, V., et al. (2001). Accident or suicide? Predictors of coroner's decisions in suicide and accident verdicts. *Medicine, Science & the Law*, 41, 111-115.

World Health Organisation. (1992). International statistical classification of diseases and related health problems, Tenth Revision [ICD 10]. Geneva, Switzerland: WHO.

*Chapter 21*

# SUICIDE IN SRI LANKA

## *Waltraud Bolz*

In recent decades, Sri Lanka has had one of the highest rates of suicide in the world (Annual Health Bulletin, 2006). This is a major health and social problem (Bolz, 2002; Somasundaram, et al., 1995). From 1930 to 1960 there was a slow but steady increase in the suicide rate. Rates from that time were comparatively low (5.2 per 100,000 in 1930 and 9.9 in 1960) (Somasundaram, et al., 1995). However, in the 1970s, the rate rose to a high level (about 20). The trend continued during the 1980s, unfortunately making Sri Lanka rank first among all nations, with a rate of 47 (Somasundaram, 1993). In 1982, the suicide rate in Jaffna, the former capital of the Tamil area, was 53.5, the highest ever heard of (Ganeswaran, et al., 1984). In 1990, the rate was about 45, while in 1995 it was 47.3 (WHO, 2004). This represented an increase of more than 700% during fifty years of independence. The latest rate is 30.1 in 1998 (Annual Health Bulletin, 2000) and 25.1 in 2004 (men 39.6 and women 10.9) (Annual Health Bulletin, 2006) which still give Sri Lanka the dubious distinction of having one of the highest suicide rates in the world. The significant reduction in suicide rates might be due to excluding the North-East Province, which has one third of the population and was the area of a civil war.

## SOME ASPECTS OF SUICIDE RESEARCH IN SRI LANKA

Primary healthcare records indicate that the death rate from attempted suicide is 10%-30% in Sri Lanka (Eddleston, et al, 2006), compared to 1% in European countries. Roughly three times more men than women die by suicide. Nonetheless, the suicide rate among women is high in absolute terms, being second only to that of women in China. It is highest for teenage girls and young women, a pattern seen also in India and China. Among children under the age of 16, more than four times more girls than boys inflict self-harm (male-female ratio = 1.6:7). Thus, it is not young people in general who are at risk, but rather young women and girls (Marecek, 2003).

Suicides are concentrated in rural areas and among economically disadvantaged groups, particularly affecting young adults between the ages of 20 and 30 (Van der Hoek & Konradsen, 2006). In rural Sri Lanka, suicidal acts are not seen as "mad behavior," but as "bad behavior," a sign of impulsiveness, a hot temper or a rebellious character.

Poisoning with pesticides and herbicides (Konradsen, et al, 2003; Van der Hoek & Konradsen, 2006) is the main method for suicide in Sri Lanka, even outnumbering the casualties of the civil war. Most incidents of suicide (85%-88%) involve poisonous agricultural chemicals, plants or household substances like kerosene and paint thinner. Other methods include hanging, drowning, self burning or overdosing on medicine. "Sati" (the self-sacrifice of widows on their husband's funeral pyre) is unknown in Sri Lanka (Laloe & Ganesan, 2002).

Depression and despair, which play such a prominent role in suicidal motivation in European and American contexts, are less prevalent in suicide in Sri Lanka (Marecek, 2003; Galappatti, 2004), although common mental disorders may play a role (Sumathipala, et al., 2004). In contrast, individuals are most often driven by explosive feelings of anger, frustration and humiliation. Many acts are carried out in a dramatic fashion and often in the presence of others. In Sri Lanka, the prototype for suicide is the 'dialogue suicide.' These are communicative acts that are directed towards other people. They take place in the course of domestic disputes, quarrels between intimates and similar crises, in a desire to strike back against unfair treatment (Marecek, 2003) or to frighten or shame another person, to teach another person a lesson, for revenge, to publicly expose a wrongdoer, to protest against unfair treatment or to reestablish lost status. Sometimes they are carried out in the presence of the person who has committed the wrongdoing. Often a note is written that details exactly how others are to blame for the death.

Conflicts over sexuality and threats to sexual honor figure prominently in young women's suicide while, for men, between 60% and 70% of the suicides were under the influence of alcohol. Besides a high suicide rate, Sri Lanka also has a high level of alcohol and drug dependency, although exact figures cannot be given due to an estimated high rate of unreported cases. Children's suicide attempts are often connected to their father's drinking, whether because of violence, sexual abuse or shame.

# AN ANALYTICAL APPROACH TO THE CULTURAL AND SOCIETAL SETTING OF SUICIDE

## Culture-Specific Practices

Reasons for such a high suicide rate can be explained in part by an analysis of cultural factors like 'collectivism,' 'distance of power,' and religion (Bolz, 2002). Civilizations can be distinguished from one another by the manner in which they evaluate and deal with conflicts. A useful tool to understand the different ways of dealing with conflicts are the factors developed by Hofstede (2005), especially the dimension of "collectivism vs. individualism." Sri Lanka puts a very high emphasis on collectivism. In individualistic civilizations, conflicts are, above all, evaluated in terms of individual tensions that may also play a positive role (e.g. to achieve certain goals). They may be solved directly. In collectivistic civilizations, indirect, multilateral and non-confrontational methods are usually preferred, since conflict in such a system is regarded as a threat to the social system. The main goal is to preserve the given social structure and to prevent any humiliation.

Emotional restraint and an outward pose of equanimity and self-control are highly valued, but then often lead to inner tensions. When people cannot direct their tensions and aggressions outwardly against the cause of conflict, they direct a large part of their aggression against themselves. This results in dissatisfaction or self-destruction through suicide. In many cases, a rather 'banal' incident will be the turning point toward a suicide attempt. In doing this, people can also frighten or shame other person and, thus, through suicide, the aggression is then, at least in part, directed outwardly.

Hofstede (2005) also examines the manner in which societies habitually deal with inequality. "Distance of Power" expresses the emotional distance that exists between managers and their employees, teachers and students, and parents and children. Despite a certain social mobility, people live and work within hierarchical structures in which degradation can be a big threat. In accordance with the high esteem attached to collectivism, people try to avoid being singled out or having their subordinate position questioned. For most Sri Lankans their position on several social hierarchies, including familial structures (e.g., generation, age and gender) or larger community structures (e.g., caste, class and occupation), is a central component of their personal identity. Their identity and self-esteem depend, therefore, on others recognizing and acknowledging their rightful status.

The traditional and rather repressive education system in Sri Lanka is closely connected with 'distance of power.' Due to very low prospects of a professional career and a high rate of unemployment among the academic elite (official figures are about 20% for all professions), there is extreme pressure both on learning and efficiency. Students do not learn to discuss problems with their parents or peers. Thus, poor problem-solving skills may also be a contributing factor.

Social transformations and the influence of foreign cultures through foreign media, migration, seeking asylum or obtaining temporary employment overseas may trigger a clash between traditional and foreign values and norms. Other important factors include the high rate of people traumatized by the civil war and the religious belief in re-birth and karma, the latter facilitating beliefs that one can put an end to one's life and not regard it as the final step.

## The Societal Setting of Suicide

The peak rates recorded in the 1980s and 1990s represent an increase of more than 700 percent compared to 1950. This implies that high rates of suicidal behavior are not only an outgrowth of primordial beliefs or traditional culture, but are also connected to strains in the social fabric and disruptions in living, which resulted from economic changes, political turmoil and social transformations.

Sri Lanka has a total population of 20,743,000 and a GDP per capita of 3,800 USD, which varies greatly between the capital and rural areas (GDP of 70 USD) (WHO, 2004). Since its independence, Sri Lanka has witnessed social unrest, inter-group tension and high levels of violence. During the civil war, persisting for more than twenty years, more than 70,000 people have been killed and large numbers of refugees produced. Many individuals have been subjected to harassment, disappearances, torture and long periods of imprisonment, or living in displaced person camps (about 100,000). The tsunami of December 2004, which left 31,000 dead and one million people (roughly 5% of the population) homeless, was an additional blow to a country already in turmoil.

At a collective level, Sri Lanka's current high incidence of suicide is a measure of its social problems, including unemployment, the frustrated expectations of rural youth and severe economic strains associated with a globalizing economy. These troubles have produced personal and familial suffering. Social unrest has also undermined people's sense of personal security and physical safety and placed strains on family and community relations.

## SERVICES AVAILABLE

Sri Lanka is a poor country with no adequate facilities for preventing and solving personal conflicts that can lead to suicide. With countless traumatized or mentally ill people, there are only five clinical psychologists, about thirty psychiatrists, no educational psychologists and hardly any therapeutic facilities at a grass-roots level, such as youth clubs that could, in time, prevent negative developments. Suicide attempts tend to be fatal, especially in the rural areas, because emergency medical rescue facilities are seldom available.

There are at least two organizations in Sri Lanka that deal with clients with suicidal ideation:

- Sahanaya Institute of Mental Health (www.sahayana.org)
- Sri Lanka Sumithrayo (www.srilankasumithrayo.org).

The program designed by Sumithrayo (which means "friend"), a rural suicide initiative, was designed to prevent suicide in rural villages. This program has had positive effects (Marecek, 2001), showing that it is possible to prevent suicides using psychosocial interventions.

## RECOMMENDATIONS

Sri Lanka needs a far more intense and efficient network of psychiatric care facilities. An immediate measure should be the establishment of psychosocial care facilities throughout the country, as well as the provision of fast rescue services for attempted suicides. Moreover, in the short-term, it is essential to make people aware of the problem of suicide. This will require qualified people in key positions, such as teachers, doctors, social workers and monks. Ongoing pilot studies indicate that actions to control access to pesticides are effective and work best when integrated into comprehensive community education programs (Konradsen, et al., 2003). Collaboration among community groups can thus be crucial to furthering the cause of suicide prevention. When attempting to create a more complex account of suicide in Sri Lanka, we should always look at individual psychology, culture-specific factors and large social and economic forces. Such accounts give evidence that suicide prevention requires more than individual coping skills and improved self-esteem. It also requires a focus on social justice, economic equity and human rights.

## REFERENCES

Annual Health Bulletin. (2000). Colombo, Sri Lanka: Department of Health Services.
Annual Health Bulletin. (2006). Colombo, Sri Lanka: Department of Health Services.
Berger, L. R. (1988). Suicides and pesticides in Sri Lanka. *American Journal of Public Health*, 78, 826-828.
Bertolote, J.M., Fleischmann, A., Butchart, A., et al. (2006). Suicide, suicide attempts and pesticides: a major hidden public health problem. *Bulletin of the World Health Organisation*, 84, 260.
Bolz, W. (2002). Psychological analysis of the Sri Lankan conflict culture with special reference to the high suicide rate. *Crisis,* 23, 167-170.
De Silva, D. (2003). Suicide prevention strategies in Sri Lanka: the role of socio-cultural factors and health services. *Ceylon Medical Journal*, 48, 68-70.
De Silva, H. J., Kasturiaratchi, N., Seneviratne, S. L., et al. (2000). Suicide in Sri Lanka: points to ponder. *Ceylon Medical Journal*, 45, 17-24.
Desapriya, E. B., Joshi, P., Han, G., et al. (2004). Demographic risk factors in pesticide related suicide in Sri Lanka. *Injury Prevention*, 10, 125.
Eddleston, M., Sheriff, M. H., & Hawton, K. (1998). Deliberate self-harm in Sri Lanka: an overlooked tragedy in the developing world. *British Medical Journal*, 317,133-135
Eddleston, M., Buckley, N. A., Gunnell, D., et al. (2006). Identification of strategies to prevent death after pesticide self-poisoning using a Haddon matrix. *Injury Prevention*, 12, 333-337.
Eddleston, M., Sudarshan, K. Senthilkumaran, M., et al. (2006). Patterns of hospital transfer for self-poisoned patients in rural Sri Lanka: implications for estimating the incidence of self-poisoning in the developing world. *Bulletin of the World Health Organization*, 84, 260.
Galappatti, A. (2004). Suicide in Sri Lanka: in search of theoretical frameworks. Unpublished.
Ganeswaran, T., Subramaniam, S., & Mahadevan, K. (1984). Suicide in a northern town of Sri Lanka. *Acta Psychiatrica Scandinavica*, 69, 420-425.
Hofstede, G. (2005). *Culture's consequences.* Thousand Oaks, CA: Sage.
Konradsen, F., van der Hoek, W., Cole, D. C., et al. (2003). Reducing acute poisoning in developing countries – options for restricting the availability of pesticides. *Toxicology*, 192, 249-261.
Laloe, V., & Ganesan, M. (2002). Self-immolation a common suicidal behaviour in eastern Sri Lanka. *Burns*, 28, 475-480.
Marecek J. (1998). Culture, gender, and suicidal behavior in Sri Lanka. *Suicide & Life-Threatening Behavior*, 28, 69-81
Marecek J., & Ratnayeke, L. (2001). Suicidal behavior in rural Sri Lanka: assessing a prevention program. In O. T. Grad (Ed.) *Suicide risk and protective factors in the new millennium,* pp. 215-220. Ljubljana, Slovenia: Cankarjew Dom.

Marecek, J. (2003). Young women's suicide in Sri Lanka: cultural, ecological and psychological factors. Paper presented at the Meetings of the American Anthropological Association, Chicago, IL.

Ratnayeke, L. (1996). Suicide and crisis intervention in rural communities in Sri Lanka. *Crisis,* 17, 149-51, 154.

Ratnayeke, L. (1998). Suicide in Sri Lanka. In R. J. Kosky, H. S. Eshkevari, R. D. Goldney, et al. (Eds.) *Suicide prevention: The global context*, pp. 139-42. New York: Plenum.

Somasundaram, D. (1993). Psychiatric morbidity due to war in Northern Sri Lanka. In J. P. Wilson & B. Raphael (Eds.) *Psychological debriefing: Theory, practice and evidence*, pp. 333-348. New York: Plenum.

Somasundaram, D., & Rajadurai, S. (1995). War and suicide in northern Sri Lanka. *Acta Psychiatrica Scandinavica*, 91, 1-4.

Sumathipala, A., Siribaddana, S., & Samaraweera, S.D. (2004). Do patients volunteer their life weariness and suicidal ideations? A Sri Lankan study. *Crisis*, 25, 103-107.

The World Health Report. (2004). Geneva, Switzerland, WHO.

The World Health Report. (2006). Geneva, Switzerland, WHO.

Van der Hoek, W., & Konradsen, F (2005). Risk factors for acute pesticide poisoning in Sri Lanka. *Tropical Medicine & International Health*, 10, 589-596.

Van der Hoek, W., & Konradsen, F (2006). Analysis of 8000 hospital admissions for acute poisoning in a rural area of Sri Lanka. *Clinical Toxicology,* 44, 225-231.

**Chapter 22**

# SUICIDE IN THE FORMER SOVIET UNION (USSR)

## *Airi Värnik*

Large variation exists between the suicide mortality rates of different countries as presented in WHO *Health for all database*. Various explanations have been proposed for these differences in national rates.

A major contribution to the theory of suicide was made by Émile Durkheim. He found suicide to be correlated with social phenomena such as family, politics, economy and religion. He postulated that each society has a constant collective inclination toward suicide, determined by social integration, reflecting the degree to which members of a society or group are bound together, and social regulation, which characterizes the strengths of the norms and rules between the individual and the society or group. The change in suicide rates is a symptom of the breakdown of the collective conscience, which depends on the structure of the society (Durkheim, 2002/1897).

The history of the former Soviet Union provides an interesting resource for investigating suicide mortality given its huge territory of 22.4 million square kilometers (one-six of the land territory on Earth) and a population of nearly 263 million according to the 1989 Census. It also provides rather well-defined socio-political time-periods and regions varying considerably in culture, religion, family traditions, nativity and pattern of alcohol consumption, although it was governed by a uniform totalitarian socio-political regime.

The Soviet Union, established in 1922 after a civil war, consisted of the Slavic (Russia, Ukraine, Belarus) and Caucasian republics (Georgia, Armenia, Azerbaijan). The Central Asian republics (Kazakhstan, Uzbekistan, Tajikistan, Turkmenistan and Kyrgyzstan) were incorporated in 1924-1925. The Baltic States (Lithuania, Latvia and Estonia) and Moldova (part of Romania before World War II) were occupied in 1940. Thus, the USSR comprised 15 republics.

The aim of this chapter is to describe and analyze the pattern of suicide distribution among both sexes and different age groups in the regions of the former USSR, and investigate the effect of rapid socio-political changes on suicide mortality during and after *Perestroika* (restructuring).

## MATERIAL AND METHODS

The database includes suicides for the USSR during 1970-1990, separately for the 15 republics in 1984-1990 and for Baltic States and Slavic republics in 1991-2002. The method for obtaining material, data sources, registration and coding of violent deaths is described elsewhere (Wasserman, et al., 1998a; Wasserman, et al., 1998b; Värnik, 1997; Värnik, et al., 2001). In the USSR, 433,020 suicides occurred between 1984-1990.

The material has been analyzed and presented in the collaborative series of studies between 1991-2006 by the Estonian-Swedish Mental Health and Suicidology Institute (principal investigator A. Värnik) and the Swedish National and Stockholm County Council's Centre for Suicide Research and Prevention of Mental Ill-Health, Karolinska Institute (principal investigator D. Wasserman).

## RESULTS

### Study Period

The period studied can be divided into three time-periods: stagnation (1965/1970-1984), Perestroika (1985-1990) and post-soviet years (since 1991). Stagnation meant highly centralized politics, continuing isolation from the other countries, low GDP, curbs on creative freedom, strict censorship and also a strongly controlled system of mortality registration all over the USSR.

In psychiatric textbooks, suicidal behavior was described solely as a symptom of mental (mainly endogenous) illness on par with psychosis. Psychological and social factors were disregarded. Suicidal patients were treated involuntarily in psychiatric hospitals with strong medication regimes. Low ethics and standards of psychiatric treatment tended to deter people from seeking help. People responded to problems of identity crisis, mistrust and fear with passive resistance and alcoholism (Mokhovikov, 1994; Värnik, 1997; Värnik & Wasserman, 1992).

Period of reforms (Perestroika) began in 1985 after Gorbachev came to power. Political changes came first, which promised spiritual liberation, democracy and a hope of higher living standards, causing optimism. Simultaneously a strict anti-alcohol policy was imposed (Värnik, 1997; Värnik, et al., 1998b).

Since 1989, epidemiological suicide research, which was prohibited in the former Soviet Union for political reasons, became possible. The top-secret archives included mortality data on suicide, murder, cholera and pestilence, while demographic data were also opened up for researchers. The Wasserman-Värnik research group began systematic suicide studies of the USSR.

The post-Soviet period started in 1991, when three Baltic States restored their independence and another 12 republics formed the Newly Independent States (NIS). After dissolution of the Soviet Union, the new liberal market economy called for completely different values, attitudes and professional expertise. There was a need for initiative taking, self-realization and responsibility, in contrast to former obedience. The degree of adaptive capacity determined one's position and even survival in this completely new situation. There were no purchase limits on alcohol sales (Buckley, 1997; Leon, et al., 1997). Psychological and psychiatric aid was not prepared to help people, and so the reforms in this field have only started.

## Suicide Rates in Different Regions of the Former USSR

The total crude average suicide rate between 1984-1990 in the USSR was 22.0, while the standardized rate by the European standard population was 23.8 and, by population of the USSR, 21.9.

The mean rates observed in the 15 republics in 1984-90 varied widely, from 2.2 in Armenia to 29.2 in Lithuania. Throughout the period studied, suicide rates were low in the Caucasus (3.5) and Central Asia (11.8) while, in the Slavic (25.6) and Baltic (28.0) republics, they were high. Central Asia differed greatly in its population composition, which was reflected in the suicide rates. In Kazakhstan, inhabited by 42% of Muslim native-borns with a large majority of Russians, the suicide rate was 19.6. In Tajikistan, inhabited by 88% of Muslim native-borns, the suicide rate was 4.9 (Wasserman, et al., 1998a; Värnik & Wasserman, 1992).

## Male and Female Suicide Rates

The highest average male suicide rates between 1984-1990 were observed in the Baltic (45.9) and in the Slavic region (42.2) while the lowest were in the Caucasus region (4.9). Female suicide rates were also the highest in the Baltic (12.3) and in the Slavic region (10.9), with the lowest in the Caucasus regions (2.1).

The variation in suicide rates between different republics within the same region was small. The exception was the Central Asian republics, where male rates ranged from 6.3 in Tajikistan to 31.0 in Kazakhstan and females rates from 3.6 in Tajikistan to 8.9 in Kazakhstan. Male to female ratios ranged from 1.9 in Tajikistan to 4.9 in Belarus. Male suicides exceeded female suicides 4.6 times in the Slavic region, and 4.1 times in the Baltic region. The smallest male to female ratios were observed in Caucasus (2.7) (Buckley, 1997; Wasserman, et al, 1998a).

## Trends

The suicide rate in the former USSR rose during the stagnation period, from 17.1 in 1965 to 29.6 in 1984 (Postovalova, 1989). Between 1984 and 1986-88 suicide rates showed a sharp fall in all republics with the exception of Armenia. This decrease ranged from 5.9% in Turkmenistan to 38.1% in Belarus, and for the whole USSR it was 35.2%.

The suicide rates fell in the Slavic region by 40.7% for men and 17.9% for women and in the Baltic region by 29.8% for men and 15.7% for women. In Central Asian republics suicide rates decreased by 36.7% for men and 15.8% for women, in the Caucasus 16.1% and 14.9%, respectively (Värnik, et al., 1998b).

Beginning in 1989, the suicide rates started to rise. The highest rates for Baltic and Slavic republics, higher than ever during the stagnation period, were registered between 1993-1995, followed by decline, thus forming an S-shape (fall-rise-fall) curve (Buckley, 1997; Gailiene, et al., 1995; Rancans, et al., 2001; Wasserman & Värnik, 1994).

## Age

Age-specific groups were studied for the Slavic republics during 1984-1990 and the Baltic countries between 1984-2004. The increase varied directly with age for women, from 5.5 per 100,000 in the age group 15-24 to 31.5 for ages 75 and over. Men's rates showed a bimodal distribution, peaking for the 45-54 (76.3) and 75+ (90.3) age groups. Between 1984 and 1986-1988, the decrease in suicide rates was particularly marked for both men and women aged 25-54, at 45% and 33%, respectively. The highest suicide rates and the largest fluctuations were observed in males aged 45-54 during the study period (Wasserman, et al., 1998b).

## DISCUSSION

Suicide rates in the former Soviet Union 1984-1990 varied widely, from 3.5 in the Caucasus to 28.0 in the Baltics. This seems to be related to different cultures and lifestyles of people inhabiting different regions, in spite of the having same socio-political and economic structure applied by the Soviet regime. High suicide rates and male-female ratios in Slavic and Baltic regions were characterized by high alcohol consumption (Nemtsov, 1998; Wasserman, et al., 1994; Wasserman, et al., 1998c), urbanization, nuclear families, a low birth rate and a high divorce rate (Goskomitet USSR, 1989).

Christianity was banned during the Soviet occupation, and active promotion of atheism took place. The low suicide rates were registered in Caucasus and Central Asia regions with stable lifestyles in large families, well-defined gender roles and long-standing traditions, which can afford protection both against everyday stress as well as against stress connected with socio-political changes. Islam, which was the basis of the life-style in Central Asia and Azerbaijan, was not influenced by atheism even under the Soviet regime. Suicide rates and male to female ratios were smaller in Central Asian republics with higher proportions of natives in the population (Buckley, 1997; Durkheim, 2002/1897; Hoyer & Lund, 1993; Lester, 1992; Värnik, 1998).

Similar factors appear to have worked simultaneously in all the republics of the former USSR causing the significant decrease of 35.2% in suicide rates that took place during *Perestroika*. The fall in suicide mortality, when the social and political climate became exceptionally hope-inspiring and a strict anti-alcohol policy was introduced, was observed in all republics and in both genders, although it was more pronounced for men than women. A sharp rise of suicides beginning in 1989 could be explained by adaptation shock caused by rapid implementation of the new socio-political and economic system and an end to the strict anti-alcohol policy. The suicide curves turned down again from 1995 after the stabilization of the society and the reorganization of medical and psychiatric services (Värnik, et al., 2000).

The role of socio-political aspects in suicide is illustrated by the highest suicide rates and the largest fluctuations in suicide rates among middle-aged men, the group considered most sensitive to social change, and who also show the greatest tendency towards alcohol abuse. The age distribution of suicide rates for females was similar to that in Europe (Gailiene, et al., 1995; Värnik, et al., 1998a).

Attitudes toward suicidal persons had been extremely harsh in the USSR (Mokhovikov, 1994; Värnik & Wasserman, 1992), and so psychiatric aid could have been one of the components influencing suicides. Changing attitudes and improvements in the quality of psychiatric services coincided with the falling suicide rates beginning in the mid-1990s (Värnik, et al., 2000).

One limitation here is the reliability and validity of suicide statistics. In the Soviet Union, qualitative and quantitative investigations have shown that procedures for reporting and registering death were the same throughout the country and strongly controlled, with no instructions to falsify data given and only secrecy stressed (Leon, et al., 1997; Wasserman & Värnik, 1998). Nevertheless, bias at the primary level could have occurred. Another limitation concerns the study design. At the individual level, only alcohol as a suicide risk factor was investigated (Värnik, et al., 2007), and other possible explanations could be influential at the aggregate level.

# REFERENCES

Buckley, C. (1997). Suicide in post-soviet Kazakhstan: role stress, age, and gender. *Central Asian Survey*, 16, 45-52.

Durkheim, E. (2002/1897). *Suicide: a study in sociology.* London, UK: Routledge.

Gailiene, D., Domanskiene, Y., & Keturakis, Y. (1995). Suicide in Lithuania. *Archives of Suicide Research*, 1, 149–158.

Goskomitet USSR (1989). Naselenie USSR 1988. In *Statisticheskij jezjegodnik (Statistical yearbook)*. Moscow, USSR: Finansy i Statistika.

Hoyer, G., & Lund, E. (1993). Suicide among women related to number of children in marriage. *Archives of General Psychiatry*, 50, 134-137.

Leon, D. A., Chenet, L., Shkolnikov, V. M., et al. (1997). Huge variation in Russian mortality rates 1984-94: artefact, alcohol, or what? *Lancet*, 350, 383-388.

Lester, D. (1992). Religiosity, suicide and homicide: a cross-national examination. *Psychological Reports*, 71, 1282.

Mokhovikov, A. N. (1994). Suicide in the Ukraine. *Crisis*, 15, 137.

Nemtsov, A. V. (1998). Alcohol-related harm and alcohol consumption in Moscow before, during and after a major anti-alcohol campaign. *Addiction*, 93, 1501-1510.

Postovalova, L. (1989). Rasprostranennost samoubijstw w SSSR (Suicide in the USSR). In L. Postovalova (Ed.) *Srawnitelno-vozrastnyje issledovanija w suicidologij*, pp. 24–34. Moskva, USSR: Moskowskij Institut Psihiatrii.

Rancans, E., Salander Renberg, E., & Jacobsson, L. (2001). Major demographic, social and economic factors associated to suicide rates in Latvia 1980-98. *Acta Psychiatrica Scandinavica*, 103, 275-281.

Wasserman, D., & Värnik, A. (1994). Increase in suicide among men in the Baltic countries. *Lancet*, 343, 1504-1505.

Wasserman, D., & Värnik, A. (1998). Reliability of statistics on violent death and suicide in the former USSR, 1970-1990. *Acta Psychiatrica Scandinavic,a* Supplement 394, 34-41.

Wasserman, D., Värnik, A., & Dankowicz, M. (1998a). Regional differences in the distribution of suicide in the former Soviet Union during perestroika, 1984-1990. *Acta Psychiatrica Scandinavica,* Supplement 394, 5-12.

Wasserman, D., Värnik, A., Dankowicz, M., et al. (1998b). Suicide-preventive effects of perestroika in the former USSR: the role of alcohol restriction. *Acta Psychiatrica Scandinavica,* Supplement 394, 1-44.

Wasserman, D., Värnik, A., & Eklund, G. (1994). Male suicides and alcohol consumption in the former USSR. *Acta Psychiatrica Scandinavica*, 89, 306-313.

Wasserman, D., Värnik, A., & Eklund, G. (1998c). Female suicides and alcohol consumption during perestroika in the former USSR. *Acta Psychiatrica Scandinavica,* Supplement 394, 26-33.

Värnik, A. (1997). Suicide in the Baltic countries and in the former republics of the USSR [doctoral dissertation]. Stockholm, Sweden: Karolinska Institute.

Värnik, A. (1998). Suicide in the former republics of the USSR. *Psychiatria Fennica*, 29, 150-162.

Värnik, A., Kõlves, K., Väli, M., et al. (2007). Do alcohol restrictions reduce suicide mortality? *Addiction*, 102, 251-6.

Värnik, A., Tooding, L.-M., Palo, E., et al. (2000). Suicide Trends in the Baltic States, 1970-1997. *Trames*, 4, 79-90.

Värnik, A., & Wasserman, D. (1992). Suicides in the former Soviet republics. *Acta Psychiatrica Scandinavica*, 86, 76-78.

Värnik, A., Wasserman, D., Dankowicz, M., et al. (1998a). Age-specific suicide rates in the Slavic and Baltic regions of the former USSR during perestroika, in comparison with 22 European countries. *Acta Psychiatrica Scandinavica,* Supplement 394, 20-25.

Värnik, A., Wasserman, D., Dankowicz, M., et al. (1998b). Marked decrease in suicide among men and women in the former USSR during perestroika. *Acta Psychiatrica Scandinavica,* Supplement 394, 13-19.

Värnik, A., Wasserman, D., Palo, E., et al. (2001). Registration of external causes of death in the Baltic States 1970-1997. *European Journal of Public Health*, 11, 84-88.

In: Suicide from a Global Perspective: Psychosocial Approaches    ISBN 978-1-61470-965-7
Editors: A. Shrivastava, M. Kembrell et al. 165-168    © 2012 Nova Science Publishers, Inc.

Chapter 23

# SUICIDE IN THE PEOPLE'S REPUBLIC OF CHINA

## Colin Pritchard

The suicide rate and the rate of undetermined 'Other External Cause Deaths' (OECD) of the majority of Islamic and Latin American countries suicide are markedly different from the Major Developed Countries (MDC). In particular, there is a likely possibility of a substantial number of hidden suicides in their OECD rates, which reflects their traditional cultural anathema to suicide. Indeed, the only consistent similarity between the two cultural groups and the MDC is that male suicide, across all age bands, is much higher than for women.

This leads to considering the other 'Non-Western' major culture for which fairly recent WHO data is available, namely the People's Republic of China (PRC). In 1997, there was a window of opportunity as for the first time the PRC had reported their mortality rates to the WHO for the years 1990, 1992 and 1994 using the ICD $9^{th}$ edition (WHO 1997). The data were based upon samples from "selected Rural and Urban zones", with representative populations from Rural and Urban areas of 52.03 million and 61.23 million respectively. Unfortunately there were no data available for the undetermined category, and so no estimate can be made of any possible hidden suicides. A detailed methodology and literature review can be found elsewhere (Pritchard, 1996; Lau & Pritchard, 2001; Pritchard & Baldwin, 2002).

Sufficient to say however, the earlier results challenged a number of stereotypical beliefs about Chinese culture, and this reworking and new analysis of the data highlight previously missed variations from the dominant Western model.

## RESULTS

The first notable difference was that, unlike the MDC, there were more males in the two PRC regions general populations than women. Table 23-1 shows the general data, which covers the age bands of Younger [15-34] and Senior [65+] aged people in order to tease out some of the complex findings that reflect markedly different patterns of suicide than those found in the MDC. Another immediate difference was that suicide rates were considerably higher in Rural than Urban zones, which is largely at odds with the majority of MDC.

Strikingly, the All Age female suicide rates were higher compared to men in both areas; 224 per million for males to 286 for females in Rural areas and 74 to 85 respectively in the Urban zones. This variation to the expected gender pattern was further emphasized by the fact that proportionately more Younger Aged [15-34] women died from suicide than their male counterparts, for example a ratio of 2.10:1 for Youth [15-24] in Rural areas and 1.48:1 in Urban regions, which highlights even further the Rural and Urban divide.

A key difference from MDC patterns is with regard to Senior suicide rates. Despite the traditional regard and veneration for elderly people, PRC Rural rates for 65+ exceeded the world's highest rates previously found in Austria, Finland and Hungary (WHO, 2005). Currently the world's highest rates of Elderly [75+] suicide is in Hungary, at 1,211 per million for males and 346 females (WHO 2006). Both PRC regions were higher than Hungary's female rate, while the Rural Chinese Elderly male rate was 18% higher than Hungary's. The PRC ratios are in stark contrast to that found in 3-year average MDC rates and ratios, as shown in Table 23-2.

The MDC Senior suicide rates were significantly higher than All Age rates, but in some MDC this is no longer the case (Pritchard & Hansen, 2005b). Current MDC Older [65-74] to All Age rates produced a ratio of 1.06:1 for males and 1.62:1 females and for male Elderly 2.42:1 and 2.03:1 for females. However, both Older and Elderly ratios to All Age rates in Rural and Urban China had significantly wider ratios than the MDC. Indeed, exploring Chinese and MDC suicide patterns further, when including Youth [15-24], Young Adult [25-34] as well as the Senior age bands, the Chinese results were significantly different from patterns of MDC suicide.

**Table 23.1. Suicide in PRC China - Selected Rural and Urban Regions: Rates per Million**

| Region ICD 9 | All Age M- F | 15-24 M - F | 25-34 M - F | 65-74 M –F | 75+ M – F |
|---|---|---|---|---|---|
| Rural | | | | | |
| 1990 Suicide | 203 – 246 | 162- 361 | 191 – 217 | 800- 510 | 1395-743 |
| 1992 Suicide | 232 – 306 | 174 – 367 | 215-385 | 975-743 | 1457-1026 |
| 1994 Suicide | 237 – 305 | 167- 330 | 219 – 420 | 1015 – 747 | 1426-1005 |
| Average | 224 –286 | 168- 353 | 210 – 341 | 930 – 667 | 1426- 925 |
| Ratio M:F | 1.28 | 2.10 | 1.62 | 0.72 | 0.65 |
| Urban | | | | | |
| 1990 Suicide | 81 – 91 | 61 – 103 | 76- 93 | 252 –201 | 589-463 |
| 1992 Suicide | 77- 93 | 56 - 106 | 70 - 85 | 238- 222 | 415 - 419 |
| 1994 Suicide | 65- 70 | 36-64 | 63- 71 | 169 – 159 | 382-328 |
| Averages S | 74 – 85 | 61 – 91 | 70- 83 | 220 – 208 | 462 –403 |
| Ratio M:F | 1.14 | 1.48 | 1.19 | 0.95 | 0.87 |

While the focus is upon the PRC, earlier work showed an apparent Chinese cultural influence when comparing other Asian countries with the MDC (Lua & Pritchard, 2001; Pritchard & Baldwin, 2002). The Asian countries for which comparable data were available were the two PRC zones, Singapore, Hong Kong, the Republic of Korea (South) and Japan. These countries All Age to Senior Aged suicide rates were significantly different than the majority of the 40 'Western' countries. The PRC zones, Hong Kong and Singapore, with their very high proportion of Chinese populations, had the biggest Senior to All Age ratios in the world, in excess of 4.6:1 (Lau & Pritchard, 2001). A further comparison was made across all age bands with Asian and the English-speaking countries, which again found more Asian women and Senior suicides occurring (Pritchard & Baldwin, 2002).

**Table 23.2. Suicide in Rural and Urban PRC and Average MDC by Age and Gender: Rates per Million**

| Country | All Age M - F | 15-24 M - F | 25-34 M - F | 65-74 * M - F | 75+ * M - F |
|---|---|---|---|---|---|
| MDC | 186 - 61 | 135 -36 | 207- 56 | 197 – 99 | 450 -124 |
| All Age ratios |  | 0.73 – 0.59 | 1.11- 0.92 | 1.06- 1.62 | 2.42- 2.03 |
| Rural PRC | 224 – 286 | 168 -353 | 210 -341 | 930 – 667 | 1426 -925 |
| All Age ratios |  | 0.75 –1.23 | 0.94-1.19 | 4.15- 2.33 | 6.64- 3.23 |
| Urban PRC | 74 – 85 | 61 – 91 | 70 – 83 | 220 – 208 | 462 – 403 |
| All Age ratios |  | 0.82 -1.07 | 0.95- 0.98 | 2.97 – 2.45 | 6.24- 4.74 |

Source Pritchard & Hansen 2005b) All X2 3 d/f.
For $X^2$ by All Age, by Age Bands by Gender and all 4 combinations p <0.00001.

## DISCUSSION

These findings from China, the Islamic and Latin American countries are an indication of the pervasive influence of culture upon suicide. Clearly patterns of suicide in the Major Developed Countries, as well as the majority of other European and Western countries, appear at odds with the majority of the world's population. It is argued that patterns of mortality reflect the nature of a society. This includes not only economic, technical and medical factors, but also psychosocial and cultural factors. What can be inferred from these PRC results?

The first surprising finding is that Chinese senior suicide rates challenge their traditional reputation of the veneration of the elderly. We can only speculate, but does this reflect something of the sense of family responsibility felt by senior aged people who do not wish to be a burden on their family in their old age? Second was the pattern of Chinese younger-aged women's suicide, which was unlike any other country reporting to the WHO. Bearing in mind the major declines in female suicides throughout the MDC, which have never been lower, these results probably reflect the position of women in China. Finally, the Rural-Urban divide may possibly have something to do with the differential availability of psychiatric services in Rural and Urban China (Pritchard & Baldwin, 2002). Of course, we do not know for sure, but these queries require an answer if the tragedy of suicide is to be reduced.

Of utmost concern from these findings is the recent apparent vulnerability of younger-aged men in Latin America and the West and of younger-aged Chinese women, whose suicide rates exceed the majority of national rates throughout the world. It is easy to forget that these statistics concern people, and the nightmare of every parent is that their children might predecease them. Consequently, these figures represent tens of thousands of parents who face an almost insurmountable loss. Ultimately, governments in the majority of the world's countries should begin to take seriously their expressed commitment to reduce the tragic, and often unnecessary, toll of suicide (Goldney, 1998).

## REFERENCES

Goldney, R. D. (1998). The International Association for the Prevention of Suicide: the Adelaide Declaration. *Crisis,* 19, 50-52

Lau, B. W. K., & Pritchard, C. (2001). Suicide of older people in Asian societies: an international comparison. *Australasian Journal on Ageing,* 20, 196-202.

Pritchard, C. (1996). Suicide in the People's Republic of China categorised by age and gender: evidence of the influence of culture upon suicide. *Acta Psychiatrica Scandinavia.* 93, 362-367.

Pritchard, C., & Baldwin, D. S. (2002). Elderly suicide in Asian and English speaking countries. *Acta Psychiatrica Scandinavia.* 105, 271-275.

Pritchard, C., & Hansen L (2005a). An analysis of suicide in people aged 65-74 and 75+ in England & Wales and the Western world 1997-2000. *International Journal of Geriatric Psychiatry,* 210, 17-25

Pritchard, C., & Hansen, L. (2005b) Adolescent and youth suicide in England & Wales: an international comparison. *International Journal of Adolescent Medicine & Health,* 17, 239-253.

World Health Organization. (1996). *Annual statistics.* Geneva, Switzerland: WHO.

Chapter 24

# SUICIDE IN JAPAN

## *Mutsuhiro Nakao*

Although Japan's population has the greatest longevity in the world (Mathers, et al., 1999), its suicide rate is high (24.1 per 100,000), ranking 9th in the world (Bertolote, 1999; WHO). The incidence of reported suicide has risen dramatically from 22,000 suicides to 32,000 for the years 1995-2004 (WHO) (Figure 24-1). In 2004, suicide ranked 6th as a cause of death among the Japanese population as a whole (6th in men and 8th in women) (Community Safety Bureau, National Police Agency, 2003). Some studies have reported that this dramatic increase is closely related to the Japanese economic depression that occurred during the same decade (Yamasaki, et al, 2004). Many employees are being forced to work harder because of ongoing business restructuring, and a number of workers who committed suicide have been officially acknowledged as victims of depression caused by overwork over the past ten years. The main reasons for suicide are health-related problems, followed by financial or living problems, and family problems (Japan Ministry of Health, Labor and Welfare, 1994). The numbers of suicides specifically related to financial and living problems, work-related problems and unemployment have been increasing in recent years.

## DEPRESSION-RELATED SUICIDE IN JAPAN

The incidence of depression has been rapidly increasing in Western countries. In Japan, too, the number of people diagnosed with depression increased from 100,000 to 430,000 between 1984 and 1998 (Watanabe, 1999). Although depression is generally more common in women than in men (Kuehner, 2003), the most dramatic increase has occurred in the middle-aged male population group (40-60 years old). A similar trend has been observed in Japanese suicides (Yamasaki, et al., 2004). When the suicide population is divided into six groups by working condition (i.e., unemployed, employer, employee, homemakers, students, and "unknown"), unemployed and employee are the leading groups for suicide (Community Safety Bureau, National Police Agency, 2003). Therefore, one strategy to prevent suicide in

Japan may be to target middle-aged men who are either unemployed or employees as a way to identify individuals who may potentially experience depression.

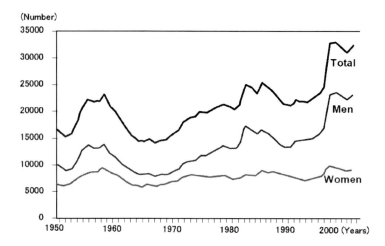

Figure 24-1. Number of Suicides in Japan.

## CURRENT STATUS OF THE LITERATURE

An examination of the literature for research on suicide in Japan during the forty year period of 1966-2006 resulted in 243 articles, of which 198 are written in English. With regard to psychiatric factors for suicide, according to a six-year cohort study in 5,352 Japanese male workers aged 40 to 54 years (Tamakoshi, et al., 2000), the odds ratio for suicide associated with depression was 9.95. It was reported that, among those visiting the hospitals or clinics because of suicide attempts in Japan, 75% had psychiatric disorders including schizophrenia, depression, alcohol problems and drug abuse (Japanese Committee for Prevention of Suicide, 2002). According to a community survey (Ono, et al., 2001), 12% of elderly people had experienced thoughts of death or suicide, and 3% had such thoughts persistently for more than two weeks. Among those elderly people with such thoughts, 23% had consulted physicians and 20% had asked family members for help. Several studies (Otsu, 2004; Yamasaki, et al., 2005) have reported that socioeconomic factors affect the suicidal mortality in Japan, with low income and conditions created by economic depression being major factors. Recent studies have also shown that a suicide prevention campaign has been effective in reducing the number of suicides in local areas of Japan, including the Akita Prefecture, among others (Oyama, et al., 2006).

## OBSERVATIONS FROM THE AUTHOR'S OWN RESEARCH

In a Japanese psychosomatic clinic (Nakao, et al., 2002), 863 outpatients were studied to examine associations between suicidal ideation, somatic symptoms and mood states. All outpatients were diagnosed using multi-axial assessments of the Diagnostic and Statistical

Manual of Mental Disorders (DSM-III-R and DSM-IV). They completed the Cornell Medical Index Questionnaire to assess suicidal ideation and somatic symptoms. Mood states were rated using the Profile of Mood States (POMS). It was found that 266 patients (31%) reported suicidal ideation. As reported in the DSM-III-R and DSM-IV, those with personality disorders, higher psychosocial stress and lower psychosocial functioning tended more often to have suicidal ideation. Using multiple regression analysis, it was found that the total number of somatic symptoms and the POMS depression scale predicted suicidal ideation. It appears that evaluation of somatic symptoms and depressive moods might be important in assessing suicidal ideation in a mind/body clinical population.

Based on this clinical study, this line of research was continued in the workplace (Nakao & Yano, 2003, 2006; Isshiki, et al., 2004). At annual health check-ups, the DSM-IV interviews were performed on 991 male workers, and 24 (2.4%) were diagnosed with major depression. In line with previous studies (Nakao, et al., 2001a, 2001b) and Western studies among primary care patients (Kroenke, et al., 1994; Marple, et al., 1997), the following twelve common major somatic symptoms were simultaneously assessed: fatigue, headache, insomnia, back pain, abdominal pain, joint or limb pain, dizziness, chest pain, constipation, palpitation, nausea and shortness of breath. The somatic symptoms were defined as positive when they occurred once a week or more frequently. It was found that 665 subjects had none of these somatic symptoms, and none of them were identified as having major depression (Nakao & Yano, 2003). The prevalence of a major depressive disorder was positively associated with the total number of somatic symptoms, and the area under the receiver operator characteristic (ROC) curve was 0.92, which showed the sensitivity and specificity of the total number of somatic symptoms with respect to detecting major depression. In the total sample, 5% had suicidal thoughts, and no one with such thoughts reported somatic symptoms. It was also found that the use of one or two items listed on annual medical check-ups could be an effective way to screen for major depression and suicidal thoughts in a Japanese working population. Selected items would not necessarily be limited to psychological discomforts as a number of common somatic symptoms could be useful as screening items as well.

## STRATEGY FOR SUICIDE PREVENTION IN JAPAN

In 2000, the Japanese government declared its intention to reduce the annual number of suicides to 22,000 by 2010 (Tatara, 2001). In 2002, the National Committee reported possible strategies for the prevention of suicide (Japanese Ministry of Health, Labor, and Welfare, 2004), emphasizing the importance of pre-intervention (assessment of factors affecting suicide), intervention (identification of high-risk persons in order to prevent suicide) and post-intervention (social support for bereaved families and friends). On the basis of such ideas, two manuals on the management of depression were published for healthcare professionals and public servants (Japanese Ministry of Health, Labor, and Welfare, 2004). In the manuals, a screening test for depression is recommended at health checkups, both in the workplace and in local communities. However, the recommended method of screening is based on the full criteria of DSM-IV-TR, including eight or nine items to assess depression. A simpler method is required if a screening test for depression is to be administered on a national basis. To fulfil the national goal of reducing suicide cases to 22,000 per year within the next five years, it is necessary to identify target groups and conduct extensive interventions for high-risk persons identified within these groups.

In Japan, the governmental healthcare policy recognizes mental health as an issue of top priority (Japanese Ministry of Health, Labor, and Welfare, 2004), and in 2005 organized the Strategic Research Group for Management of Depression Related to Suicide. The research group conducted two types of intervention. One assessed the prevalence of suicide attempts in local communities and developed a program for preventing suicide. The other assessed patients who have already attempted suicide and who are being treated at emergency clinics (Strategic Research Group for Management of Depression Related to Suicide, undated).

In 2006, the Fundamental Law established the Strategy for Preventing Suicide ("Jisatsu Taisaku Kihonn Hou" in Japanese). This Japanese law is intended to prevent suicide and to support family members bereaved by suicide. It also declared that national strategies are needed to increase awareness and recognition of suicide problems among the Japanese people.

## CONCLUSIONS

A systematic reduction in the incidence of suicide in Japan will first require the identification of individuals who may potentially experience depression, as most individuals who commit suicide are depressed. A simple method, such as the identification of physical discomfort, is required to enable screening for depression on a national scale (Nakao & Takeuchi, 2006). Fulfillment of the national goal will require the identification of target groups and extensive interventions for high-risk persons within these groups (e.g., middle aged men with depression). Extensive and consistent campaigns related to suicide problems are also needed to reach high-risk people whose susceptibility goes unrecognized (Nakao & Takeuchi, 2006).

## REFERENCES

Bertolote, J. M. (1999). Foreword. In *Figures and facts about suicide*, pp. iii-x. Geneva, Switzerland: World Health Organization.

Community Safety Bureau, National Police Agency. (2003). Suicide report. Accessedfrom: URL: http://www.t-pec.co.jp/mental/2002-08-4.htm (in Japanese)

Isshiki, A., Nakao, M., Yamaoka, K., et al. (20040. Application of subjective symptom checklist for screening major depression by annual health examinations: a cross-validity study in the workplace. *Journal of Medical Screening*, 11, 207-209.

Japan Ministry of Health, Labour, and Welfare. (2004). *Vital Statistics.* Tokyo, Japan: Kousei Toukei Kyoukai.

Japanese Ministry of Health, Labor, and Welfare. *A proposal for suicide prevention.* Accessed from: URL: http://www.mhlw.go.jp/houdou/2002/12/h1218-3.html (in Japanese)

Japanese Ministry of Health, Labor, and Welfare. *Manual of management of depression.* Accessed from: http://www.mhlw.go.jp/shingi/2004/01/s0126-5.html#2 (in Japanese)

Japanese Ministry of Health, Labor, and Welfare. *Manual of strategy for facilitating management of depression.* Accessed from:
http://www.mhlw.go.jp/shingi/2004/01/s0126-5.html#1 (in Japanese)

Japanese Committee for Prevention of Suicide. (2002). *A proposal for prevention of suicide: current status of suicide in Japan.* Accessed from: http://www.mhlw.go.jp/houdou/2002/12/h1218-3.html/ (in Japanese)

Kroenke, K., Spitzer, R. L., Williams, J. B., et al. (1994). Physical symptoms in primary care: predictors of psychiatric disorders and functional impairment. *Archives of Family Medicine,* 3, 774-779.

Kuehner, C. (2003). Gender differences in unipolar depression: an update of epidemiological findings and possible explanations. *Acta Psychiatrica Scandinavica,* 108, 163-174.

Marple, R. L. L., Kroenke, K., Lucey, C. R., et al. (1997). Concerns and expectations in patients presenting with physical complaints. *Archives of Internal Medicine,* 157, 1482-1488.

Mathers, C. D., Sandana, R., Salormon, J. A., et al. (1999). Healthy life expectancy in 191 countries. *Lancet,* 26, 1985-1991.

Nakao, M., & Takeuchi, T. (2006). The suicide epidemic in Japan and strategies of depression screening for its prevention. *Bulletin of the World Health Organization,* 84, 492-493.

Nakao, M., & Yano, E. (2003). Reporting of somatic symptoms as a screening marker for detecting major depression in a population of Japanese white-collar workers. *Journal of Clinical Epidemiology,* 56, 1021-1026.

Nakao, M., & Yano, E. (2006). Prediction of major depression in Japanese adults: somatic manifestation of depression in annual health examinations. *Journal of Affective Disorders,* 90, 29-35.

Nakao, M., Fricchione, G., Myers, P., et al. (2001). Anxiety is a good indicator for somatic symptom reduction through a behavioral medicine intervention in a mind/body medicine clinic. *Psychotherapy & Psychosomatics,* 70, 50-57.

Nakao, M., Yamanaka, G., & Kuboki, T. (2001). Major depression and somatic symptoms in a mind/body medicine clinic. *Psychopathology,* 34, 230-235.

Nakao, M., Yamanaka, G., & Kuboki, T. (2002). Suicidal ideation and somatic symptoms of patients with mind/body distress in a Japanese Psychosomatic Clinic. *Suicide & Life-Threatening Behavior,* 32, 80-90.

Ono Y., Tanaka E., Oyama H., et al. (2001). Epidemiology of suicidal ideation and help-seeking behaviors among the elderly in Japan. *Psychiatry & Clinical Neuroscience,* 55, 605-611.

Otsu, A., Araki, S., Sakai, R., et al. (2004). Effects of urbanization, economic development, and migration of workers on suicide mortality in Japan. *Social Science & Medicine,* 58, 1137-1146.

Oyama, H., Ono, Y., Watanabe, N., et al. (2006). Local community intervention through depression screening and group activity for elderly suicide prevention. *Psychiatry & Clinical Neuroscience,* 60, 110-114.

Strategic Research Group for Management of Depression Related to Suicide. *Two research tasks to be performed.* Accessed from: http://www8.ocn.ne.jp/~seishin/strategy2.html (in Japanese)

Tamakoshi, A., Ohno, Y., Yamada, T., et al. (2000). Depressive mood and suicide among middle-aged workers: findings from a prospective cohort study in Nagoya, Japan. *Journal of Epidemiology,* 10, 173-178.

Tatara, K. (2001). Guideline of "Health in Japan toward the 21st century (Kenko-Nippon-21)". Tokyo, Japan: Gyousei. (in Japanese)

Watanabe Y. (Ed.). (1999). *Patient survey 1.* Tokyo: Health and Welfare statistics Association, (in Japanese).

World Health Organization. *Prevention of suicidal behaviors: a task for all.* Accessed from: http://www.who.int/mental_health/prevention/suicide/supresuicideprevent/en/ (in Japanese)

Yamasaki, A., Morgenthaler, S., Kaneko, Y., et al. (2004). Trends and monthly variations in the historical record of suicide in Japan from 1976 to 1994. *Psychological Reports*, 94, 607-612.

Yamasaki, A., Sakai R., & Shirakawa, T. (2005). Low income, unemployment, and suicide mortality rates for middle-age persons in Japan. *Psychological Reports,* 96, 37-48.

*Chapter 25*

# SUICIDE IN ISRAEL

## *Eliezer Witztum and Daniel Stein*

"The universality of suicidal behavior across all societies and cultures is well-documented. Attitudes toward suicide vary with time and place, reflecting the ideologies of each society for the value of life and concept of death" (Stengel, 1975).

## SUICIDE IN JUDAISM

In Judaism, the duty of preserving life, including one's own, is considered a paramount injunction (Cohn, 1972). Nevertheless, Jewish tradition emphasizes that one should let himself be killed rather than violate three cardinal rules - against idol worship, murder and incest. In the Bible, although no explicit command forbidding suicide is given, the sovereignty of God and not of man over life and death is repeatedly emphasized: "It is I who put to death and give life" (Dt. 32:39). Although God is equally sovereign over the deaths of all humans, those of his own people touch him deeply: "Precious in the sight of the Lord is the death of His godly ones" (Ps. 116:15).

Six suicides are recorded in the Bible: Samson, Avimelech, King Saul and his arm bearer, Ahitophel and Zimri. In every case, mitigating circumstances for the suicidal act exist, that is, to account for one's sins or to avoid captivity. For example, the account of King Saul's death reads: "And the battle went heavily against Saul, and the archers hit him; and he was badly wounded by the archers. Then Saul said to his armor bearer: Draw your sword and pierce me through with it, lest these uncircumcised come and pierce me through and make sport of me. But his armor bearer would not, for he was greatly afraid. So Saul took his sword and fell on it. And when his armor bearer saw that Saul was dead, he also fell on his sword and died with him" (1 Sam. 31:1-6 and 1 Chron. 10:1-6).

A typology relevant in Judaism is the heroic suicide, demonstrated, for example, in the story of Samson, who was ready to kill himself and not be captured by the Philistines. Samson's death is thus recorded: "And Samson grasped the two middle pillars on which the house rested, and braced himself against them…. and he bent with all his might so that the house fell on the lords and all the [Philistine] people who were in it." (Jdg. 16:25-30).

Heroic suicide is particularly noteworthy in the narrative of Masada, the most famous case of collective suicide in Jewish history (Zerubavel, 1994). The fortress of Masada in the Judean desert was the last stronghold against the Roman Empire at the end of the Jewish revolt of 66-73 A.D. After a long siege, the Romans succeeded in demolishing the walls of the fortress. It was a profound religious conviction and an equally strong sense of freedom that led the leader of the rebels, Elazar Ben-Yair, and the 960 surviving defenders of Masada to kill their wives and children and then each other rather than surrender to the Romans. This heroic tradition continued throughout the two thousand years in which the Jewish nation was in exile, from the readiness of the Jews in Medieval Spain to kill themselves rather than succumb to Christianity, to a similar readiness of the Jewish warriors in the Polish ghettos during the Second World War (Zerubavel, 1994).

Specific injunctions against suicide appeared for the first time in the Talmud, and later, in post-Talmudic writings (Cohn, 1972). It was written that no burial rites honoring the person were to be performed, and that the burial be done in a separate place, outside the cemetery. Only rites respecting mourners were permitted (Cohn, 1972). Later Jewish codes of law (those of Maimonides from the 12th Century) and the Shulhan Arukh from the 16th Century, distinguished between suicide while of sound mind, to which these restrictions apply, and suicide while of unsound mind (including suicide by minors) which is forgiven. These injunctions still apply in Modern Judaism, so that official orthodox burial ceremonies are not permitted in the case of suicide (Levav & Aisenberg, 1989). In conclusion, there is an inherent duality in the way Judaism perceives suicide, namely, as sinful and forbidden in general, but allowing, if not worshiping, the readiness of the individual to die when it comes to protecting the existence of the Jewish religion or nation (Stein, et al., 1989; Zerubavel, 1994).

## SUICIDE IN MODERN ISRAEL

Israel presents ample motives for the study of suicide, undergoing major socio-economic and socio-cultural changes both before and since its independence in 1948. This is relevant since social instability may increase the risk of suicide (Levav & Aisenberg, 1989). Other important relevant socio-cultural factors include the considerable ethnic diversity in Israeli society, the influence of the never-ending immigration to Israel and the repeated switches between war and peace conditions within a brief period of time (Levav & Aisenberg, 1989). In this respect, Lester (2006) has shown a significant inverse correlation between the number of suicide terrorist attacks and number of people killed in these attacks and suicide rates in Israel from 1983-1999, supporting indirectly the association between war conditions and reduced suicide risk.

Suicide rates for Jews are consistently lower than those of Protestants and mostly also lower in comparison to Catholics (Levav & Aisenberg, 1989). In keeping with these trends, suicide rates in Israel are also relatively low. In the most updated report of the World Health Organization (WHO) of suicide rates in 110 countries in the 1990's (WHO, 2003), Israel ranks in the 73rd and 76th place for males (10.5 per 100,000) and females (2.6), respectively. Suicide rates in Israel are lower than those in most European and North American countries, in the range of South and Central American countries, but considerably higher than most Muslim countries.

This low rate of suicide is found in Jewish Israelis of all ages, including adolescents (Kohn, et al., 1997), in contrast to the sharp rise in adolescent suicide rates from the 1970's to the 1990's in many Western industrialized countries (Spirito & Esposito-Smythers, 2006). The average suicide rate between 1975-1989 for 15-19 year old Israeli Jewish males (5.3) and females (1.9) is among the lowest in the world (Kohn, et al., 1997). Among other likely protective factors in addition to the influence of Judaism is the low rate of suicides in Israeli youth performed under the influence of alcohol and drugs (Stein, et al., 1998).

One exception to this finding is the high suicide rate in 18-21 year old Israeli males, being significantly higher than that of both 15-17 and 21-29 year olds (Kohn, et al., 1997; Lubin, et al., 2001). A considerable increase in suicide rate occurred in 18-21 year old males from 1984-5 to 1992-4 (3.9 versus 18.2), coupled with a dramatic rise in the use of firearms in completed suicides (11% vs. 77%, respectively) (Lubin, et al., 2001). As most 18-21 year old Israeli males serve in the army, the high suicide rate in this age group likely reflects the considerable psychosocial distress and the availability of firearms during service (Kohn, et al., 1997; Lubin, et al., 2001). The rise in the suicide rate in male soldiers from 1984 to 1994 may reflect a potential increase in overall distress associated with army service after the first Palestinian uprising in 1987 (Lubin, et al., 2001). In a study of Israeli soldiers who killed themselves during service, most were above average in intelligence, physical fitness and measures predictive of successful adaptation to military service, and their performance during service was generally satisfactory. Their suicide was unexpected, apparently a result of a narcissistic failure related to service that led to the development of depression, but was not communicated to significant others (Apter, et al., 1993).

The high suicide rates in 18-21 year old Israeli males are even higher in immigrants from the former USSR. Immigration is known to be associated with an increase in suicide risk, particularly in younger immigrants. The elevated suicide risk in Russian-born youngsters has been related primarily to identity crises, loss of familial and social support, severe intergenerational conflicts, social isolation and a sense of estrangement in the new country (Ponizovsky & Ritsner, 1999).

Additional support for the association of immigration with increased suicide risk comes from two studies assessing temporal trends in completed and attempted suicides during the 1980's and 1990's. Nachman, et al. (2002) found an overall increase in the rate of suicide from 1987 to 1992, stabilizing thereafter to 1997. Stein, et al. (2002) have shown high rates of attempted suicide from 1990-1992, with a constant decrease thereafter to 1998. Both studies relate these temporal changes to the massive immigration of around 400,000 Jews from the former USSR to Israel during the late 1980's and early 1990's. Indeed, Russian-born individuals have been found to be over-represented among suicide completers and attempters in relation to their overall population. Additionally, the suicide rate among Russian immigrants to Israel has been shown to be significantly higher in comparison to that of natives born in both Russia and Israel (Ponizovsky & Ritsner, 1999). Similar trends have been shown for Ethiopian immigrants to Israel (Arieli, et al., 1994).

Several factors may account for the relatively low suicide rate in Israel in addition to the influence of Judaism (Levav & Aisenberg, 1989; Kohn, et al., 1997). The tendency towards secularization and social alienation, which likely increases the risk of suicide, is more pronounced in Western industrialized countries than in Middle-Eastern or North-African countries (Beit-Hallahmi, 1975). Currently, more than a half of Israel's Jewish citizens are of Middle-Eastern or North-African descent who tend to adhere to their traditional religious values, an inclination potentially reducing suicide risk (Beit-Hallahmi, 1975).

The highest suicide rates in Israel have been found in the early 1950's (around 18), decreasing to 11-14 in the 1960's. From 1970 to the latest recordings in 2003, there has been a remarkable stability in suicide rates in Israel, ranging from 6 to 9 (Statistical Abstracts of Israel, 1973-2006). Although these temporal changes may be influenced by methodological inconsistencies, they may nevertheless reflect several important socio-demographic processes. First, the high suicide rates in the early years of Israel might have been related to the highly unstable socio-political and economic condition at that time (Levav & Aisenberg, 1989; Nachman, et al., 2002). Second, the majority of the Jewish population in the early years of Israel was of Jewish Ashkenazi (i.e., Eastern-European descent). By contrast, immigration in the 1950-1960's brought to Israel mostly Non-Ashkenazi Jews from North Africa and Middle-Eastern countries (Levav & Aisenberg, 1989). Jews born in Europe may have brought to Israel the proneness for suicide present in many of their native countries, in contrast to the low rate of suicide in many Muslim North-African and Middle-Eastern countries, whereas the heterogeneously constituted group of Israeli-born stands in-between (Levav & Aisenberg, 1989).

The issue of suicidal behavior among Israeli Arabs, of whom the vast majority are Muslims, and the rest Christians and Druses (Levav & Aisenberg, 1989), is also important to explore. The attitude of Islam towards suicide is more condemning than that of Christianity and Judaism (Dublin, 1963). Indeed, the finding of exceptionally low suicide rates in many Muslim countries is replicated in Israel. Although differences may exist between Israeli Jews and Arabs in the disclosure of information relevant to suicide (Levav & Aisenberg, 1989; Goffin, et al., 2000), the suicide rates of Israeli Muslims are consistently lower in comparison to Jews (Levav & Aisenberg, 1989; Kohn, et al., 1997; Lubin, et al., 2001). Additional socio-demographic factors likely reducing the suicide risk in Israeli Arabs in comparison to Jews include lower rates of urbanization, greater social and religious cohesion, a greater inclination to live in groups (extended families and tribes) and less self-injurious behaviors (Goffin, et al., 2000).

## CONCLUSION

Judaism has firm attitudes against suicide, although not negating it in specific circumstances. The impact of this religious-socio-cultural construction is expressed in the low rate of suicide in modern Israeli Jews. Important exceptions are male Israeli soldiers and new immigrants. These are specific high-risk populations, which ultimately require early identification of distress associated with lack of adjustment to their specific circumstances as well as the tailoring of adequate interventions.

# REFERENCES

Apter, A., Bleich, A., King, R. A., et al. (1993). Death without warning? A clinical postmortem study of suicide in 43 Israeli adolescent males. *American Journal of Psychiatry,* 50, 138-142.

Arieli, A., Gilat I., & Aycheh, S. (1994). Suicide by Ethiopian immigrants to Israel. *Harefuah,* 127, 65-70 (in Hebrew).

Beit-Hallahmi, B. (1975). Religion and suicidal behavior. *Psychological Reports,* 37, 1303-1306.

Cohn, H. C. (1972). Suicide. In *Encyclopedia Judaica.* Vol. 15. Jerusalem, Israel: Keter.

Dublin, L. I. (1963). Suicide: a sociological and statistical study. New York: Ronald.

Goffin, R., Avitzour, M., Haklai Z., et al. (2000). Intentional injuries among the young: presentation to emergency rooms, hospitalization, and death in Israel. *Journal of Adolescent Health,* 27, 434-442.

Kohn, R., Levav, I., Chang, B., et al. (1997). Epidemiology of youth suicide in Israel. *Journal of the American Academy of Child & Adolescent Psychiatry,* 36, 1537-1542.

Lester, D. (2006) Suicide attacks in Israel and suicide rates. *Perceptual & Motor Skills,* 102, 104.

Levav, I., & Aisenberg, E. (1989). Suicide in Israel: cross-national comparisons. *Acta Psychiatrica Scandinavica,* 79, 468-473.

Lubin, G., Glasser, S., Boyko, V., et al. (2001). Epidemiology of suicide in Israel: a nationwide population study. *Social Psychiatry & Psychiatric Epidemiology,* 36, 123-127.

Nachman, R., Yanai, O., Goldin, L., et al. (2002). Suicide in Israel: 1985-1997. *Journal of Psychiatry & Neuroscience,* 27, 423-428.

Ponizovsky, A. M., & Ritsner, M. S. (1999). Suicide ideation among recent immigrants to Israel from the former Soviet Union: an epidemiological survey of prevalence and risk factors. *Suicide & Life-Threatening Behavior,* 29, 376-392.

Rosen G. (1971). History in the study of suicide. *Psychological Medicine,* 1, 267-285.

Spirito, A., & Esposito-Smythers, C. (2006). Attempted and completed suicide in adolescents. *Annual Review of Clinical Psychology,* 2, 237-266.

Central Bureau of Statistics. (1970-2006). *Statistical Abstracts of Israel.* Jerusalem, Israel: Central Bureau of Statistics.

Stein, D., Witztum, E., & Kaplan De-Nour A. (1989). Attitudes of adolescents to suicide. *Israel Journal of Psychiatry,* 26, 58-68.

Stein, D., Apter, A., Retzoni, G., et al. (1998). The association between recurrent suicidal behavior and negative affective conditions among adolescents. *Journal of the American Academy of Child & Adolescent Psychiatry,* 37, 488-494.

Stein, D., Asherov, J., Lublinsky, E., et al. (2002). Sociodemographic factors in attempted suicide in two cities in Israel, between 1990- 1998. *Journal of Nervous & Mental Disease,* 190, 115-118.

Stengel, E. (1975). *Suicide and attempted suicide.* Harmondsworth, UK: Penguin Books.

World Health Organization. (2003). *Mental health resources: Suicide rates.* Geneva, Switzerland: WHO.

Zerubavel, Y. (1994). The death of memory and the memory of death: Masada and the Holocaust as historical metaphors. *Representations,* 45, 72-100.

*Chapter 26*

# SUICIDE IN INDIA

## *G. Gururaj*

Suicide is a major public health problem in every country of the world and even more so in India and other Low and Middle Income Countries (LMIC). In recent years, it has increasingly been recognized that suicides result in considerable loss of precious human resources at a young age (DeLeo, 2002). With increasing globalization, industrialization and urbanization, as well as changing values and lifestyles in society, the problem of suicide has been increasing at a phenomenal pace. Suicides lead to significant mortality, morbidity, huge socio-economic losses, psychosocial disability, and poor quality of life among survivors (DeLeo, 2002). A major barrier to understanding suicide phenomena in many countries of the world has been the unavailability of reliable and representative national and regional data. This is due in part to the absence of surveillance systems and good reporting practices. Consequently, efforts and initiatives towards the prevention of suicide have been limited and unsatisfactory.

India, with a population of more than a billion, is going through a major socio-demographic and epidemiological transition, with new challenges confronting policy makers and professionals. The population is spread over 600 districts, 4,378 towns and 638,365 villages, as well as 35 cities (with a million plus people) with varying population densities (Census, 2001). Notably, nearly half the population is comprised of children (42%) and elderly (7%). Increasing literacy levels, declining poverty levels (26%), growing urbanization (28%) (Central Statistical Organization, 2004), escalating migration (29%) and greater media presence (60%) (NFHS, 1999) are some hallmark features of changes in recent years. The declining infant mortality rate, maternal mortality rate, under-5 mortality rate and a marginal improvement in living standards has reduced the burden of communicable and infectious diseases during the last two decades. Correspondingly, noncommunicable diseases and injuries have been on the increase in the same period (Reddy, et al., 2005; Gururaj, 2005a). This demographic and epidemiological transition has brought suicide to the forefront of the healthcare delivery system. Apart from being a major public health problem, suicide is also a social, economic, cultural and developmental problem in India.

There is an increasing recognition that suicide prevention policies and programs should be developed based on epidemiological knowledge and understanding. Various problems linked with data availability, analysis and proper understanding have hampered the development of such prevention programs in India and other developing countries (Vijayakumar, et al., 2005a). The only nationally representative data are available from the National Crime Records Bureau (NCRB), which in turn receives information from several states and union territories (NCRB, 2003). As suicide is a medico-legal problem under the Indian Penal Code section 309/305/306 (NCRB, 1999), information on completed suicides is generally collected by the police. This information flow is subject to the proper reporting of suicides at different levels from villages, taluks, districts and states. In addition, the investigating agencies often lack analytical and interpreting skills. Thus, the available data provide information only on time trends and broad sociodemographic characteristics (Gururaj, 2005a). Hospitals do not report attempted suicides to any central agency and, hence, information from the health sector is non-existent.

Despite this deficiency in officially reported figures, several epidemiological studies have been undertaken in different parts of India, beginning with the first study in 1961 (Satyavathi & Rao, 1961; Ganapathy & Rao, 1966; Badrinarayana, 1977; Nandi, 1978; Ponnudurai & Jayakar, 1979; Sarma & Sawang, 1993; Hegde, 1993; Gururaj & Isaac, 2001a). The majority of these studies have been undertaken by individual researchers based on their area of interest, and all have used police data as the basis combined with hospital investigations. In general, hospital-based studies (Latha, et al., 1996; Kandamurthan, 1998; Narang, 2000) and population-based studies (Gururaj & Isaac, 2001a; Aaron, et al., 2004; Bose, et al., 2006) have been few and limited, while larger surveillance systems on suicide are nonexistent in India. Thus, the under-reporting of suicide is a significant problem due to medico-legal aspects, social stigma and police and hospital reporting practices (Gururaj, 2005a; Gururaj & Isaac, 2001a).

## THE MAGNITUDE OF THE PROBLEM

During the year 2003, 110,851 persons ended their lives by completing suicide, with a rate of 10.4 per 100,000 (NCRB, 2003). Suicides increased from nearly 40,000 in 1980 by more than 2.5 times in the last 25 years. During the period 1993-2003, the incidence of suicide increased by 8.9%, while the population registered an increase of 20.8%.

The survey of causes of death covering 26 states revealed that suicides accounted for 3.2% of total deaths, 25% of total injury deaths, and was the $9^{th}$ leading cause of death in India (RGI, 1998a). The Medical Certification of Causes of Death survey, covering nearly 498,586 medically certified deaths, revealed that suicides accounted for 1% of total deaths (RGI, 1998b) and 8% of injury deaths. In a review of cause of death data for 13 major states of India, an analysis of the Years of Life Lost (YLL) showed that suicide was one among the top nine causes of death (Indrayan, et al., 2002).

Suicidal behavior has three dimensions related to degree of medical lethality and suicidal intent, broadly classified as completed suicide, attempted suicide, and those with suicidal ideation. The similarities between the three overlap with each other with few differences (Vijayakumar, et al., 2004). Independent studies from different parts of the country by individual researchers have reported higher incidence rates of suicides in different places. Several Independent studies from different parts of the country have different rates of suicide by region, with rates ranging from 8 to 95 (Bose, et al., 2006; Gururaj & Isaac, 2001a). A recent study in rural Tamil Nadu reported a rate of 92 (Prasad, et al., 2006), while an urban study from Bangalore reported a rate of 35 (Gururaj & Isaac, 2001a). Studies from Tamil Nadu have reported rates of 82 and 92 for the period 1998-2004 and 2000-2002, respectively (Bose, et al., 2006; Prasad, et al., 2006). Wide variations in suicide rates across the country are due to inclusion and exclusion criteria, the source of information, the sample size and the statistical technique. No specific causes have been attributed to the higher rates of suicides in different regions, and are thought to be linked to reporting and local sociocultural practices.

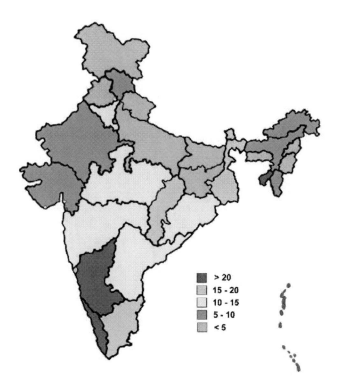

Figure 26-1. Suicide rate per 100,000 population across various States and Union Territories of India, 2003. (National average: 10.4 per 100,000 population).

Hospital-based information is the only source for estimating the burden of attempted suicides. Various hospital-based studies have revealed that the incidence of suicides among hospital-based admissions varies from 5% to 15% of the total emergency and medical admissions (Gururaj & Isaac, 2001a; Kandamurthan, 1998; Latha, et al., 1996; Baby, et al., 2006). A comparative study of completed and attempted suicides reported a ratio of 1:8 between the two, with an incidence rate of 35 and 200-325 respectively (Gururaj & Isaac, 2001a). A recent population-based survey in Bangalore reported that the incidence of attempted suicides varies from 3%-9%, with higher rates in villages and towns compared with urban Bangalore (Gururaj, et al., 2004a).

The extent of suicidal ideation in the general population is not known. A recent study from Bangalore surveyed a population of 10,134 individuals from different town, rural, slum and urban communities and reported suicide ideation (for frequent, repetitive and intense thoughts) to be present among 8%, 12%, 7% and 5%, respectively with 8%-10% having attempted suicide in the past year (Gururaj, et al., 2004a). Sidhartha and Jena (2006) recently reported that the prevalence of ideation (lifetime), ideation (last year), attempts (lifetime) and attempts (last year) among adolescents in Delhi were 21.7%, 11.7%, 8% and 3.5%, respectively.

**Table 26.1. Indian Studies on Suicide**

| Sl. No. | Author | Year | Place | Incidence rate |
|---|---|---|---|---|
| 1. | Satyavathi & Murthy Rao | 1961 | Bangalore | 8.1 |
| 2. | Ganapathy & Venkoba Rao | 1966 | Madurai | 43.0 |
| 3. | Nandi, et al. | 1979 | West Bengal (rural) | 26.5 |
| 4. | Hegde | 1980 | North Karnataka (rural) | 9.3 |
| 5. | Ponnudurai, et al. | 1986 | Chennai | 14.1 |
| 6. | Gauranga, Banerjee, et al. | 1990 | West Bengal | 43.4 |
| 7. | Shukla, et al. | 1990 | Jhansi (1986-87) | 29.0 |
| 8. | Gopal, Sarma, & Gautam Sawang | 1993 | Rural Andhra Pradesh | 22.8 |
| 9. | India | 1999 | National level data | 11.0 |
| 10. | Gururaj & Isaac | 2000 | Bangalore | 34.0 |
| 11. | Joseph, et al. | 2003 (1994 – 99) | Vellore, South India | 95.2 (83.7 – 106.3) |
| 12. | Bose, et al. | 2006 (1998 – 2004) | Vellore, South India | 82.2 |
| 13. | NCRB | 2003 | National average | 11.0 |

## REGIONAL DISTRIBUTION

Among the 28 states and 7 union territories of India, the southern and western parts of India (the progressively forward states of Karnataka, Tamil Nadu, Andhra Pradesh, Kerala and Maharashtra) have registered a significant increase in suicide and, together, contribute more than two-thirds of total suicides. These states have consistently remained in the top ten places during the last ten years. Among the Union Territories, the Union Territory of Pondicherry has remained in first place with 582 completed suicides during 2003 (NCRB, 2003).

It is interesting to note that the share of 35 cities (with a population of more than one million) is only 11% of the total suicides, with the remaining occurring in the vast rural and semi-urban parts of India. According to the NCRB (2003), the increase among the cities was 5.1% during the year 2003, compared with the national average increase of 4% during the same period. Among the metropolitan cities, the cities of Bangalore, Chennai, Mumbai and Delhi have reported higher number of suicides, contributing to nearly 40% of the total number of suicides. Smaller cities have also begun to report more suicides in recent years. It is unclear what the contributory factors for the increase in suicide in selected states and cities are, but they may be linked to better reporting practices. the phenomenon of globalization, industrialization, changing values, and local sociocultural issues.

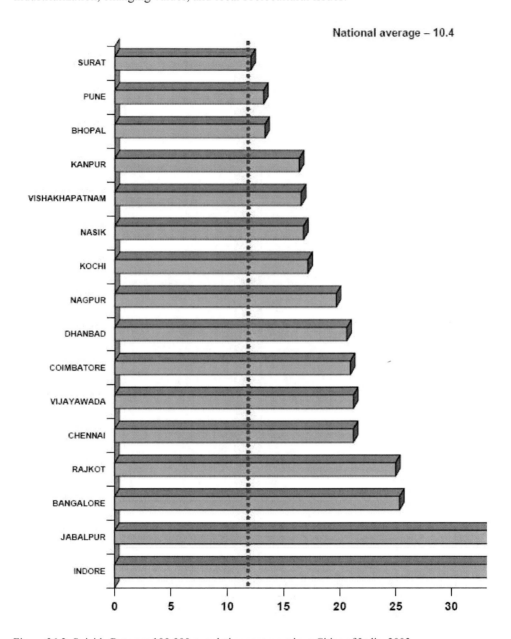

Figure 26.2. Suicide Rate per 100,000 population across various Cities of India, 2003.

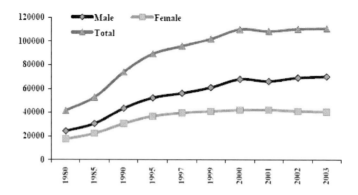

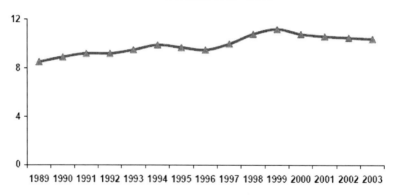

Figure 26.3. Changing pattern and rate of suicides in India..

## SOCIODEMOGRAPHIC CORRELATES

In sharp contrast to the phenomenon observed in high-income countries where suicides are a problem of older age groups, suicide in India is a problem of the young and middle-age groups. At the national level, the male to female ratio was 2:1, with 63% suicides occurring among men. Among the suicides, 36% were in the age group of 15 to 29 years and 34% in the age group 30 to 44, with higher number of males in both groups (NCRB, 2003). Significant variations are noticed across different states and union territories in the country. An important observation has been a greater occurrence among women 15 – 29 years of age compared with other age groups. A population-based study from Vellore, Tamil Nadu, revealed the annual suicide rate to be 148, 58 and 189 per 100,000 among males, females and those under 55 years of age, respectively (Joseph, et al., 2003). The high frequency among men and younger age groups is similar to reports from other parts of India (Gururaj & Isaac, 2001a; Aaron, et al., 2004).

The overall literacy rate in India is 64%, with variations across geographical regions (Census, 2001). More than 90% of completed suicides were recorded in individuals with no or low levels of education. Nearly 70% of suicides were married, and 21% were unmarried. The incidence of suicide among the unmarried was found to be high in some of the states of India (NCRB, 2003). No definite associations have been established, as marriage seems to serve both a protective and stressful role. Similarly, 57% of suicides among women and 21% of total suicides were housewives. At the national level, students and unemployed individuals constitute 6% and 9% (NCRB, 2003). Data available from selected cities indicate that the proportion of educated beyond graduate levels was high in cities compared with rural areas. Fifteen percent of total suicides occurred among people engaged in farming or agricultural activities. Recent studies and anecdotal media reports have reported high level of suicidal ideation and behaviors among farmers (Patil, 2002), students (Sidhartha & Jena, 2006) and women (Tousignant, et al., 1998; Mayer, 2002, 2003). Suicides among agricultural communities have been a cause of concern in recent years as a result of crop failures and economic deprivation among farmers (Patil, 2002).

## SUICIDE METHODS

A wide variety of suicide methods are used in India in sharp contrast to the methods in the West. Hanging and poisoning contributed 29% and 38% of total suicides during 2003 (NCRB, 2003). Apart from these methods, other lethal methods were jumping into a well, self-immolation, jumping from moving vehicles, electrification and being hit by a vehicle. This pattern of suicides has not registered a major change during the last decade. The northeastern states of India have a higher rate of hanging compared to other parts, where self-poisoning with overdose of alcohol, drugs and organophosphorus compounds have predominated. The unique pattern of suicides in India through self-immolation accounted for 10% of the suicides, with nearly 66% in the age group of 15 to 44 years (NCRB, 2003).

## CAUSES OF SUICIDE

The absence of analytical studies in the area of suicide epidemiology has clearly hindered a proper understanding of causal mechanisms. The causes of suicide have their origin in the social, economic, cultural, psychological and health status of an individual. The information available at the national level is clearly not of any value as causes were not clearly known in two thirds of completed suicides (other causes 25%, causes not known 16% and illness 23%). Among the causes, the most common were family problems (24%), unemployment (2.3%), poverty (2.4%), sudden economic crisis (2.6%) and love affairs (3.6%) (NCRB, 2003). No clear pattern of causation can be established with such information. Even though a large number of precipitating events have been listed, no information on the association and interaction of these factors is known. In addition, the causes for completed and attempted suicides are likely to be different (Gururaj & Isaac, 2001a).

Suicide is multi-factorial, cumulative and progressive in nature (Gururaj & Isaac, 2001b). Several risk factors have been implicated in the causation of suicide. They can be broadly grouped under sociocultural, environmental, health-related and biological. Disturbed family relationships have been recognized as one of the major social factors contributing for nearly 10% to 50% of suicides (Gururaj, 2005a). Economic factors such as unemployment, sudden economic bankruptcy and chronic economic deprivation have been found to be responsible for nearly 15% to 25% of suicides, especially among men. Dowry disputes and issues related to childbirth have been found to be both directly and indirectly responsible for suicide among young married women, especially in rural areas (INCLEN, 2000; Planning Commission, 2004).

Among the major mental health problems identified in those who have attempted or completed suicide are depression (14%-67%), schizophrenia (2%-12 %), alcohol abuse by the suicide or by the spouse (7%-35%), affective disorders, drug dependence, adjustment disorders and mood and personality problems (Rao & Madhavan, 1983; Vijayakumar & Rajkumar, 1999; Krishnamurthy, et al., 2000; Gururaj & Isaac 2001a; Chandrashekaran, et al., 2003; Gururaj, 2004b; Baby, et al., 2006). Depression is the most common risk factor, but difficulties in early recognition and management, cultural meanings and interpretation are major barriers. Similarly, even though alcohol use is widely prevalent (as more than one-third adult men consume alcohol), well-established community programs are widely lacking (Gururaj, et al., 2006 a & b). The existing addiction services do not reach the vast majority of those who need the services.

Two case-control studies in Chennai and Bangalore have established the role of some clear factors. In Chennai, the presence of an Axis I mental disorder, a family history of psychopathology, the presence of negative life events in the previous 12 months and personality disorders, along with previous suicidal attempts, were found to be the major risk factors (Vijayakumar & Rajkumar, 1999). A case-control study from Bangalore revealed that a combination of risk factors and absence of protective factors was responsible for suicide (Gururaj, et al., 2004b). Unresolved family conflicts, the presence of negative life events, sudden economic bankruptcy, the presence of domestic violence, alcohol consumption by the self or the spouse, a previous history of suicidal attempts and the presence of mental disorder were the major risk factors identified. Accompanying these factors was the absence of protective factors such as the presence of a positive outlook, problem-solving skills, coping abilities, help in crisis situations and communication. In Pondicherry, Srivastava, et al. (2004) observed major risk factors including unemployment, lack of formal education, stressful life events, physical disorders and presence of idiopathic pain. A recent study found that the causes of suicide were multiple and operate in an interactive, progressive and cumulative nature for the majority of suicides (Gururaj, et al., 2001b).

## SERVICES FOR SUICIDE SURVIVORS AND AT-RISK INDIVIDUALS AND FAMILIES

The organization and delivery of services range from identifying at risk individuals and families to crisis management and early intervention for suicide attempters and long-term care. Services are required for family members of completed suicides, survivors of suicide attempts, and those with suicidal ideation. The availability, accessibility, affordability and awareness are major determining factors influencing service delivery patterns. The current healthcare delivery in India is shared between organized public and unorganized private healthcare agencies (including private teaching and non-teaching hospitals, local nursing homes and a wide range of private healthcare providers) with more than 70% being delivered by the latter (NSSO, 1998). Qualified mental health professionals, such as psychiatrists, psychologists and social workers, are limited in India (Gururaj, et al., 2005b). Mental health professionals in medical colleges and in selected district hospitals are the only source of help for much of the country. The quality of mental healthcare is also debatable in terms of the nature and pattern of services delivered. The availability of emergency, pre-hospital and acute care is limited, especially in rural parts of the country, while it is increasingly becoming expensive in urban areas (Joshipura, 2003). Crisis management is often undertaken by a few non-governmental organizations (NGOs), whose focus is mainly in urban areas through the networking of professionals and trained volunteers. These NGOs are sometimes the "Port of call" for local communities and provide emotional and psychosocial support via counseling and referrals (Vijayakumar, et al., 2005c). Families often cope with the crisis in their own ways, primarily through traditional and spiritual practices. Thus, with limited resources and an absence of professional manpower and direction, only a fraction of the people in need get necessary services.

Suicide prevention needs to incorporate and integrate a large number of strategies delivered with an inter-sectoral approach and delivered through short-term, medium-term and long-term activities, based on a policy framework. Because of the reasons cited earlier, suicide prevention has not gained firm ground in India. Recent initiatives such as the report of the National Commission on Farmers[1] and The Protection of Women from Domestic violence Act 2005[2] are two major steps aimed at improving conditions for farmers and women. Social empowerment programs need more rigorous evaluation to assess their impact. Many initiatives by NGOs and professionals to increase awareness and reduce stigma are restricted to local places, not continuous, and currently limited to initiatives.

## CHALLENGES FOR SUICIDE PREVENTION

The challenges in suicide prevention are several and exist at different levels. Compared to efforts in developed countries, suicide prevention is at an infant stage in India and many other LMICs (Vijayakumar, 2005c). In addition, interventions that have been promising in developed countries cannot be easily implemented in India and other developing countries because of variations in the epidemiological pattern of suicides and changes in healthcare delivery practices (Gururaj, et al., 2001). Lack of knowledge about potentially modifiable risk factors has been a major stumbling block, as all possible risk factors cannot be targeted at once due to lack of resources. At the national level, some of the major challenges include absence of proper surveillance and information systems, non-recognition of suicide as a public health problem, lack of a central coordinating agency to implement and monitor interventions, lack of an inter-sectoral approach and absence of a policy framework. The absence of institutions, competent researchers (amidst pockets of excellence) and funding opportunities is another major stumbling block for the growth of suicide prevention research

---

[1] krishakayog.gov.in/4threport.pdf
[2] www.prsindia.org/pdfs/Acts/2005/THE_PROTECTION_OF_WOMEN_FROM_DOM.pdf

(Gururaj, 2005a). Any prevention program should be driven by good-quality, unbiased research on a long-term basis, with well-designed scientific studies.

The health sector has often considered suicide to be a social and economic problem, while communities consider it to be a cultural problem and welfare agencies consider it to be a health problem. Within the health sector, suicide is considered to be primarily a mental health problem. The absence of linkages between sectors is a major barrier. The growth of mental health services in the Indian region has been patchy, fragmented and, thus, suicide prevention has often been neglected. The presence of stigma has concealed the problem at local levels, resulting in under-reporting, misclassification and an absence of analysis. As suicide is considered to be a medico-legal issue, the complexities of law result in concealment and, hence, suicide is not considered a public health issue. The sensational publicity and attribution of suicide to flimsy reasons by the media has resulted in an increase in suicide and copycat acts.

Difficulties in recognizing who is at risk and who is likely to attempt or complete suicide has resulted in a lack of focus in organization and delivery of services for prevention and early management. The rapid expansion of the private health sector has shifted the responsibility equally to both public and private sectors. Crisis management is often the responsibility of NGOs in India, resulting in the organization of services for individuals and their families via telephone helpline services (in selected cities), counseling services, after-care services and regular clinical services, amid increasing healthcare costs.

## FUTURE DIRECTIONS

As suicides are multi-factorial in nature, a multi-pronged strategy is essential. A public health approach to suicide should have four components: identifying the problem, delineating risk factors, implementing interventions, and evaluating what works. A national policy framework for suicide prevention is required, and initial attempts in this direction have just begun in India (Manoranjitham, et al., 2005; Vijayakumar, 2006; NIMHANS, 2006). Converting this policy into deliverable programs requires strengthening the ability of policy makers, program managers, professionals, communities and the media. The various strategies that are likely to deliver results include limiting and regulating the easy availability of organophosphorus compounds and drugs; enhancing the skills of primary care and family physicians for early recognition and treatment of mental health problems (primarily depression and alcoholism); crisis and long-term support for suicide attempters; prevention of violence against women and children; increasing social support systems especially for people in high-risk situations; responsible media reporting practices; increasing counseling facilities in all healthcare and educational institutions and workplaces; measures towards destigmatization of suicide; decriminalization of suicide; and community awareness programs. However, for these programs to be really effective, it is essential to incorporate them into a larger socioeconomic and cultural perspective through targeted programs aimed at modifiable risk factors. This also requires an inter-sectoral approach at national, state and provincial levels, with clearly defined roles and a lead agency responsible for implementation. The programs need to be cost-effective, culturally-specific, sustainable and deliverable, and delivered through short-term and long-term programs. Ultimately, it is surveillance and research which are crucial to driving interventions and measuring the impact.

## REFERENCES

Aaron, R., Joseph, A., Abraham, S., et al. (2004). Suicides in young people in rural southern India. *Lancet*, 3, 1-4.

Baby, S., Manju, P., Haridas, M., et al. (2006). Psychiatric diagnosis in attempted suicide. *Calicut Medical Journal*, 4, 1-5.

Badrinarayana, A. (1977). Suicidal attempt in Gulbarga. *Indian Journal of Psychiatry*, 19, 69-70.

Banerjee, G., Nandi, D. N., Nandi, S., et al. (1990). The vulnerability of Indian women to suicide. A field study. *Indian Journal of Psychiatry*, 32, 305-308.

Bose, A., Konradsen, F., John, J., et al. (2006). Mortality rate and years of life lost from unintentional injury and suicide in South India. *Tropical Medicine & International Health*, 11, 1553-1556.

Central statistical Organisation. (2004). *Select socioeconomic statistics of India, 2002*. New Delhi, India: Ministry of Statistics & Programme implementation, Government of India.

Census of India 2001. (2001). Delhi, India: Registrar general of India.

Chandrashekaran, R., Gyanashelan, J., Sahai, A., et al. (2003). Psychiatric and personality disorders in survivors following their first suicide attempt. *Indian Journal of Psychiatry*, 2, 45-48.

DeLeo, D. (2002). Struggling against suicide: the need for an integrative approach. *Crisis*, 23, 23-31.

De Leo, D., Bertolote, J., & Lester, D. (2002). Self-directed violence In E. G. Krug, L. L. Dahlberg, J. A. Mercy, et al. (Eds.) *World report on violence and health*, pp.185-239. Geneva, Switzerland: World Health Organization.

Ganapathy, M. N., & Venkoba, R. A. (1966). A study of suicide in Madurai. *Journal of Indian Medical Association*, 46, 18-23.

Gururaj, G. (2005a). Injuries in India: a national perspective. Burden of disease in India, National Commission on Macroeconomics and Health, pp. 325-347. New Delhi, India: Ministry of Health & Family Welfare, Government of India.

Gururaj, G., Ahsan, M. N., Issac, M. K., et al. (2001c). *Suicide prevention: Emerging from darkness*. Geneva, Switzerland: World Health Organization.

Gururaj, G., Girish, N., & Benegal, V. (2006a). *Burden and socio-economic impact of alcohol: The Bangalore study*. Geneva, Switzerland: World Health Organization.

Gururaj, G., Girish, N., Benegal, V., et al. (2006b). *Public health problems caused by harmful use of alcohol: Gaining less or losing more?* Geneva, Switzerland: World Health Organization.

Gururaj, G., Girish, N., & Isaac, M. K. (2005b). Mental, neurological and substance abuse disorders: strategies towards a systems approach. *Burden of disease in India: National Commission on Macroeconomics and Health*, pp. 226-250. New Delhi, India: Ministry of Health & Family Welfare, Government of India.

Gururaj, G., Girish, N., Isaac, M. K., et al. (2004a). *Final report of the project Health behaviour surveillance*. Ministry of Health and Family Welfare, Government of India.

Gururaj, G., & Isaac, M. K. (2001a). *Epidemiology of suicides in Bangalore, Publication No.43*. Bangalore, India: National Institute of Mental Health and Neurosciences.

Gururaj, G., & Isaac, M. K. (2001b). *Suicides: beyond numbers. Publication No.44*. Bangalore, India: National Institute of Mental Health and Neurosciences.

Gururaj, G., Isaac, M. K., Subbakrishna, D. K., et al. (2004b). Risk factors for completed suicides: a case-control study from Bangalore, India. *Injury Control & Safety Promotion*, 11, 183-191.

Hegde, R. S. (1993). Suicide in a rural community of North Karnataka. *Indian Journal of Psychiatry*, 22, 368-370.

Indrayan, A., Wysocki, M.J., Kumar, R., et al. (2002). Estimates of the years-of-life-lost due to the top nine causes of death in rural areas of major states in India in 1995. *National Medical Journal of India*, 15, 7-13.

International Clinical Epidemiologists Network. (2000). India safe: studies of abuse in the family environment in India: A summary report.

Joseph, A., Abraham, S., Muliyil, J. P., et al. (2003). Evaluation of suicide rates in rural India using verbal autopsies, 1994-99. *British Medical Journal*, 326, 1121-1122.

Joshipura, M.K., Shah, H.S., Patel, P.R., et al. (2003). Trauma care systems in India. *Injury*, 34, 1-8.

Kandamurthan, M. (1998). Preliminary findings on the psychosocial factors for attempt of suicide in Kerala. *NIMHANS journal*, 261-270.

Krishnamurthy, K., Khan, F.A., Gowri, D.M., et al. (2000). Suicidal intent in schizophrenic patients: a serious risk. *Journal of Postgraduate Psychiatry*, 59-67.

Latha, K. S., Bhat, S. M., & D'Souza, P. (1996). Suicide attempters in a general hospital unit in India: their sociodemographic and clinical profile: emphasis on cross-cultural aspects. *Acta Psychiatrica Scandinavia*, 94, 26-30.

Manoranjitham, S., Abraham, S., & Jacob, K. S. (2005). Towards a national strategy to reduce suicide in India. *National Medical Journal of India*, 18, 118-122.

Mayer, P. (2003). Female equality and suicide in the Indian states. *Psychological Reports*, 92, 1022-1028.

Mayer, P., & Ziaian, T. (2002). Suicide, gender, and age variations in India. *Crisis*, 23, 98-103.

Nandi, D.N., Banerjee, G., & Boral, G.C. (1978). Suicide in West Bengal: a century apart. *Indian Journal of Psychiatry*, 20, 155-160.

Nandi, D.N., Mukherjee, S.P., Banerjee, G., et al. (1979). Is suicide preventable by restricting the availability of lethal agents? A rural survey of West Bengal. *Indian Journal of Psychiatry*, 21, 251-255.

Narang, R.L., Mishra, B.P., & Mohan, N. (2000). Attempted suicide in Ludhiana. *Indian Journal of Psychiatry*, 42, 83-87.

National Crime Records Bureau. (1999). *Accidental deaths and suicides in India*. New Delhi, India: Ministry of Home affairs, Government of India.

National Crime Records Bureau. (2003). *Accidental deaths and suicides in India*. New Delhi, India: Ministry of Home Affairs, Government of India.

National Institute of Mental Health and Neurosciences. (2006). *Towards suicide prevention in Karnataka: strategies and an action plan*. Government of Karnataka.

National Sample Survey Organization. (1998). *Morbidity and treatment of ailments: NSS 52$^{nd}$ round report no 441/25.0/1*. New Delhi, India: National Sample Survey Organization, Department of statistics, Government of India.

Patil, R. R. (2002). An investigative report on circumstances leading to death among Indian cotton farmers. *International Journal of Occupational Medicine & Environmental Health*, 15, 405-407.

Planning Commission. (2004). Study of the nature, extent, incidence and impact of domestic violence against women in the states of Andhra Pradesh, Chattisgarh, Gujarat, Madhya Pradesh and Maharashtra. Nagpur, India: Yuganthar Education Society.

Ponnudurai, R., & Jayakar, J. (1979). Suicide in Madras. *Indian Journal of Psychiatry*, 22, 203-205.

Prasad, J., Abraham, V. J., Minz, S., et al. (2006). Rates and factors associated with suicide in Kaniyambadi Block, Tamil Nadu, South India, 2000-2002. *International Journal of Social Psychiatry*, 52, 65-71.

Rao, V., & Madhavan, T. (1983). Depression and suicide behaviour in the aged. *Indian Journal of Psychiatry*, 4, 251-259.

Reddy, K. S., Shah, B., Varghese, C., et al. (2005). Responding to the threat of chronic disease in India. *Lancet*, 366, 1744-1749.

Registrar General of India. (1998a). *Medical certification of causes of death*. New Delhi, India: Ministry of Home Affairs.

Registrar General of India. (1998b). *Survey of causes of death (rural)*, vital statistics division. Series 3, no 31. New Delhi, India: Ministry of Home Affairs.

Registrar General of India. (2003). *Census of India 2001*. New Delhi, India: Ministry of Home Affairs, Government of India.

Sarma, G. P., & Sawang, G. D. (1993). Suicides in rural areas of Warangal District. *Indian Journal of Behavioural Science*, 3, 79-84.

Satyavathi, K., & Murthy Rao, D. L. N. (1961). A study of suicides in Bangalore. *Transactions of All India Institute of Mental Health*, 2, 1-19.

Shukla, G. D., Verma, B. L., Mishra, D. N., et al. (1990). Suicide in Jhansi city. *Indian Journal of Psychiatry*, 32, 44-51.

Sidhartha, T., & Jena, S. (2006). Suicidal behaviors in adolescents. *Indian Journal of Pediatrics*, 73, 783-788.

Srivastava, M. K., Sahoo, R. N., Ghotekar, L. H., et al. (2004). Risk factors associated with attempted suicides: a case-control study. *Indian journal of Psychiatry*, 46, 33-38.

Tousignant, M., Seshadri, S., & Raj, A. (1998). Gender and suicide in India: a multiperspective approach. *Suicide & Life-Threatening Behavior*, 28, 50-62.

Vijayakumar, L. (2006). Suicide prevention strategy: a framework for India. Unpublished.

Vijayakumar, L., John, S., Pirkis, J., et al. (2005b). Suicide in developing countries (2) Risk factors. *Crisis*, 26, 112-119.

Vijayakumar, L., Nagaraj, K., & John, S. (2004). Suicide and suicide prevention in developing countries. Working paper No. 27, Disease Control Priorities Project.

Vijayakumar, L., Nagaraj, K., Pirkis, J., et al. (2005a). Suicide in developing countries (1) Frequency, distribution and association with socioeconomic indicators. *Crisis*, 26, 104-111.

Vijayakumar, L., Pirkis, J., & Witeford, H. (2005c). Suicide in developing countries (3) Prevention efforts. *Crisis*, 26, 120-124.

Vijayakumar, L., & Rajkumar, S. (1999). Are risk factors for suicide universal? A case control study in India. *Acta Psychiatrica Scandinavica*, 99, 407-411.

*Chapter 27*

# SUICIDE IN SUB-SAHARAN AFRICA

## *Sussie Eshun and Paul Bartoli*

Suicide, the deliberate act of harming oneself with the intention of ending one's life, has been described by the World Health Organization (WHO, 2004) as a "huge but preventable health problem." It is the cause of one-half of all violent deaths in our world today, with the rates continuing to rise. Although there is a vast amount of literature on suicide in most parts of the world, particularly developed countries, there is a lack of information on suicide among less developed countries, many of which are in Sub-Saharan Africa. Sub-Saharan Africa is comprised of 42 countries and 6 islands, and is home to over 700 million people. It includes many of the least developed countries in the world and is a region that faces challenges that are overwhelming enough to place individuals at risk for suicide.

The lack of information on the cause of death in many developing countries and the need to address it have been documented in recent studies (Sibai, 2004). In fact, the WHO list of world suicide rates only includes one country (Zimbabwe) from the Sub-Saharan African region. The most recent data from 2005 regarding causes of death worldwide indicated that of the 42 countries in the region, only one had complete data on cause of death; 16 had no data since 1990; and the remaining 25 had no data available (Mathers, et al., 2005). In addition to the lack of data, there is information that indicates that, compared to developed countries, countries in Sub-Saharan Africa tend to have lower rates of mental illnesses (World Health Organization Consortium, 2005). Although the latter may be factual, it gives the impression that suicide and mental illness are not problems facing people in Sub-Sahara Africa. However, there are also data available that suggest that suicide poses more of a problem to developing countries than has been portrayed over the years. A WHO report in 2000 indicated that of the estimated 725,000 people who died from injuries, 27,000 (4%) were completed suicides. Other reports have implied that, compared to the developed world, young females from developing countries have a higher risk for suicide among youths 5-24 years of age (World Conference of Ministers Responsible for Youth, undated). Even more disheartening is the estimation that, by 2020, depression, which is a strong predictor of suicide, will be the third leading cause of disability in the developed world, and the leading cause of death in less developed countries such as those in Sub-Saharan Africa (Murray & Lopez, 1997). Thus, it is imperative that health policy makers and practitioners focus on establishing measures for accurate data collection as well as culturally-sensitive suicide prevention programs for this region.

Suicide is the result of a complex interaction between personal predispositions and environmental stressors such as social and economic factors. Even without data or accurate records on suicide rates, Sub-Saharan Africans are constantly faced with challenges that increase their risk for depression, anxiety and suicide. These factors include chronic poverty and unemployment, loss of loved ones and social isolation as a result of displacement and marginalization from wars and political unrest. According to the World Bank, in addition to severe poverty, one in four African countries suffers from the effects of war. This often results in millions of people being displaced and seeking refuge in other countries (World Bank, 2006). Thus, in addition to experiencing social isolation and losing loved ones, many of these people are forced to face the challenges involved in acculturation. One additional pressing factor that increases the suicide risk for people in this region is the AIDS epidemic. The UNAIDS program has emphasized that, although only 10% of the world's population live in Africa, it is estimated that an overwhelming number (64%) of all HIV infections are in Africa (UNAIDS, 2006a). These percentages imply that a significant proportion of people in Sub-Saharan Africa are bound to experience the emotional turmoil, anxiety and intense depression associated with AIDS. It is also noteworthy to mention the children of people who die from AIDS-related opportunistic infections as it is estimated that eight out of ten children in the world whose parents have died from AIDS-related complications live in Sub-Saharan Africa (UNAIDS, 2006b). These are only a few examples of the harsh conditions under which many people in this region live. These factors and others significantly increase their risk for depression and underscore their perpetual feeling of desperation that can lead to suicide.

For any suicide prevention endeavor to be successful in the Sub-Saharan African region, it is necessary that plans and programs be developed within a cultural context. Historically there has been a general negative attitude towards suicide and suicide ideation among various cultural groups in Africa. Approximately 4 decades ago, Orley (1970) reported that among the Baganda people of Uganda, suicide is seen as a "terrible act," to the extent that the body of a suicide is buried without respect, and no one is allowed to inherit the dead person's possessions. Recent studies among diverse groups in Africa suggest that negative attitudes about suicide still persist (Peltzer & Cherian, 1998; Eshun, 2003; Lester & Akande, 1994). The stigma associated with suicide and mental illness in general is so strong that there have been reports that, in some Sub-Saharan African countries, suicide attempts are seen as a criminal offense (Njenga, 2006). These negative sanctions make it even more difficult for suicidal individuals to seek help.

There is a critical need for establishing suicide prevention programs and initiating or continuing existing preventive measures, with an emphasis on a multi-system approach that focuses on the following issues.

## MASS HEATH EDUCATION ABOUT SUICIDE

One of the top priorities is to destigmatize suicide and mental illness among Africans. This effort will be successful if it includes key people in the local communities such as chiefs, sub-chiefs, extended family heads, and local government leaders. Given the reportedly extreme negative perception of suicide, it may be better to incorporate education about suicide into already existing media programs through radio and television where available, utilizing respected people in their regions and addressing the cost of suicide to the entire community. In some remote regions it may require communicating to the local chief first, and then having the chief have the "town crier" (or official announcer) go around the village announcing a town meeting at which healthcare workers share information about suicide. All these efforts constitute an initial effort to destigmatize mental illness and suicide.

## TRAINING FOR PRIMARY CARE WORKERS

It is also crucial to train primary healthcare workers in the region about the typical warning signs of suicide. Primary healthcare workers include medical practitioners, nurses, midwives, public health personnel and, where applicable, herbalists. These people are important because they are often the first point of contact for people who 'do not feel good' and who are more comfortable presenting their somatic symptoms than emotional ones. Once the key healthcare workers are trained, they may in turn be recruited to train and help disseminate information in the community, especially among teachers and others in some form of supervisory role.

## ESTABLISHMENT OF MULTI-PURPOSE CENTERS

Another important endeavor is to establish a suicide prevention center as a critical component of any multi-service health center. This may be more feasible in areas in which there is already an existing health clinic for medical problems. In this way, suicidal individuals who are identified by healthcare professionals could be referred to a counselor or appropriate practitioner within the same unit. A multiservice center will further help destigmatize the negativity associated with suicide and mental illness, while also offering some level of privacy and confidentiality. This has been done quite successfully by some non-governmental organizations (NGOs) working with survivors of sexual and gender-related violence in some East African countries and, thus, the process could be transferred to the prevention of suicide. In remote places where there are no established health clinics, the use of mobile clinics may be an alternative. Here health professionals would travel to the community on specific days to offer their services and train local people to be of assistance to individuals in need on the other days.

## ACCESSIBILITY

Training is not enough, especially if there is lack of accessibility to the needed help. The use of popular western-type preventive methods such as suicide hotlines is impractical for most communities in Sub-Saharan Africa, due to lack of telephones or reliable telephone services. Thus, it is better for suicidal individuals to have someone in their immediate environment who they can trust to help them in a time of difficulty.

The need for action is clear. The population of Sub-Saharan Africa is at critical, increasing risk for suicide due to a multiplicity of factors, not the least of which includes poverty, war, displacement and AIDS. Similar highly charged emotional issues with strongly embedded belief systems such as sexual violence have been addressed with a multi-tiered education and training model dispersed to different regions using geographically and culturally-sensitive methods. A similar approach to the issue of suicide is clearly a necessity in the high-risk region of Sub-Saharan Africa.

## REFERENCES

Eshun, S. (2003). Sociocultural determinants of suicide ideation: a comparison between American and Ghanaian college samples. *Suicide & Life-Threatening Behavior*, 33, 165-171.

Lester, D., & Akande, A. (1994). Attitudes about suicide among the Yoruba of Nigeria. *Journal of Social Psychology*, 134, 851-854.

Mathers, C. D., Ma Fat, D., Inoue, M., et al. (2005). Counting the dead and what they died from: an assessment of the global status of cause of death data. *Bulletin of the World Health Organization*, 83, 171-177.

Murray, C. J. L., & Lopez, A. D. (1997). Alternate projections of mortality and disability cause 1990-2020: global burden of disease. *Lancet*, 349, 1498-1504.

Njenga, F. G. (2006). Forensic psychiatry: the African experience. *World Psychiatry*, 5, 97.

Orley, J. H. (1970). *Culture and mental illness*. Nairobi, Kenya: East African Publishing.

Peltzer, K., & Cherian, V. L. (1998). Attitudes toward suicide among South African secondary school pupils. *Psychological Reports*, 83, 1259-1265.

Sibai, A. M. (2004). Mortality certification and cause-of-death reporting in developing countries. *Bulletin of the World Health Organization*, 82, 83.

UNAIDS. (2006). AIDS orphans in sub-Saharan Africa: a looming threat to future generations. UN News Service. Accessed at: www.undispatch.org/archives/un_news/

UNAIDS. (2006). Report on the global AIDS epidemic. Geneva, Switzerland: UNAIDS

World Bank. (2006). *Conflict and development in Africa*. Accessed at: www.worldbank.org/afr/aftsd/conflict.

World Conference of Ministers Responsible for Youth. (undated). *United Nations Report on Global Situation of Youth shows changing trend*. New York. United Nations. Accessed at: http://www.un.org/events/youth98/backinfo/yreport.htm. Retrieved on December 13, 2006.

World Health Organization. (2004). Suicide huge but preventable public health problem, says WHO (World Suicide Prevention Day – 10 September 2004). Geneva, Switzerland: WHO.

World Health Organization Consortium (2005). Prevalence, severity, and unmet need for treatment for mental disorders in the WHO World Mental Health Surveys. *Journal of the American Medical Association*, 292, 2581-2590.

Chapter 28

# SUB-SYNDROMAL SUICIDE: AN ARAB PERSPECTIVE

## *Ahmed Okasha, Aida Seif El Dawla and Tarek Okasha*

Subsyndromal disorders are defined by the absence of one of the symptoms required to meet full diagnostic criteria or by failing to meet the criterion for duration. Still, Howarth, et al. (1992) argued that subsyndromal disorders may be associated with significant associated disability. Many subsyndromal conditions eventually fulfill diagnostic criteria but, before they do this, there is frequently a varying period of *disability* that impacts the patient and the family both emotionally and socially, even if it lacks a diagnostic label.

Judging disability in a cultural context is a more sensitive and valid indicator of the need for treatment than diagnosis. Patients may meet the full diagnostic criteria but not have any disability and not require treatment; or they may have a subthreshold disorder but suffer from a high level of disability with a need for treatment.

Are subsyndromal conditions self-limiting risk factors for more severe conditions, or do they have a stable course of their own? While the answer to that question requires elaborate longitudinal research, it is safe to assume that early identification and intervention to relieve suffering and stressful symptoms are likely to have a positive effect on long-term clinical outcomes and quality of life.

Applied to the issue of suicide, it may be life itself and not merely its quality that may be at stake. However, given that many of those, if not the majority of those who attempt suicide (its completion being in many cases a matter of chance) may not fulfill the diagnostic criteria of a mental disorder, the challenge to address suicide may not lie in psychiatric clinics alone but rather in the public health system as a whole. In that regard, culture is a determining factor, not only in its permissiveness towards self-harm, but also in regard to its determination of mental health and ill health.

## SUBSYNDROMAL SUICIDE

In spite of the fact that subsyndromal psychiatric disorders do exist, and despite their burden possible equaling that of syndromal ones, as long as they are not acknowledged by international classifications, they are not included in national surveys. In this way, their exact prevalence is not known, nor are there any valid structured diagnostic systems, management plans or longitudinal outcome studies. As far as can be seen, there are no previous studies of suicide in subsyndromal disorders since nosologically they do not exist. Hence we shall deal with the issue of the suicide spectrum, addressing attempted suicide to examine "subsyndromal suicide."

The spectrum of suicide varies in intensity, where ideas and attempts of suicide may be considered subsyndromal.

## THE EPIDEMIOLOGY OF SUICIDE

According to WHO estimates, approximately one million people died from suicide in the year 2000 and 10 to 20 times more people attempted suicide worldwide. This represents an average of one death every 40 seconds and one attempt every 3 seconds. It also indicates that more people are dying from suicide than in all of the armed conflicts around the world and, in many places, about the same or more than those dying from traffic accidents.

Countries with higher rates, and more concerned by them, have a higher tendency to report on suicide mortality than countries where suicide is not perceived as a major public health problem.

The comparative analysis of number of suicides by age brings in a fresh view. One of the classic principles in suicidology is the predominance of suicide among elderly men. This is undisputable in terms of suicide rates. However, information on the number of suicides reveals a different picture: globally speaking, currently more suicides (57%) are committed by people aged 5-44 years than by people aged 45 years and more. Also the age group in which more completed suicides occur is 35-44 years, for both males and females.

Suicides are under-reported for cultural and religious reasons, as well as because of different classification and ascertainment procedures. Unfortunately, in cases of young people, death due to suicide is often misclassified or masked by other mortality diagnoses. This makes the global picture of death by suicide even graver.

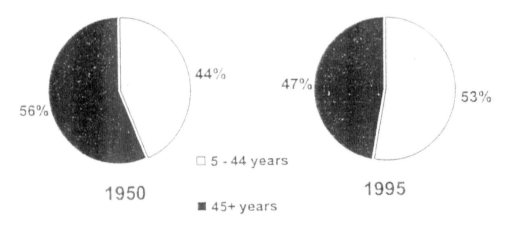

Figure 29.1. Percentage of suicide by age in 1950 and 1995 (Selected countries).

## SUICIDE AND CULTURE

In ancient Egypt, suicide meant a disaster for both the body and the soul. By destroying the body, instead of having it embalmed, the soul would lose its home. This occurs as the soul must return every night to the body to be reborn the following morning at sunrise in order to live eternally. Whether suicide is sinful though, being subject to eternal reprobation, makes this irrelevant.

Suicide is one of those issues that lie in a twilight zone between religion and psychiatry. This overlap, although separated throughout the ages, has in some cultures still retained its print on the medical profession. In Islamic culture, it is deeply imbedded that life and death are God's will. This has a protective value against suicide for those that believe our lives do not belong to us, but to God.

There are some indications that the religiousness of a person might serve as a protective factor against suicide. The data collected in the WHO SUPRE-MISS community study investigated the religious denomination of the respondents and their religiousness (Bertolote, et al., 2005). (Table 28-1)

### Table 28.1. Religious Variables in the WHO SUPRE-MISS Community Survey Study (2005)

|  | Campinas Brazil | Chennai India | Colombo Sri Lanka | Durban S. Africa | Hanoi Vietnam | Karaj Iran | Tallinn Estonia | Yuncheng China |
|---|---|---|---|---|---|---|---|---|
| **Religion** | | | | | | | | |
| Number | 516 | 500 | 683 | 497 | 2277 | 504 | 498 | 503 |
| Christian | 86% | 3% | 13% | 40% | 3% | 0% | 47% | 1% |
| Muslim | 0% | 5% | 24% | 3% | 0% | 100% | 0% | 0% |
| Hindu | 0% | 92% | 18% | 13% | 0% | 0% | 0% | 0% |
| Buddhist | 0% | 0% | 44% | 0% | 6% | 0% | 0% | 1% |
| Other | 5% | 0% | 1% | 28% | 1% | 0% | 3% | 0% |
| None | 8% | 0% | 0% | 17% | 91% | 0% | 49% | 98% |
| **Religiousness** | | | | | | | | |
| Number | 514 | 499 | 659 | 484 | 2106 | 502 | 492 | 503 |
| Yes | 1% | 92% | 96% | 51% | 34% | 80% | 37% | No data |

Religious families assess the quality of life according to adherence to religious rituals regardless of symptomatology. Negative symptoms may be perceived by a great group of Islamic followers as piousness and deeper contemplation about God and, hence, considered virtuous. Positive symptoms are sometimes perceived as gifted from God by extraordinary perception and are, therefore, considered special. The comparison of Egyptian, Indian and British depressive patients revealed that Egyptians have a significant increase in suicidal tendencies but not in actual suicide or attempted suicide (Okasha, 2000).

Table 28-2 shows that WHO region (EMRO), which is dominantly Islamic, has the lowest rate of suicide expressed in DALY'S percentages (in 2002 0.7 %).

**Table 28.2. Health Burden due to Suicide Expressed in DALY (%)**

| Region | 1998 | 1999 | 2000 | 2001 | 2002 |
|---|---|---|---|---|---|
| Africa | 0.2 | 1.0 | 0.2 | 0.2 | 0.2 |
| America | 1.2 | 1.7 | 1.1 | 1.1 | 1.0 |
| EMRO | 1.0 | 0.9 | 0.5 | 0.7 | 0.7 |
| Europe | 2.2 | 2.9 | 2.5 | 2.3 | 2.3 |
| SE Asia | 1.3 | 1.3 | 1.2 | 1.6 | 1.7 |
| W Pacific | 3.6 | 3.3 | 2.8 | 2.5 | 2.6 |
| World | 1.6 | 1.7 | 1.3 | 1.4 | 1.4 |

Table 28-3 shows the low reported suicide rates in some Islamic countries.

**Table 28.3. Reported Numbers of Suicides in some Islamic Countries (WHO, 2004)**

|  | Year | Males | Females | Total |
|---|---|---|---|---|
| Bahrain | 1988 | 13 | 1 | 14 |
| Egypt | 1987 | 14 | 8 | 22 |
| Iran | 1991 | 91 | 20 | 111 |
| Kuwait | 2001 | 26 | 8 | 34 |
| Syria | 1985 | 10 | 0 | 10 |
| Jordan | 1979 | 0 | 0 | 0 |
| Bosnia | 1991 | 457 | 74 | 531 |
| Turkmenistan | 1998 | 322 | 84 | 406 |
| Uzbekistan | 2000 | 1455 | 464 | 1919 |

Personal and family problems constitute the main trigger for suicide and attempted suicide in traditional societies. In industrial societies, work-related problems are more prevalent among suicide attempters. In traditional societies, social networks prevent the overtaxing of patients and decrease demands on patients until functional recovery. Critical comments in particular are usually balanced by the family's warmth and positive regard.

## ATTEMPTED SUICIDE: A SUBSYNDROMAL DISORDER?

There is considerable confusion between the concepts of suicidal behavior and deliberate self-harm. They overlap, with clear suicidal intent at one end and acts of self-mutilation on the other.

Feelings of hopelessness and the intention to kill oneself are rare among Muslim depressed patients where losing hope in relief by God and self-inflicted death are considered blasphemous and punishable. However, the rates of suicidal attempts (parasuicide), which result in more care-elicitation than death intentions, had no significant associations with religiosity (Okasha & Lotaif, 1979).

An Egyptian investigation of parasuicide in Cairo revealed a crude rate of 38.5 per 100,000. There was a high rate among the age group 15-44 years with no major difference between the two sexes. Single patients constituted 53% of the total, with students showing the highest risk (40%) (Okasha, et al., 1988).

Another study in Cairo showed that attempters were mostly young women (age 15-34 years) belonging to large overcrowded families. They had a higher tendency to be single, literate and unemployed than the corresponding age group in the general population. Some 97% of the sample expressed feelings of social isolation, and so their attempt can be taken as a cry for help (Okasha, 1984). Another more recent investigation in Egypt revealed that 37% of attempters had no psychiatric morbidity. They attempted suicide as a result of familial difficulties (Okasha, et al., 2006).

In Kuwait, attempted suicide constituted more than one quarter of 219 consecutive liaison referrals from all general hospitals (Al-Ansari, et al., 1990). Around 1.1% of suicide attempters eventually killed themselves (Kuey and Gulec, 1989). In the Eastern province of Saudi Arabia the rate of attempting self-harm was 20, well below the rate of 100-200 reported in Western countries (Daradkeh & Al-Zayer, 1988). The act of deliberate self-harm followed an acute stress reaction associated with interpersonal strains and frustration. Serious suicidal intent correlated with antecedent feelings of hopelessness and helplessness.

## Conclusion

The decision to attempt suicide reflects more than a symptom. It reflects an attitude, a belief in the futility of life. Between the development of that feeling and the actual carrying out of a suicide attempt lies a spectrum that ranges from distress to disease. As mental health professionals, we are met with the challenge of identifying potential suicides before they reach the end of the spectrum.

We can observe that a great proportion of suicidal attempts are secondary to family and financial situations and without a "syndromal" psychiatric disorder. Even those suicidal acts associated with psychiatric symptoms show a high prevalence of atypical or subsyndromal disorders.

The keys to successful management include knowledge about the religious, cultural and socioeconomic background of a patient and careful evaluation and follow-up to observe symptom progression and the effect on functioning and decision-making. Religious and cultural belief systems then may ultimately provide understandable explanations for traumatic life events or provide meaning for survival.

## References

Al-Ansari, E. A., El-Hilu, M. A., & Hassan, K. I. (1990). Patterns of psychiatric consultations in Kuwait general hospitals. *General Hospital Psychiatry,* 12, 257-263.

Bertolote, J. M., Fleischmann, A., de Leo, L., et al. (2005). Suicide attempts, plans, and ideation in culturally diverse sites: the WHO supre-miss community survey. *Psychological Medicine*, 35, 1457–1465.

Bertolote, J. M. (2001). Suicide in the world: an epidemiological overview, 1959-2000. In D. Wasserman (Ed.) *Suicide: An unnecessary death*, pp.5-10. London, UK: Dunitz.

Daradkeh, T. K. & Al-Zayer, N. (1988). Parasuicide in an Arab industrial community: the Arabian-American oil company experience, Saudi Arabia. *Acta Psychiatrica Scandinavica*, 77, 707- 711.

Howarth, E., Johnson, J., Klerman, G. L., et al. (1992). Depressive symptoms as relative and attributable risk factors for first-onset major depression. *Archives of General Psychiatry*, 49, 817-823.

Kuey, L., & Gulec, C. (1989). Depression in turkey in the 1980's: epidemiological and clinical approaches. *Clinical Psychopharmacology*, 12 supplement 2, s1-s12.

Okasha, A. (1984). Depression and suicide in Egypt. *Egyptian Journal of Psychiatry*, 7, 33-45.

Okasha, A., & Lotaif, F. (1979). Attempted suicide: an Egyptian investigation. *Acta Psychiatrica Scandinavica*, 60, 69-75.

Okasha, A., Khalil, A. H., El-Fiky, M. R., et al. (1988). Prevalence of depressive disorders in a sample of rural and urban Egyptian communities. *Egyptian Journal of Psychiatry*, 11, 167-181.

Okasha, A. (2000). Global burden of depression. Paper read at the meeting on Globalization of Psychiatry, International Perspectives. Cairo, Egypt.

Okasha, A., Bassim, R., & Okasha, T. (2006). Epidemiology and psychiatric morbidity in suicide attempters at the poison control center, Ain Shams University Hospital. MD thesis, Ain Shams University, Institute of Psychiatry, Cairo, Egypt.

Wasserman, D. (2001) *Suicide: An unnecessary death.* London, UK: Dunitz.

World Health Organization. (1999). *Figures and facts about suicide.* WHO/MNH/MBD/99. Geneva, Switzerland: WHO.

In: Suicide from a Global Perspective: Psychosocial Approaches   ISBN 978-1-61470-965-7
Editors: A. Shrivastava, M. Kembrell et al. 205- 214   © 2012 Nova Science Publishers, Inc.

Chapter 29

# OUTCOME AND IMPLICATIONS OF RESEARCH IN SUICIDOLOGY FROM DEVELOPING COUNTRIES

*Anju Kuruvilla and K. S. Jacob*

Suicide rates in developing countries have been on the rise (WHO, 2001). Consequently there has been considerable research and systematic investigation into the phenomenon in recent years. Investigations have focused mainly on epidemiological data, risk factors and proposals for national and global initiatives.

## EPIDEMIOLOGICAL RESEARCH

### Suicide Rates

There have been several studies that have investigated suicide in different parts of the developing world. The rates that have been reported vary from 0.2 in Iran to 29.6 per 100,000 in Ukraine (WHO, 2003). Some countries have no or little official data on death by suicide (Eshun, 2003; Khan & Hyder, 2006). However, available research reports an increasing rate over the years in many of these countries (WHO, 2001).

Researchers acknowledge that suicide deaths are often underreported (Joseph, et al., 2003; Manoranjitham, et al., 2005; Vijayakumar, et al., 2005; Prasad, et al., 2006; Khan & Hyder, 2006) for reasons which are discussed below. Therefore, there are differences between officially available statistics and reality. Recent reports from India exemplify this (Joseph, et al., 2003; Aaron, et al., 2004). The average suicide rate from a community covered by a comprehensive health program, with extensive and accurate data, was 8-10 times higher than the reported national average (Murthy, 2000).

## Methods of Suicide

Methods used for suicide are similar across nations. The most common are poisoning and hanging (Fleischmann, et al., 2005; Prasad, et al., 2006; Khan & Hyder, 2006; Dzamalala, 2006; Tamosiunas, et al., 2006). Among females, burning (Marchesan, et al., 1997; Sukhai, et al., 2002; Ahmadi, 2007) and drowning are common (Prasad, et al., 2006), while hanging and shooting are more common in males (Khan & Hyder, 2006; Meel, 2006). Ingestion of agricultural pesticides such as organophosphorous was the most common method of self-poisoning employed, although prescription drugs such as paracetamol (acetaminophen), with benzodiazepines and tricyclic antidepressants also being used (Gunnell & Eddleston, 2003; Paudyal, 2005; Khan & Hyder, 2006). The easy accessibility to highly toxic agents, such as organophosphorous compounds, ensures a high fatality rate, even if the attempt was impulsive and with low intentionality (Gunnell & Eddleston, 2003).

## POPULATIONS AT RISK

### Age and Gender

Western research documents higher suicide rates in men than women. In most developing nations this is the same, although the ratios vary and are sometimes close to one (Mayer & Ziaian, 2002; Joseph, et al., 2003; Khan & Hyder, 2006). China is significantly different reporting a male to female ratio of 1:3 (Pritchard, 1996; Phillips, et al., 2002). Many reasons have been postulated for this, including the relative powerlessness of women, restrictions on their choices and ability to negotiate, and the perceived social and economic burden of being female (Phillips, et al., 2002; Vijayakumar, et al., 2005).

Similar to Western statistics, the risk of suicide shows an increase with age. (Mayer & Ziaian, 2002; Phillips, et al., 2002; Vijayakumar, et al., 2005; Eddleston, 2005; Rodrigues & Werneck, 2005; Abraham, et al, 2005). Rates among young people have also been increasing in developing countries (Gunnell & Eddleston, 2003; Flisher, et al., 2004; Aaron, et al., 2004; Vijayakumar, et al., 2005; Centers for Disease Control & Prevention, 2007). Among the younger population, the rates in young women, aged 15-24, has been shown to be high compared to young men in many regions (Phillips, et al., 2002, Joseph, et al., 2003; Aaron, et al., 2004; Eddleston, et al., 2005). Risk factors appear to vary in importance for different age groups. Youth suicide is more highly associated with impulsiveness than for other age groups; older people have more serious intent (Eddleston, et al., 2005).

### Marital Status

Marital status by itself has not shown to be predictive of suicide in developing countries (Phillips, et al., 2002; Vijayakumar, et al., 2005). However, conflicts and distress in marital and family relationships are associated with suicide risk (Khan, 2002; Gururaj, et al., 2004).

## Residence

Limited data are available regarding differential suicide rates based on place of residence. Reports from China, Lithuania and the Ukraine suggest that the number of suicides is higher in rural areas than in urban areas (Kryzhanovskaya & Pilyagina, 2006; Yip, 2001; Phillips, et al., 2002; Kalediene & Petrauskiene, 2004).

## Socioeconomic Factors and Education

Low socioeconomic status has been identified as a major correlate for suicide in developing nations. Poverty, bankruptcy and unemployment have been cited as proximal causes for suicide (Phillips, et al., 2002; Gururaj, et al., 2004). While lower levels of education are generally associated with a greater risk of suicide (Gururaj, et al., 2004), some reports find a reversal, with higher education levels associated with high male suicide rates, attributed to the pressures of modernization (Vijayakumar, et al., 2005).

# PSYCHIATRIC AND PSYCHOLOGICAL RISK FACTORS

## Psychiatric Disorders

Western studies report that about 90% of suicides are associated with mental illness, especially depression (Goldsmith, et al., 2002). Although limited, data from the developing world also indicate that persons with psychiatric disorders are at a greater risk of suicide (Eferakeya, 1984; Nwosu & Odesanmi, 2001; Phillips, et al., 2002; Kebede, et al., 2003; Chakrabarti & Devkota, 2004; van der Hoek & Konradsen, 2005; Moreno & Andrade, 2005; Parkar, et al., 2006; Agoub, et al., 2006; Mert & Bilgin, 2006). Psychiatric disorders reported include depression, bipolar disorder, schizophrenia, substance use disorders (predominantly alcohol) and dual diagnoses. Those with a history of previous attempts are also at a greater risk (Phillips, et al., 2002). Significant numbers are also identified as having adjustment disorders or psychosocial stressors (Parkar, et al., 2006). There are no available data on the association between personality factors and suicide in developing countries.

Compared to Western data, however, the overall reported prevalence of serious mental illness among people who commit suicide in developing countries is less. Some suggest that these lower rates may be a result of under-diagnosis secondary to the lack of availability of mental health services (Vijayakumar, et al., 2005) and various other cultural factors discussed below. However, workers in the field agree that, while important, mental illness is not necessary, nor the most common, correlate of suicidal behavior in the developing world.

## Patterns of Distress

Depressive and anxiety symptoms, physical symptoms of distress, anger and frustration are the common presenting symptoms (Liu, et al., 2005; Kinyanda, 2005; Parkar, et al., 2006).

## BIOLOGICAL FACTORS

There are few reports on the possible biological factors related to suicide in the developing world. A genetic study from China reported the possibility that TPH1, a rate-limiting enzyme in serotonin biosynthesis, may play a significant role in the etiology of suicidal behavior (Liu, et al., 2006). Others have investigated a polymorphism in the serotonin transporter gene (5-HTTLPR) for its association with suicidal behavior. The association was reported as unlikely in schizophrenic patients (Chong, et al., 2000), while the risk among depressed patients bearing SS or LS genotypes was higher (Segal, et al., 2006).

## SOCIETY AND CULTURE

Culture strongly influences suicidal behavior. Society determines the nature of stress and coping, views, proscriptions and prescriptions regarding suicidal behavior, and the availability of means and access to treatment (Goldsmith, 2002). As a consequence, suicidal behavior varies in different cultures. As mentioned earlier, Western research attributes most suicides to mental disorders, while researchers in many developing nations in Asia, Africa and Latin America identify psychosocial context and stress as the most common correlates of suicide. Commonly reported stressors include family conflict (with spouses and in-laws or between parent and child), sexual conflicts, substance abuse by the spouse, illicit relationships, serious illness, financial hardship, failures in exams and in love, lower education, unfulfilled expectations at work, humiliation, and shame (Odejide, et al., 1986; Queralt, 1993; Khan, 2002; Pearson, 2002; Gururaj, et al., 2004; Chakrabarti & Devkota, 2004; Vizcarra, et al., 2004; Ndosi, et al., 2004; Manoranjitham, et al., 2005; Parkar, et al., 2006; Groohi, et al.,2006; Prasad, et al, 2006).

The high rates of suicide in the unemployed and marginalized and those subject to rapid and significant social change (Kondrichin & Lester, 2002; Schlebusch, et al., 2003; Vijayakumar, et al., 2005) is explained by the fact that suicide has been interpreted, not only as a gesture of despair, but also a means by which to express a deeply felt sense of having been wronged. Thus, it may seem an option to those who perceive themselves as wielding little power in order to make a change (Pearson, 2002). While the cultural script in some areas may include suicide as a solution, in others, such as some subcultures in Africa, less suicide ideation may be a reflection of the negative social sanctions that exist (Eshun, 2003).

Research in the developing world thus highlights the fact that suicide is a behavior that results from a variety of factors. It is important to understand the interaction of these factors and realize the contribution of culture and society, as well as psychopathology (Phillips, et al., 1999).

## MEDICAL AND PSYCHOTHERAPEUTIC INTERVENTION

In a study from India, 13% of 269 suicides had made at least one previous attempt, but 82% of these had not received any care. Only 24% had been in contact with a mental health professional or family physician or were in treatment before the suicide (Gururaj, et al.,

2004). Although studies have shown the effectiveness of both pharmacological and psychological therapies in developing countries (Patel, et al., 2003; Bass, et al., 2006), there is a paucity of research in this area. Literature from the West reports a higher risk for suicide in people with mental illness currently admitted to a hospital, those recently discharged from such facilities and those attending crisis intervention centers. There are no formal data on this from the developing nations.

## PREVENTION STRATEGIES

### Programs for Suicide Prevention

Suicide prevention programs in developing countries are scarce. Sri Lanka is the only developing country to have formulated a specific national suicide prevention plan (Vijayakumar, et al., 2005). Some countries, such as India, do have national mental health plans that have been instituted to varying degrees (Jacob, 2001). However, there is little ongoing evaluation of existing programs. Many developing countries have non-governmental organizations involved in suicide prevention work in the form of crisis centers or hotline services. While useful, these are not without limitations, including variability in the quality of services provided. There are also community suicide programs that respond to local needs in which suicide prevention activities are incorporated into other health and social programs (Vijayakumar, et al., 2005).

### Reduction in Access to Means of Suicide

Self-poisoning with pesticides accounts for a large number of suicides in the developing world. There are recent efforts in some of these countries to reduce access to these agents, as well as to reduce their toxicity, by various strategies such as using a double-locked box and government regulation (Bertolote, et al., 2006). The feasibility and effectiveness of such strategies remain to be evaluated.

## BARRIERS TO RESEARCH AND PROMISING APPROACHES

The problems for suicide research in the developing world are myriad (Murthy, 2000; Gururaj & Isaac, 2001) and include the following.

### Data Collection

There often is ambiguity and misclassification of deaths, which affects the accuracy of reporting and quality of information available. There is a lack of uniformity, and inconsistencies exist in the terminology and definitions of suicide and suicide attempts, just as they do in other parts of the world. Inefficient civil registration systems exist, with variable standards in certifying and investigating death. These compound the problem of the non-reporting of deaths as a result of the legal and social consequences of suicide, religious condemnation of suicide, concerns regarding post-mortems and a mistrust of police and legal authorities (Vijayakumar, et al., 2005; Khan & Hyder, 2006; Prasad, et al., 2006; Parkar, et al., 2006). Consequently, death by suicide is often reported as an illness or accident and, therefore, leads to an underestimate of the extent of the problem in many developing countries (Joseph, et al., 2003).

## Financial Considerations

Monetary issues influence public and government priorities. Many developing nations struggle to deal with infectious diseases, malnutrition, infant and maternal mortality, and other major health problems. In situations where physical health needs are dominant, there is often a limited demand for mental health services. As a result, mental health and suicide prevention receive scant attention from governments (Prasad, et al., 2006).

## Access to Mental Health Services

Cultural models of illness often attribute depression, anxiety and unexplained somatic symptoms to life events, fate, supernatural causes and physical diseases rather than to mental illness, thus reducing the demand for mental health care (Jacob, 2001). Stigma is a significant barrier to reducing suicide (Goldsmith, 2002). It results in diminished self esteem, reduced help-seeking behavior and reduced opportunities for people with mental illness (Parkar, et al., 2006). There is a gross inadequacy in the number of researchers trained in mental health (Manoranjitham, et al., 2005). Available mental health professionals are most often located in urban areas, making access to treatment difficult for the vast majority of the population, which is rural. While the recognition of psychiatric syndromes in primary care is low, even those who are identified often receive inadequate treatment.

## Suicide Rates

The low base rate of suicide exacerbates the above problems since large sample sizes are required to provide statistical power for studies of such infrequent events. While most investigations focus on the proximal risk factors, these are not always predictive of suicide. Thus, distal factors also need to be studied (Goldsmith, 2002).

# CONCLUSIONS

Research in suicide has increased in the developing world. However, there are many gaps. Several suggestions have been made by researchers for future investigation. These include increased uniformity in classification, more ethnographic and qualitative methods to give a greater understanding of the process, more psychological autopsy studies, and more longitudinal and prospective studies. Suggested reforms to improve the availability and quality of data on suicide rates from developing countries include the decriminalization of both suicide and attempted suicide, improvements in the surveillance systems to study and monitor rates, and measures to establish the cause of death as accurately as possible.

Research needs include focusing on risk factors, both individual and community and proximal and distal, the feasibility and practicality of programs and specific intervention strategies, and an interdisciplinary approach to the problem. There is a need to design studies to understand the potential of pharmacological and psychotherapeutic interventions in reducing suicidal behavior, as well as long-term follow-up studies

Suicide research should be considered a priority issue that should be tackled at the central, state and local levels, with cooperation between academic and clinical professions and partnerships between public and private enterprises and government and non-governmental organizations.

## REFERENCES

Aaron, R., Joseph, A., Abraham, S., et al. (2004). Suicides in young people in rural southern India. *Lancet,* 363, 1117-1118.

Abraham, V. J., Abraham, S., & Jacob K. S. (2005). Suicide in the elderly in Kaniyambadi block, Tamil Nadu, South India. *International Journal of Geriatric Psychiatry*, 20, 953-955.

Ahmadi, A. (2007). Suicide by self-immolation: comprehensive overview, experiences and suggestions. *Journal of Burn Care & Research*, 28, 30-41.

Agoub, M., & Moussaoui, D., & Kadri, N. (2006). Assessment of suicidality in a Moroccan metropolitan area. *Journal of Affective Disorders*, 90, 223-226.

Bass, J., Neugebauer, R., Clougherty, K. F., et al. (2006). Group interpersonal psychotherapy for depression in rural Uganda: 6-month outcomes: randomised controlled trial. *British Journal of Psychiatry,* 188, 567-573.

Bertolote, J. M., Fleischmann, A., Eddleston, M., et al. (2006). Deaths from pesticide poisoning: a global response. *British Journal of Psychiatry*, 189, 201-203.

Centers for Disease Control and Prevention (CDC). (2007). Suicide trends and characteristics among persons in the Guarani Kaiowa and Nandeva communities--Mato Grosso do Sul, Brazil, 2000-2005. *Morbidity & Mortality Weekly Report*, 56, 7-9.

Chakrabarti, K., & Devkota, K. C. (2004). Retrospective study of suicide cases admitted in Nepal Medical College Teaching Hospital. *Nepal Medical College Journal*, 6, 116-118.

Chong, S. A., Lee, W. L., Tan, C. H., et al. (2000). Attempted suicide and polymorphism of the serotonin transporter gene in Chinese patients with schizophrenia. *Psychiatry Research*, 97, 101-106.

Dzamalala, C. P., Milner, D. A., & Liomba, N. G. (2006). Suicide in Blantyre, Malawi (2000-2003). *Journal of Clinical Forensic Medicine*, 13, 65-69.

Eddleston, M., Gunnell, D., Karunaratne, A., et al. (2005). Epidemiology of intentional self-poisoning in rural Sri Lanka. *British Journal of Psychiatry*, 187, 583-584.

Eferakeya, A. E. (1984). Drugs and suicide attempts in Benin City, Nigeria. *British Journal of Psychiatry*, 145, 70-73.

Eshun, S. (2003). Sociocultural determinants of suicide ideation: a comparison between American and Ghanaian college samples. *Suicide & Life-Threatening Behavior*, 33, 165-171.

Fleischmann, A., Bertolote, J. M., De Leo, D., et al. (2005). Characteristics of attempted suicides seen in emergency-care settings of general hospitals in eight low- and middle-income countries. *Psychological Medicine*, 35, 1467-1474.

Flisher, A. J., Liang, H., Laubscher, R., et al. (2004). Suicide trends in South Africa, 1968--90. *Scandinavian Journal of Public Health*, 32, 411-418.

Goldsmith, S. K., Pellmar, T. C., Kleinman, A. M., et al. (2002). *Reducing suicide: A national imperative*. Washington, DC: The National Academic Press.

Groohi, B., Rossignol, A. M., Barrero, S. P., et al. (2006). Suicidal behavior by burns among adolescents in Kurdistan, Iran: a social tragedy. *Crisis*, 27, 16-21.

Gunnell, D., & Eddleston, M. (2003). Suicide by intentional ingestion of pesticides: a continuing tragedy in developing countries. *International Journal of Epidemiology*, 32, 902-909.

Gururaj, G., Isaac, M. K., Subbakrishna, D. K., et al. (2004). Risk factors for completed suicides: a case-control study from Bangalore, India. *Injury Control & Safety Promotion*, 11, 183-191.

Ikealumba, N. V., & Couper, I. D. (2006). Suicide and attempted suicide: the Rehoboth experience. *Rural & Remote Health*, 6, 535.

Jacob, K. S. (2001). Community care for people with mental disorders in developing countries: problems and possible solutions. *British Journal of Psychiatry*, 178, 296-298.

Joseph, A., Abraham, S., Muliyil, J. P., et al. (2003). Evaluation of suicide rates in rural India using verbal autopsies. *British Medical Journal*, 326, 1121-1122.

Kalediene, R., & Petrauskiene, J. (2004). Inequalities in daily variations of deaths from suicide in Lithuania: identification of possible risk factors. *Suicide & Life-Threatening Behavior*, 34, 138-146.

Kebede, D., Alem, A., Shibre, T., et al. (2003). Onset and clinical course of schizophrenia in Butajira-Ethiopia: a community-based study. *Social Psychiatry & Psychiatric Epidemiology*, 38, 625-631.

Khan, M. M. (2002). Suicide on the Indian subcontinent. *Crisis*, 23, 104-7.

Khan, M. M., & Hyder, A. A. (2006). Suicides in the developing world: case study from Pakistan. *Suicide & Life-Threatening Behavior*, 36, 76-81.

Kinyanda, E., Hjelmeland, H., & Musisi, S. (2005). Psychological factors in deliberate self-harm as seen in an urban African population in Uganda: a case-control study. *Suicide & Life-Threatening Behavior*, 35, 468-477.

Kondrichin, S. V., & Lester, D. (2002). Suicide in the Ukraine. *Crisis*, 23, 32-33.

Kryzhanovskaya, L., & Pilyagina, G. (1999). Suicidal behavior in the Ukraine, 1988-1998. *Crisis*, 20, 184-190.

Liu, X., Tein, J., Sandler, I. N., et al. (2005). Psychopathology associated with suicide attempts among rural adolescents of China. *Suicide & Life-Threatening Behavior*, 35, 265-276.

Liu, X., Li, H., Qin, W., et al. (2006). Association of TPH1 with suicidal behaviour and psychiatric disorders in the Chinese population. *Journal of Medical Genetics*, 43, e4.

Manoranjitham, S., Abraham, S., & Jacob K. S. (2005). Towards a national strategy to reduce suicide in India. *National Medical Journal of India*, 18, 118-122.

Marchesan, W. G., da Silva, F. F., Canalli, J. E., et al. (1997). Suicide attempted by burning in Brazil. *Burns*, 23, 270-271.

Mayer, P., & & Ziaian, T. (2002). Suicide, gender, and age variations in India: are women in Indian society protected from suicide? *Crisis*, 23, 98-103.

Meel, B. (2006). Epidemiology of suicide by hanging in Transkei, South Africa. *American Journal of Forensic Medicine & Pathology*, 27, 75-78.

Mert, E., & Bilgin, N. G. (2006). Demographical, aetiological and clinical characteristics of poisonings in Mersin, Turkey. *Human & Experimental Toxicology*, 25, 217-223.

Miller, G. (2006). Mental health in developing countries. *Science*, 311, 464-465.

Moreno, D. H., & Andrade, L. H. (2005). The lifetime prevalence, health services utilization and risk of suicide of bipolar spectrum subjects, including subthreshold categories in the Sao Paulo ECA study. *Journal of Affective Disorders*, 87, 231-241.

Murthy, R. S. (2000). Approaches to suicide prevention in Asia and the Far East. In K. Hawton & K. van Heeringen (Eds.) *The international handbook of suicide and attempted suicide*. Chichester, UK: John Wiley.

Ndosi, N. K., Mbonde, M. P., & Lyamuya, E. (2004). Profile of suicide in Dar es Salaam. *East African Medical Journal*, 81, 207-211.

Nwosu, S. O., & Odesanmi, W. O. (2001). Pattern of suicides in Ile-Ife, Nigeria. *West African Journal of Medicine*, 20, 259-262.

Odejide, A. O., Williams, A. O., Ohaeri, J. U., et al. (1986). The epidemiology of deliberate self-harm. The Ibadan experience. *British Journal of Psychiatry*, 149, 734-737.

Parkar, S. R., Dawani, V., & Weiss, M. G. (2006). Clinical diagnostic and sociocultural dimensions of deliberate self-harm in Mumbai, India. *Suicide & Life-Threatening Behavior*, 36, 223-238.

Patel, V., Chisholm, D., Rabe-Hesketh, S., et al. (2003). Efficacy and cost effectiveness of drug and psychological treatments for common mental disorders in general health care in Goa, India: a randomised, controlled trial. *Lancet*, 361, 33–39

Paudyal, B. P. (2005). Poisoning: pattern and profile of admitted cases in a hospital in central Nepal. *Journal of the Nepal Medical Association*, 44, 92-96.

Pearson, V. (2002). Ling's death: an ethnography of a Chinese woman's suicide. *Suicide & Life-Threatening Behavior*, 32, 347-358

Phillips, M. R., Liu, H., & Zhang, Y. (1999). Suicide and social change in China. *Culture, Medicine & Psychiatry*, 23, 25-50.

Phillips, M. R, Yang, G., Zhang, Y., et al. (2002). Risk factors for suicide in China: a national case-control psychological autopsy study. *Lancet*, 360, 1728-1736.

Phillips, M. R., Li, X., & Zhang, Y. (2002). Suicide rates in China, 1995–99. *Lancet*, 359, 835-840.

Prasad, J., Abraham, V. J., Minz, S., et al. (2006). Rates and factors associated with suicide in Kaniyambadi Block, Tamil Nadu, South India, 2000-2002. *International Journal of Social Psychiatry*, 52, 65-71.

Pritchard, C. (1996). Suicide in the People's Republic of China categorized by age and gender: evidence of the influence of culture on suicide. *Acta Psychiatrica Scandinavica*, 93, 362-367

Queralt, M. (1993). Risk factors associated with completed suicide in Latino adolescents. *Adolescence*, 28, 831-850.

Rodrigues, N. C., & Werneck, G. L. (2005). Age-period-cohort analysis of suicide rates in Rio de Janeiro, Brazil, 1979-1998. *Social Psychiatry & Psychiatric Epidemiology*. 40, 192-196.

Segal, J., Pujol, C., Birck, A., et al. (2006). Association between suicide attempts in south Brazilian depressed patients with the serotonin transporter polymorphism. *Psychiatry Research*, 143, 289-291.

Schlebusch, L., Vawda, N. B., & Bosch, B. A. (2003). Suicidal behavior in black South Africans. *Crisis*, 24, 24-28.

Sukhai, A., Harris, C., Moorad, R G., et al. (2002). Suicide by self-immolation in Durban, South Africa: a five-year retrospective review. *American Journal of Forensic Medicine & Pathology*, 23, 295-298.

Tamosiunas, A., Reklaitiene, R., Virviciute, D., et al. (2006). Trends in suicide in a Lithuanian urban population over the period 1984-2003. *BioMed Central Public Health*, 6, #184.

van der Hoek, W., & Konradsen, F. (2005). Risk factors for acute pesticide poisoning in Sri Lanka. *Tropical Medicine & International Health*, 10, 589-596

Vijayakumar, L., John, S., Pirkis, J., et al. (2005). Suicide in developing countries (2): risk factors. *Crisis*, 26, 112-119.

Vijayakumar, L., Nagaraj, K., Pirkis, J., et al. (2005). Suicide in developing countries (1): frequency, distribution, and association with socioeconomic indicators. *Crisis*, 26, 104-111.

Vijayakumar, L., Pirkis, J., & Whiteford, H. (2005). Suicide in developing countries (3): prevention efforts. *Crisis*, 26, 120-124.

Vizcarra, B., Hassan, F., Hunter, W. M., et al. (2004). Partner violence as a risk factor for mental health among women from communities in the Philippines, Egypt, Chile, and India. *Injury Control & Safety Promotion*, 11, 125-129.

World Health Organization. (2001). *World health report 2001: mental health: new understanding, new hope*. Geneva, Switzerland: World Health Organization.

World Health Organization.2003 Mortality Database. Geneva. WHO. www.who.int/mental_health/ prevention/suicide/suiciderates/en/

Yip, P. S. (2001). An epidemiological profile of suicides in Beijing, China. *Suicide & Life-Threatening Behavior*, 31, 62-70.

Yip, P. S., & Liu, K. Y. (2006). The ecological fallacy and the gender ratio of suicide in China. *British Journal of Psychiatry*, 189, 465-466.

# INDEX

## A

Abraham, 20, 231, 232, 233, 250, 256, 257, 258, 259
abuse, 12, 37, 39, 42, 59, 60, 62, 63, 64, 66, 67, 69, 74, 232
academic difficulties, 38
access, 41, 77, 112, 114, 115, 116, 119, 136, 137, 158, 189, 252, 254, 255
accessibility, 115, 116, 228, 238, 250
acculturation, 22, 134, 136, 137, 236
acetaminophen, 250
acid, 70, 76
acute stress, 48, 158, 246
adaptation, 134, 197, 215
adjustment, 45, 112, 114, 217, 227, 252
adolescent suicidal ideation, 29
adolescents, 10, 17, 18, 21, 25, 26, 34, 35, 38, 57, 63, 77, 119, 135, 136, 137, 138, 156, 160, 162, 215, 218, 222, 234, 257, 258, 259
adrenocorticotropic hormone, 46
adult psychiatric inpatients, 10
adulthood, 42, 66, 75
adults, 20, 21, 24, 26, 35, 38, 39, 60, 63, 67, 69, 89, 142, 210
advancement, 95
adverse conditions, 22
adverse effects, 134, 135
affective disorder, 33, 61, 75, 79, 80, 151, 154, 227
Afghanistan, 53, 154

Africa, ix, 45, 48, 49, 51, 52, 235, 236, 238, 239, 243, 244, 253
African Americans, 73
aggregation, 34
aggression, 47, 48, 55, 56, 61, 62, 63, 65, 68, 69, 75, 76, 80, 149, 153, 156, 169, 170, 171, 187
aggressive behavior, 67, 68, 76
aggressive personality, 60, 63
aggressiveness, 47
agriculture, 116
AIDS, 52, 236, 238, 239
Alaska, 22, 77, 78
Albania, 179
alcohol abuse, 40, 49, 74, 94, 147, 197, 227
alcohol consumption, 94, 100, 109, 193, 197, 198, 199, 227
alcohol dependence, 80
alcohol problems, 206
alcohol use, 94, 227
alcoholics, 60, 79
alcoholism, 72, 74, 80, 94, 166, 195, 230
aldosterone, 46
alienation, 216
allele, 64
alternative hypothesis, 88
ambivalence, 55
American culture, 148
American Psychological Association, 16, 17, 150
anatomy, 122

anger, 12, 13, 20, 55, 62, 186, 252
anthropologists, 121
anthropology, 172
antidepressants, 49
antisocial behavior, 22, 69
anxiety, 13, 16, 20, 26, 59, 67, 75, 85, 94, 100, 133, 155, 168, 236, 252, 255
anxiety disorder, 16, 68
Argentina, 177, 178, 180
armed conflict, 242
Armenia, 193, 195, 196
arousal, 46, 151
Ashkenazi Jews, 216
Asia, 195, 197, 244, 253, 258
Asian Americans, 73
Asian countries, 202
aspiration, 146, 148
assault, 67, 175
assessment, 39, 41, 51, 66, 158, 208, 238
assimilation, 22
asylum, 188
attachment, 61
attacker, 154
attribution, 230
Austria, 99, 139, 202
authorities, 5, 59, 175, 254
authority, 94, 175
autobiographical memory, 11, 17
autonomic nervous system, 46
autonomy, 14, 167, 168, 169, 172
autopsy, 19, 41, 114, 256, 259
aversion, 168
avoidance, 13
awareness, 5, 13, 32, 136, 208, 228, 229, 230
Azerbaijan, 178, 194, 197

**B**

BAC, 49
back pain, 207
bad behavior, 186
Bahrain, 177, 178, 245
Balkans, 154
Bangladesh, 53
bankruptcies, 89
bankruptcy, 86, 227, 251
barriers, 13, 14, 124, 135, 227
base, 14, 255
base rate, 255
Beck Depression Inventory, 31
behavior therapy, 14, 16
behavioral disorders, 19
behavioral dispositions, 169
behavioral medicine, 210
behavioral sciences, 25
behaviors, 9, 12, 13, 16, 19, 38, 40, 47, 60, 61, 62, 85, 114, 138, 146, 147, 149, 210, 217, 226, 234
Beijing, 260
Belarus, 193, 196
Belgium, 106
belief systems, 238, 246
benefits, 10, 74, 100, 102, 103
bias, 198
Bible, 176, 182, 213
biological psychiatry, 121
biosynthesis, 252
bipolar disorder, 39, 43, 51, 67, 72, 74, 102, 151, 166, 251
birth rate, 86, 87, 197
blame, 169, 170, 186
blood, 49
bonds, 20, 100, 123, 157
borderline personality disorder, 14, 15, 16, 33, 63
Bosnia, 179, 245
brain, 45, 48, 61, 72, 74, 156
brain structure, 48
Brazil, 177, 178, 180, 243, 256, 258, 259
breakdown, 154, 168, 193
breeding, 49
Britain, 132, 137
Buddhism, 175
burdensomeness, 11, 13, 15, 16, 28, 29, 30, 32, 34, 35
burn, 58
burnout, 156

business cycle, 102
Butcher, 46, 50

# C

Cairo, 2, 246, 247
Cambodia, 154
campaigns, 209
case studies, 124
case study, 182, 258
Catholics, 215
Caucasians, 73
Caucasus, 195, 196, 197
causality, 101
causation, 97, 165, 227
CDC, 256
cell death, 34
censorship, 194
Census, 135, 138, 193, 219, 226, 231, 233
Central Asia, 127, 194, 195, 196, 197, 198
central nervous system, 68, 69
central planning, 124
cerebrospinal fluid, 70, 76
certification, 233, 239
challenges, 71, 94, 124, 131, 133, 219, 229, 235, 236
chemicals, 186
Chicago, 190
chicken, 166
child abuse, 49
child maltreatment, 59
childhood, 20, 21, 23, 37, 39, 42, 47, 59, 60, 61, 62, 63, 64, 65, 66, 67, 68, 69, 75, 135, 156, 167
childhood sexual abuse, 60, 64, 68, 69
children, 21, 22, 30, 35, 60, 63, 64, 73, 77, 79, 87, 135, 156, 167, 186, 187, 198, 204, 214, 219, 230, 236
Chile, 177, 181, 260
China, viii, 53, 56, 58, 72, 111, 115, 117, 118, 123, 128, 129, 133, 148, 151, 152, 185, 201, 202, 203, 204, 243, 250, 251, 252, 258, 259, 260
Chinese women, 204

cholera, 195
cholesterol, 47, 51, 72, 76, 79, 80
Christian Bible, 176
Christianity, 175, 197, 214, 217
Christians, 216
chronic diseases, 5
cigarette smoking, 47
cities, 106, 114, 148, 218, 219, 223, 226, 230
citizens, 105, 109, 131, 132, 216
City, 140, 143, 257
civil war, 185, 186, 188, 193
classification, 183, 243, 256
clients, 14, 24, 136, 189
climate, 132, 156, 197
clinical disorders, 29
clinical interventions, 77
clusters, 55, 85
CNS, 66
cocaine, 60, 69
coding, 194
cognition, 10, 12, 16, 146
cognitive dissonance, 146, 150
cognitive dysfunction, 40, 75
cognitive function, 43
cognitive perspective, 9
cognitive process, 11, 13
Cognitive risk, 10, 15, 17
cognitive style, 10, 47
cognitive theory, 13
cognitive therapy, 14, 169
collectivism, 148, 187
college students, 15, 16, 42
colleges, 228
Colombia, 177, 180
color, iv
common presenting symptoms, 252
communication, 46, 228
communication skills, 46
communities, 5, 50, 57, 77, 85, 94, 111, 112, 113, 114, 115, 116, 124, 131, 191, 208, 222, 226, 228, 229, 230, 237, 238, 247, 256, 260

community, 12, 17, 22, 26, 34, 59, 60, 66, 67, 69, 72, 73, 77, 93, 111, 112, 113, 114, 115, 116, 119, 135, 153, 154, 155, 187, 188, 189, 206, 210, 227, 230, 232, 237, 238, 243, 247, 249, 254, 256, 258
community relations, 188
community support, 77
comorbidity, 114
comparative analysis, 103, 242
competition, 49, 114, 124
complexity, 54, 55, 115
complications, 49, 236
composition, 86, 112, 113, 114, 115, 195
compounds, 116, 226, 230, 250
conceptual model, 12
conceptualization, 94, 168
concordance, 76
conference, 15
confidentiality, 96, 238
conflict, 38, 77, 145, 187, 190, 239
conflict resolution, 77
confounders, 107
Confucianism, 148
CONGRESS, iv
consciousness, 12
constipation, 207
construction, 96, 217
contemporary suicidology, 121, 126
contingency, 14
controlled trials, 14
controversial, 75
controversies, 150, 172
convergence, 132
conversations, 26
conviction, 39, 214
cooperation, 256
coping skills, 85, 189
coping strategies, 14, 48, 158
copyright, iv
*Copyright*, iv
correlation, 20, 66, 88, 89, 94, 123, 126, 127, 214
correlations, 31, 61, 62, 97
cortex, 48

corticosteroids, 46
corticotropin, 46
cortisol, 46, 48, 51, 61, 69
cost, 154, 230, 237, 259
cost effectiveness, 259
Costa Rica, 178, 181
cotton, 124, 233
counseling, 228, 230
counterbalance, 71
country of origin, 132, 133
covering, 139, 221
criminal behavior, 149
criminal justice system, 171
criminal violence, 156
criminality, 67
crises, 13, 149, 186, 215
crisis management, 228
criticism, 56, 89, 122
Croatia, 123, 128
crop, 124, 226
cross-cultural differences, 165
cross-cultural sensitivity, 50
CSF, 61, 65, 68, 69, 76, 80
Cuba, 177, 181
cultural heritage, 134
cultural influence, 202
cultural norms, 133, 165
cultural tradition, 122, 134
cultural values, 146
culture, 19, 20, 22, 23, 26, 49, 77, 134, 147, 151, 156, 165, 166, 170, 171, 173, 188, 189, 190, 193, 201, 203, 204, 241, 243, 253, 259
Czech Republic, 35

**D**

daily living, 105
damages, iv
danger, 115, 161
data analysis, 126
data availability, 220
data collection, 236
database, 129, 193, 194

death rate, 185
deaths, 56, 117, 119, 121, 124, 157, 182, 183, 194, 213, 221, 233, 235, 249, 254, 258
decision makers, 6
decision-making process, 61
deconstruction, 13
defense mechanisms, 22
deficiencies, 11, 48, 146
deficiency, 220
degradation, 155, 187
dehumanization, 155
delinquency, 63, 150
delusion, 81
delusional thinking, 75
delusions, 80
dementia, 47
democracy, 195
demographic change, 116
demographic data, 195
demographic factors, 75, 154, 217
demonstrations, 32
denial, 168
Denmark, 2, 80, 101, 106, 113, 114, 118, 132, 138
Department of Health and Human Services, 81, 162
dependent variable, 107
depressive symptomatology, 24, 49
depressive symptoms, 38, 65, 137
deprivation, 90, 106, 125, 148, 226, 227
depth, 54
despair, 133, 157, 170, 186, 253
detachment, 12
developed countries, 167, 183, 229, 235
developing brain, 61
developing countries, 48, 73, 115, 148, 168, 173, 175, 176, 182, 190, 220, 229, 234, 235, 239, 249, 250, 251, 252, 253, 254, 256, 257, 258, 260
developing nations, 250, 251, 253, 255
Diagnostic and Statistical Manual of Mental Disorders, 207
diagnostic criteria, 241

diathesis, 46, 47, 50, 60, 72
diet, 76
differential rates, 122, 136
disability, 5, 219, 236, 239, 241
disaster, 154, 155, 156, 158, 159, 160, 161, 243
disaster area, 154
disclosure, 217
discomfort, 209
discrimination, 115, 134, 148
diseases, 122, 183, 220, 255
disorder, 17, 19, 26, 43, 46, 47, 49, 51, 60, 63, 67, 74, 102, 119, 145, 147, 155, 159, 168, 227, 241, 246
displaced persons, 154
displacement, 156, 236, 238
dissatisfaction, 23, 187
dissociation, 12, 69
dissonance, 146, 150, 151
distress, 13, 23, 109, 127, 132, 136, 155, 175, 210, 215, 217, 246, 251, 252
distribution, 65, 112, 118, 194, 196, 197, 199, 234, 260
diversity, 37, 114
divorce rates, 116, 141
dizziness, 207
doctors, 56, 176, 189
domestic violence, 37, 56, 59, 155, 227, 233
dominance, 28
Dominican Republic, 178
dose-response relationship, 114
drug abuse, 19, 114, 122, 159, 206
drug dependence, 166, 227
drugs, 63, 215, 226, 230, 250
duality, 214
dysfunctional assumptions, 10
dysphoria, 13

# E

earthquakes, 153, 155, 156
Eastern Europe, 123, 128
ecological data, 95, 110

ecology, xi, 126
economic change, 188
economic crisis, 161, 227
economic development, 128, 210
economic disadvantage, 166
economic growth, 124, 125
economic integration, 105
economic losses, 219
economic problem, 229
economic status, 105, 106, 107, 108, 109, 110, 125
economic theory, 90
economic welfare, 100
Ecuador, 178, 180
education, 6, 49, 54, 61, 101, 106, 107, 108, 109, 114, 116, 157, 166, 187, 189, 226, 237, 238, 251, 253
educational attainment, 106, 108
educational institutions, 230
educational psychologists, 189
egalitarianism, 148
egg, 166
Egypt, 2, 177, 178, 182, 243, 245, 246, 247, 260
El Salvador, 177, 181
elderly population, 126
emergency, 117, 189, 208, 217, 222, 228, 257
emotion, 55, 171
emotional state, 55
emotionality, 13
empathy, 169
employees, 187, 205, 206
employers, 109
employment, 49, 101, 102, 103, 105, 109, 116, 125, 133, 147, 188
employment status, 101
empowerment, 229
endocrine, 46
energy, 159
England, 106, 114, 117, 118, 119, 131, 132, 136, 137, 183, 204
environment, xi, 25, 40, 43, 45, 64, 65, 77, 114, 133, 167, 169, 238

environmental factors, 41, 47, 122
environmental influences, 68
environmental stress, 236
enzyme, 252
epidemic, 89, 127, 210, 236, 239
epidemiologic studies, 68, 80
epidemiology, 127, 128, 226, 259
epilepsy, 72
epinephrine, 46
equal opportunity, 148
equality, 57, 233
equity, 189
Estonia, 3, 123, 129, 194, 243
estrangement, 12, 216
ethics, 171, 194
ethnic diversity, 214
ethnic groups, 22, 77, 132, 134, 136
ethnic minority, 25, 132, 136
ethnicity, 107, 112
etiology, 90, 122, 165, 252
Europe, 123, 127, 129, 139, 166, 197, 216, 244
euthanasia, 57, 182
everyday life, 23, 155, 157
evidence, 14, 15, 27, 28, 29, 32, 40, 42, 49, 50, 65, 66, 75, 79, 97, 101, 109, 114, 118, 123, 124, 125, 126, 128, 143, 155, 159, 161, 162, 168, 176, 189, 191, 204, 259
evolution, 27, 33, 34
examinations, 54, 209, 210
exclusion, 124, 221
executive function, 48
executive functioning, 48
exile, 214
experimental manipulation, 30
expertise, 195
exposure, 49, 72, 114, 153, 154, 156
extreme poverty, 159

# F

fairness, 171
faith, 175

families, 5, 22, 25, 77, 85, 175, 197, 208, 217, 228, 230, 244, 246
family conflict, 134, 227, 253
family environment, 232
family history, 11, 60, 75, 118, 227
family income, 28, 107
family interactions, 16, 33
family life, 20
family members, 30, 33, 59, 88, 149, 155, 206, 208, 228
family physician, 230, 253
family relationships, 87, 227, 251
family violence, 49
farmers, 114, 117, 119, 124, 226, 229, 233
fear, 12, 14, 22, 195
feelings, 13, 22, 23, 186, 246
female rat, 186, 196, 197, 202, 225, 250
fertility, 28, 33
fertility rate, 33
financial, 25, 27, 31, 33, 38, 39, 109, 134, 154, 205, 246, 253
financial difficulty, 39
Finland, 42, 90, 106, 112, 113, 118, 202
firearms, 95, 114, 116, 215
first aid, 158, 160, 161
fitness, 27, 28, 29, 32
fixation, 13
flight, 46
floods, 153, 155, 156
fluctuations, 13, 123, 124, 196, 197
fluid, 13, 78
force, 88, 94, 125
formal education, 228
formation, 11, 146
France, 103, 177, 183
fraternal twins, 76
freedom, 194, 214
Freud, 20, 151, 153, 159, 160, 170
Freud, Sigmund, 151, 170
frontal lobe, 45
funding, 229

# G

gay men, 26
GDP, 188, 194
GDP per capita, 188
gender differences, 64, 72
gender role, 197
general practitioner, 161
genes, 27, 28
genetic components, 47
genetic factors, 50, 72, 76, 134
genetic predisposition, 64
genotype, 43, 65
geography, 117
Georgia, 193
German suicide rate, 102
Germany, 1, 95, 102, 103, 125, 128, 139, 140, 177, 183
gestures, 19
gifted, 244
global economy, 124
globalization, 122, 123, 126, 153, 219, 223
goal-directed behavior, 48
God, 169, 213, 243, 244, 245
governments, 204, 255
grass, 189
Great Britain, 118, 175
Great Depression, 101, 139
Greece, 102, 112, 119, 175
Greeks, 172
group interests, 94
growth, 5, 124, 171, 229
Guatemala, 178, 180
guidance, 169
guidelines, 142
guilt, 21, 157, 167, 170, 171, 173
guilty, 170, 171
Guyana, 178, 180

# H

happiness, 31, 77
harassment, 188

harbors, 46
hate crime, 134, 135
hazards, 107, 108
head injury, 48
headache, 207
health care, 112, 137, 259
health insurance, 102
health practitioners, 115
health problems, 122, 135, 153, 183, 232, 255
health services, 135, 190, 229, 258
health status, 226
hearing loss, 31
helplessness, 13, 246
heterosexuals, 22
high fat, 250
high school, 107, 149
higher education, 251
high-risk populations, 217
hippocampus, 48
history, 9, 11, 13, 17, 19, 49, 60, 63, 66, 76, 80, 102, 123, 128, 137, 151, 159, 182, 193, 214, 227, 252
HIV, 49, 52, 236
HIV/AIDS, 49, 52
homelessness, 166
homes, 131
homicide, 21, 49, 90, 151, 166, 181, 198
homicide rates, 90, 181
homogeneity, 97
homosexuality, 23
homosexuals, 23
Hong Kong, 55, 99, 102, 202
hopelessness, 9, 10, 11, 13, 14, 15, 16, 17, 18, 19, 20, 23, 24, 26, 29, 30, 31, 32, 40, 47, 55, 75, 100, 150, 155, 170, 245, 246
hormones, 48
hospitalization, 102, 217
host, 102, 132, 133, 135
hostilities, 156, 159
House, 35
household composition, 86
household crowding, 116

household income, 108
housing, 154
human, 45, 49, 58, 128, 153, 154, 158, 167, 168, 170, 189, 219
human behavior, 153
human development, 58
human resources, 219
human right, 49, 189
human rights, 49, 189
Hungary, 123, 129, 139, 202
Hunter, 260
hurricanes, 153, 155, 156
husband, 186
hypocrisy, 150
hypothesis, 28, 62, 64, 72, 85, 88, 101, 126

## I

ideal, 10, 24, 105, 148
identical twins, 76
identification, 20, 22, 45, 134, 140, 208, 217, 241, 258
identity, 19, 22, 23, 124, 125, 133, 137, 187, 195, 215
idiopathic, 228
imageability, 17
imitation, 85, 94, 96, 140
imitation theory, 94
immigrants, 22, 131, 132, 133, 134, 135, 136, 137, 148, 215, 216, 217, 218
immigration, 123, 131, 132, 135, 138, 214, 216
immunity, 106
imprisonment, 188
improvements, 73, 198, 256
impulses, 9, 20
impulsive, 60, 63, 65, 67, 68, 250
impulsiveness, 69, 186, 250
impulsivity, 14, 40, 43, 47, 48, 60, 61, 62, 67, 69, 75, 76, 80
in transition, 25, 125, 128

incidence, 64, 99, 114, 118, 119, 122, 125, 131, 157, 166, 170, 172, 175, 188, 190, 205, 208, 221, 222, 226, 233
income, 31, 73, 86, 88, 89, 90, 100, 106, 107, 108, 109, 112, 115, 116, 117, 127, 129, 159, 206, 211, 225, 257
income inequality, 88, 90, 116, 159
independence, 129, 168, 185, 188, 195, 214
independent variable, 30, 31
Indians, 56, 166
individual differences, 40, 165, 166
individualism, 148, 151, 187
individuality, 169
industrialization, 219, 223
industrialized countries, 215, 216
industrialized societies, 167
inefficiency, 47
inequality, 86, 88, 112, 126, 187
infant mortality, 219
inflation, 107
infrastructure, 156
ingest, 115
ingestion, 257
initiation, 135
injuries, 49, 217, 220, 235
injury, iv, 12, 14, 15, 33, 110, 154, 221, 231
inner tension, 187
innocence, 171
insanity, 94
insects, 28
insecurity, 156
insomnia, 155, 207
institutions, 128, 229
integration, 22, 79, 86, 87, 93, 94, 96, 97, 105, 122, 133, 137, 149
intellectual disabilities, xi
intelligence, 61, 215
intentionality, 250
interdependence, 126
International Classification of Diseases, 107
interpersonal events, 38

interpersonal factors, 55, 56
interpersonal interactions, 169
interpersonal relations, 38, 41, 55, 167, 170
interpersonal relationships, 38, 55, 167, 170
intervention, 5, 26, 33, 41, 66, 157, 158, 161, 172, 191, 208, 210, 228, 241, 253, 256
intervention strategies, 66, 256
intimacy, 169
intrinsic motivation, 17
investment, 5, 116, 169
ions, 129
Iran, 133, 176, 178, 243, 245, 249, 257
Iraq, 154
Ireland, 69, 78, 123, 127
Islam, 175, 176, 197, 217
islands, 235
isolation, 11, 14, 38, 86, 115, 133, 135, 168, 194, 215, 236, 246
Israel, viii, 3, 154, 213, 214, 215, 216, 217, 218
issues, 22, 39, 101, 118, 119, 132, 133, 159, 223, 227, 237, 238, 243, 255
Italy, 2, 3, 78, 100, 102, 111, 125, 177, 183

## J

Japan, viii, 2, 90, 91, 95, 97, 102, 124, 125, 127, 128, 129, 139, 171, 175, 177, 202, 205, 206, 208, 209, 210, 211
Jewish Talmud, 176
Jews, 214, 215, 216, 217
job creation, 110, 116
job dissatisfaction, 109
jobless, 99, 100
Jordan, 245
jumping, 226

## K

Kazakhstan, 125, 127, 179, 194, 195, 196, 198
Kenya, 239
kerosene, 186
kill, 85, 103, 108, 145, 151, 157, 169, 176, 213, 214, 245
Korea, 202
Kuwait, 176, 178, 179, 183, 245, 246, 247
Kyrgyzstan, 179, 194

## L

labor force, 86, 88, 90, 105, 106, 116, 125
labor force participation, 86, 88, 90, 125
labor market, 100, 125
labour market, 103, 129
language barrier, 133, 134, 136
Latin America, 176, 177, 181, 182, 183, 201, 203, 204, 253
Latinos, 136
Latvia, 123, 124, 129, 194, 198
laws, 56, 253
Le Suicide, 93
lead, 9, 13, 20, 23, 39, 40, 61, 66, 124, 125, 133, 135, 142, 147, 149, 150, 153, 154, 156, 169, 181, 187, 188, 219, 230, 236
learning, 31, 48, 140, 187
learning process, 140
Lebanon, 154
liberation, 195
life expectancy, 210
life experiences, 43, 50
lifetime, 39, 62, 76, 222, 258
light, 126, 135
literacy, 219, 226
lithium, 72, 78
Lithuania, 123, 127, 194, 195, 198, 251, 258
living arrangements, 101
local government, 237
loneliness, 20
longevity, 205
longitudinal study, 64, 137
love, 139, 227, 253
lying, 61

## M

magazines, 148
magnitude, 5
major depression, 63, 67, 70, 74, 75, 79, 80, 119, 145, 207, 209, 210, 247
major depressive disorder, 17, 51, 102, 207
majority, 53, 77, 132, 134, 145, 149, 178, 182, 195, 201, 202, 203, 204, 216, 220, 227, 228, 241, 255
malaise, 54, 55, 56, 57
Malaysia, 178
malnutrition, 255
maltreatment, 23, 63, 65, 67, 69
man, 76, 78, 159, 170, 213
management, 50, 51, 158, 208, 209, 227, 228, 230, 242, 246
MANCOVA, 30, 31, 32
manic, 151
manipulation, 30
Manju, 231
man-made disasters, 159
manpower, 228
mapping, 14
marginalization, 123, 236
marital status, 20, 43, 86, 94, 97, 107, 112
market economy, 124, 195
marriage, 73, 79, 87, 198, 226
married women, 227
masking, 55
mass, 95, 97, 142, 143, 154, 156, 157
mass media, 95, 97, 143
materials, 149
matrix, 168, 190
matter, iv, 241
media, 91, 97, 139, 140, 141, 142, 143, 159, 188, 219, 226, 230, 237
median, 65

medical, 11, 21, 42, 49, 55, 72, 80, 115, 121, 136, 145, 156, 159, 175, 189, 197, 203, 207, 221, 222, 228, 237, 243
medical care, 136
medical history, 159
medication, 194
medicine, 173, 186, 210
memory, 11, 12, 15, 16, 48, 51, 218
memory performance, 51
memory retrieval, 16
mental disorder, 5, 47, 50, 59, 61, 112, 113, 145, 147, 149, 156, 161, 181, 186, 227, 239, 241, 253, 257, 259
mental health, 29, 50, 94, 112, 115, 116, 118, 121, 127, 131, 132, 134, 135, 136, 137, 153, 155, 156, 157, 158, 159, 160, 161, 162, 165, 208, 227, 228, 229, 230, 241, 246, 252, 253, 254, 255, 260
mental health professionals, 159, 228, 246, 255
mental illness, 20, 37, 39, 40, 47, 55, 67, 115, 123, 165, 168, 173, 176, 235, 236, 237, 238, 239, 251, 252, 253, 255
mental retardation, 47
mental state, 94
mental states, 94
messages, 33
meta-analysis, 47, 50, 141
metabolism, 78
metabolites, 80
methodology, 93, 95, 118, 176, 201
metropolitan areas, 112
Mexico, 133, 178, 180
migrants, 132, 137
migration, 97, 114, 116, 126, 128, 131, 137, 154, 156, 188, 210, 219
military, 43, 215
minorities, 22, 26, 114, 131, 137, 176
minority groups, 132
minors, 214
missions, 160
misuse, 41
models, 9, 12, 46, 50, 90, 126, 172, 255
moderates, 43, 45

moderators, 39
modernization, 87, 98, 116, 123, 138, 251
mold, 72
Moldova, 194
monks, 189
Montenegro, 157, 161, 162
mood disorder, 47, 49, 68, 73, 74, 75, 76, 149
mood states, 207
moral imperative, 74
morbidity, 101, 102, 118, 138, 191, 219
mortality, 21, 54, 56, 80, 88, 89, 90, 96, 103, 106, 110, 115, 118, 119, 121, 123, 124, 125, 126, 127, 128, 129, 137, 138, 193, 194, 195, 197, 198, 199, 201, 203, 206, 210, 211, 219, 239, 242, 243, 255
mortality rate, 88, 124, 125, 128, 129, 193, 198, 201, 211, 219
Moscow, 198
motivation, 14, 27, 28, 29, 30, 31, 32, 33, 186
multidimensional, 46, 54, 57
multiple regression, 207
multiple regression analysis, 207
murder, 195, 213
Muslims, 216

## N

nation states, 94
national culture, 91
National Institute of Mental Health, 2, 75, 232, 233
National Institutes of Health, 110
national policy, 230
national strategy, 232, 258
nationalism, 154
Native Americans, 73
NATO, 157
natural disaster, 153, 155, 160
natural disasters, 153, 155
nausea, 207
needy, 31
negative attitudes, 236

negative consequences, 5, 105, 142
negativity, 238
neglect, 59, 60, 61, 62, 63, 66, 67, 69, 182
Nepal, 53, 257, 259
nervous system, 46
Netherlands, 117, 177, 183
networking, 228
neurobiology, 34, 67, 79, 80, 151
neurotransmission, 68
neurotransmitter, 45, 47
neurotransmitters, 48, 61
neutral, 38
New England, 34, 118, 160
New South Wales, 117, 126, 128
New Zealand, 24, 78, 79, 90, 117
NGOs, 228, 229, 230, 238
Nicaragua, 178, 180
Nigeria, 238, 257, 259
non-immigrant citizens, 131
non-institutionalized, 106
norepinephrine, 46
normal development, 156
North Africa, 216
North America, 68, 80, 127, 137, 151, 171, 215
Norway, 106, 113, 118
nurses, 237
nursing, 228
nursing home, 228

## O

obedience, 195
obstacles, 12, 94
offenders, 176
officials, 139
OH, 127, 129
oil, 247
old age, 27, 167, 204
opportunities, 28, 95, 109, 115, 136, 229, 255
optimism, 195
organism, 168

Organization for Economic Cooperation and Development, 103
Other External Causes of Death' (OECD), 175
outpatients, 10, 15, 24, 29, 100, 102, 207
overlap, 221, 243, 245

## P

Pacific, 1, 244
pain, 12, 14, 55, 142, 154, 161, 207, 228
Pakistan, 176, 179, 182, 258
Palestinian uprising, 215
Panama, 178, 181
panic disorder, 19
Paraguay, 180
parallel, 107
parental care, 33
parenting, 72
parents, 24, 30, 39, 59, 167, 187, 204, 236
participants, 29, 30, 31, 32
paternalism, 123
pathogenesis, 47
pathology, 74, 85, 165
pathways, 17, 26, 40, 45, 61, 93
peace, 43, 153, 160, 161, 214
peacekeepers, 154
peacekeeping, 43, 160
peer group, 167
perceived attractiveness, 31
perfectionism, 10, 16
perinatal, 21, 25
permission, iv
permit, 167
perseverance, 23
personal achievements, 169
personal autonomy, 158
personal history, 49
personal identity, 187
personal relations, 89
personal relationship, 89
personality, 22, 25, 40, 42, 47, 48, 59, 63, 68, 72, 74, 147, 156, 168, 169, 173, 207, 227, 231, 252

personality disorder, 25, 40, 42, 47, 59, 63, 68, 74, 156, 207, 227, 231
personality factors, 252
Peru, 178, 180
pessimism, 47
pesticide, 115, 190, 191, 256, 260
phenotype, 65
Philadelphia, 25, 101, 102, 128
Philippines, 260
physical abuse, 59, 60, 63, 69
physical fitness, 215
physical health, 23, 100, 109, 134, 255
physicians, 42, 159, 206
Physiological, 69
physiological arousal, 13
pilot study, 160
placebo, 52
plants, 186
plausibility, 27
playing, 48
pleasure, 6
poison, 247
Poland, 68, 123
police, 49, 220, 254
policy, 109, 116, 162, 195, 197, 208, 219, 229, 230, 236
policy makers, 219, 230, 236
political aspects, 197
political force, 134
politics, 193, 194
pollution, 156
polymorphism, 43, 64, 67, 252, 257, 259
polymorphisms, 69
population group, 205
positive correlation, 87, 89, 125
positive regard, 245
positive relationship, 29, 62, 105
posttraumatic stress, 49, 67, 154, 160
poverty, 73, 105, 148, 154, 156, 219, 226, 236, 238
praxis, 56
PRC, 201, 202, 203
predictor variables, 102
prefrontal cortex, 47, 48

pregnancy, 31, 39
preparation, iv
preservation, 16, 33, 77
preservative, 27
primate, 66, 68
principles, 14, 242
private enterprises, 256
privatization, 124
probability, 20, 76
problem solving, 14, 16, 17, 23, 40, 46
problem-solving, 11, 14, 16, 17, 61, 77, 140, 188, 228
problem-solving skills, 14, 188, 228
producers, 124
professional literature, 49
professionals, 6, 158, 159, 208, 219, 228, 229, 230, 237
prognosis, 168
project, 26, 90, 232
prolactin, 76
promoter, 64
property crimes, 147
proportionality, 107
proposition, 93, 109
protection, 169, 197
protective factors, 46, 47, 71, 77, 78, 190, 215, 227
Protestants, 215
prototype, 186
proximal risk factor, 60, 255
psychiatric diagnosis, 39
psychiatric disorders, 19, 39, 66, 71, 76, 77, 101, 123, 206, 209, 242, 251, 258
psychiatric hospitals, 114, 194
psychiatric illness, 72, 103
psychiatric morbidity, 101, 102, 246, 247
psychiatric patients, 17, 42, 51, 52, 72, 76, 146, 150, 151
psychiatry, 25, 51, 79, 80, 93, 173, 239, 243
psychodynamic (Freudian) theory, 19
psychodynamic aspects, 172
psychological distress, 153, 160
psychological pain, 9

psychological problems, 42, 100
psychological processes, 12
psychological states, 100
psychological stress, 114
psychological stressors, 114
psychological variables, 165
psychology, 34, 138, 170, 189
psychopathology, 20, 38, 40, 43, 55, 59, 68, 77, 150, 165, 168, 172, 173, 227, 253
psychopharmacology, 46
psychoses, 168
psychosis, 49, 75, 94, 119, 194
psychosocial factors, 26, 232
psychosocial functioning, 207
psychosocial interventions, 189
psychosocial stress, 207, 252
psychosocial support, 47, 228
psychosomatic, 155, 156, 173, 207
psychotherapy, 14, 25, 26, 172, 173, 256
psychotic symptoms, 75, 119
PTSD, 155, 156
puberty, 21
public health, 5, 6, 93, 116, 161, 190, 219, 220, 229, 230, 237, 239, 241, 242
public policy, 96, 109
Puerto Rico, 133
punishment, 170

## Q

quality of life, 122, 219, 241, 244
quality of service, 254
Queensland, 117
questionnaire, 143

## R

race, 107
racism, 22
radio, 148, 237
reactions, 24, 85, 155, 158
realism, 122
reality, 10, 22, 146, 148, 249

recall, 17
recession, 125, 127
recognition, 96, 208, 220, 227, 229, 230, 255
recommendations, iv, 135, 142, 158, 160
recovery, 11, 245
reform, 89, 127
reforms, 195, 256
refugees, 154, 156, 161, 188
regions of the world, xi
regression, 62, 64, 65, 67, 108, 150
regression analysis, 67, 108
regression model, 62, 150
rehabilitation, 51
rejection, 13, 21, 23, 55, 175
relatives, 19, 21, 25, 27, 76
relevance, 33, 38, 39, 41, 122
reliability, 66, 89, 181, 198
relief, 245
religion, 47, 74, 81, 147, 154, 182, 187, 193, 214, 243
religiosity, 123, 246
religious beliefs, 77
religious traditions, 175
religiousness, 243
rendition, 140
replication, 15, 24, 26
repression, 59
reputation, 203
researchers, 40, 71, 94, 95, 116, 150, 195, 220, 221, 229, 253, 255
resilience, 71, 75
resistance, 105, 166, 195
resource availability, 28
resources, 5, 45, 136, 158, 218, 228, 229
response, 30, 45, 46, 60, 61, 64, 72, 76, 127, 176, 181, 256
restrictions, 116, 199, 214, 250
restructuring, 14, 194, 205
retirement, 21
rewards, 157
rights, iv, 167, 169
risk assessment, 41
risks, 78, 106, 108

Romania, 194
romantic relationship, 21, 29, 32
root, 100
roots, 189
rules, 148, 171, 193, 213
ruminative thinking, 10
rural areas, 111, 112, 115, 116, 186, 188, 189, 226, 227, 232, 234, 251
rural women, 115, 123
rural-urban suicide, 115, 116
Russia, 126, 154, 193, 216
Rwanda, 154

## S

safety, 77, 102, 134, 188
sanctions, 157, 237, 253
Sartorius, vii, 3, 5
Saudi Arabia, 182, 246, 247
Scandinavia, 33, 182, 204, 232
schizophrenia, 19, 39, 41, 46, 47, 49, 51, 52, 69, 114, 118, 168, 206, 227, 251, 257, 258
schizophrenic patients, 39, 232, 252
school, 38, 77, 108, 135, 147, 148, 159, 239
schooling, 107, 108
science, 50, 93, 94, 95
scientific papers, 139
scope, 96, 102
seasonality, 118
second generation, 137, 148
Second World, 160, 214
secretion, 48
security, 188
selective attention, 13
self esteem, 255
self-awareness, 12
self-concept, 150
self-control, 187
self-destruction, 16, 33, 170, 172, 187
self-destructive behavior, 27, 30, 170
self-efficacy, 23

self-esteem, 20, 23, 39, 61, 100, 123, 187, 189
self-identity, 20, 22, 23
self-image, 146
self-mutilation, 245
self-perceptions, 10
senses, 12
sensitivity, 12, 22, 50, 207
Serbia, 3, 157, 161, 162
serotonin, 43, 47, 64, 65, 66, 69, 70, 76, 78, 252, 257, 259
serum, 80
services, iv, 49, 112, 115, 116, 135, 157, 162, 189, 197, 198, 204, 227, 228, 230, 238, 252, 254, 255
SES, 106
sex, 55, 107, 111, 114, 116, 118, 148, 161
sex differences, 161
sexual abuse, 59, 60, 61, 63, 64, 67, 186
sexual reproduction, 27, 31
sexual violence, 238
sexuality, 186
shame, 19, 21, 166, 170, 171, 186, 187, 253
shape, 196
shock, 197
shortness of breath, 207
showing, 106, 189, 246
signs, 162, 237
Sinai, 3
Singapore, 202
skills training, 46
sleep deprivation, 47
smoking, 74
social behavior, 34, 79
social capital, 116
social change, 58, 122, 123, 124, 126, 128, 129, 197, 253, 259
social circle, 88
social class, 105, 106
social consequences, 100, 254
social construct, 129
social context, 97, 149, 151, 153
social costs, 103

social development, 17
social environment, 97, 110, 113, 122, 127, 133
social fabric, 188
social group, 20, 93, 94, 165
social identity, 22
social infrastructure, 116
social integration, 86, 87, 89, 93, 94, 95, 98, 116, 122, 133, 134, 135, 138, 145, 147, 149, 193
social justice, 189
social learning, 140
social learning theory, 140
social network, 41, 94, 123, 134, 155, 245
social norms, 122
social organization, 134, 165
social participation, 88
social phenomena, 193
social problems, 102, 188
social programs, 254
social regulation, 122, 147, 193
social relations, 85, 86, 88, 149
social relationships, 85, 86, 88
social roles, 20
social sciences, 34, 93, 96
social services, 116
social situations, 85
social status, 28, 89, 134, 148
social structure, 58, 151, 187
social support, 41, 42, 43, 72, 86, 90, 112, 116, 117, 133, 154, 158, 168, 208, 215, 230
social support network, 133
social transition, 113, 157
social workers, 189, 228
sociocultural practices, 221
socioeconomic background, 246
socioeconomic status, 34, 73, 106, 112, 114, 251
sociology, 33, 90, 93, 95, 96, 97, 110, 127, 150, 198
solution, 146, 149, 253
Somalia, 154
somatization, 156

South Africa, 3, 48, 49, 51, 52, 239, 257, 258, 259, 260
sovereignty, 213
Soviet Union, viii, 89, 123, 125, 127, 193, 195, 197, 198, 199, 218
Spain, 178, 183, 214
species, 27, 28
speech, 134, 137
Spring, 46, 52, 157
Sri Lanka, viii, 115, 154, 162, 185, 186, 187, 188, 189, 190, 191, 243, 254, 257, 260
stability, 216
stabilization, 197
standard of living, 89
state, 13, 15, 46, 55, 94, 96, 103, 129, 146, 168, 172, 173, 230, 256
states, 40, 57, 58, 88, 95, 170, 176, 207, 220, 221, 223, 225, 226, 232, 233
statistics, 54, 56, 58, 119, 198, 199, 204, 210, 231, 233, 249, 250
stereotypes, 181
stigma, 21, 24, 59, 74, 115, 175, 220, 229, 236
stimulus, 12
stratification, 105
stress, 13, 21, 22, 23, 40, 45, 46, 47, 48, 49, 51, 52, 60, 61, 64, 67, 72, 85, 88, 90, 109, 123, 127, 134, 135, 136, 145, 146, 153, 154, 155, 156, 157, 159, 160, 168, 197, 198, 252
stress reactions, 153, 159
stressful life events, 20, 41, 42, 64, 114, 154, 157, 228
stressors, 13, 40, 45, 46, 109, 114, 153, 253
structure, 22, 193, 197
style, 55, 116, 124, 197
subgroups, 49, 123
Sub-Sahara Africa, 235
sub-Saharan Africa, 49, 239
substance abuse, 40, 47, 49, 59, 60, 61, 63, 72, 74, 77, 147, 149, 154, 155, 156, 159, 232, 253

substance use, 38, 47, 59, 94, 137, 145, 252
suicidal ideation, 9, 10, 11, 13, 15, 16, 17, 19, 20, 23, 24, 29, 31, 33, 38, 64, 78, 79, 132, 135, 136, 150, 152, 159, 162, 189, 191, 207, 210, 221, 222, 226, 228
suicidal thinking, 10, 12, 27, 28, 29
suicide attempters, 10, 16, 17, 29, 34, 43, 51, 54, 61, 62, 68, 74, 76, 78, 80, 140, 228, 230, 245, 246, 247
suicide attempts, 11, 12, 13, 14, 15, 33, 36, 38, 39, 40, 42, 43, 59, 62, 63, 64, 65, 69, 74, 78, 79, 80, 115, 131, 136, 137, 140, 186, 190, 206, 208, 228, 237, 254, 257, 258, 259
suicide bombers, 153, 154, 157, 160
suicide completers, 34, 43, 216
superego, 171
supernatural, 255
surveillance, 171, 219, 220, 229, 231, 232, 256
survival, 195, 246
survivors, 20, 21, 24, 26, 121, 156, 159, 219, 228, 231, 238
susceptibility, 12, 39, 209
Sweden, 111, 119, 125, 128, 131, 199
Switzerland, 3, 58, 106, 119, 129, 139, 141, 162, 183, 191, 204, 209, 218, 231, 232, 239, 247, 260
sympathetic subsystem, 46
symptoms, 9, 13, 14, 21, 32, 33, 35, 38, 48, 49, 59, 75, 132, 151, 155, 162, 168, 207, 209, 210, 237, 241, 244, 246, 247, 252, 255
syndrome, 20, 21, 145, 156, 158, 161
Syria, 176, 179, 245

## T

Taiwan, 102, 103, 125, 160, 162
Tajikistan, 179, 194, 195, 196
target, 20, 30, 31, 32, 146, 158, 206, 208, 209
targeting individuals, 159

taxation, 103
teachers, 77, 159, 187, 189, 237
techniques, 14, 32, 158
teenage girls, 185
teens, 21, 73, 79
telephone, 230, 238
telephones, 238
television coverage, 142
temperament, 61, 121
tension, 188
tensions, 187
terminal illness, 140
territory, 157, 193
terrorism, 35, 153, 154
terrorist acts, 153, 154
testing, 16, 95
testosterone, 68
textbook, 6, 42, 79, 90, 103, 143
textbooks, 194
Thailand, 154
therapeutic relationship, 172
therapy, 14, 15, 16, 17, 172
thoughts, xi, 13, 20, 21, 23, 134, 206, 207, 222
threatening behavior, 37
threats, 186
time-frame, 11, 37
torture, 155, 188
toxicity, 254
trade, 131
traditions, 6, 22, 170, 193, 197
trainees, 42
training, 160, 238
traits, 60, 61, 63, 123, 167
transformation, 62, 123
transformations, 122, 128, 188
transmission, 156
transportation, 153
trauma, 37, 49, 51, 59, 60, 61, 62, 63, 64, 65, 66, 67, 68, 69, 121, 154, 156
traumatic events, 61, 158
traumatic experiences, 37, 59, 66
treatment, 12, 14, 16, 33, 45, 46, 50, 51, 66, 69, 78, 80, 102, 116, 119, 126, 135,

136, 148, 151, 186, 194, 230, 233, 239, 241, 252, 253, 255
trial, 16, 256, 259
tricyclic antidepressant, 250
tricyclic antidepressants, 250
triggers, 19, 40, 46, 142
Trinidad, 125, 127
Trinidad and Tobago, 125, 127
tryptophan, 70
tuition, 109
Turkey, 154, 159, 162, 179, 258
Turkmenistan, 179, 194, 196, 245
twins, 30, 31, 60, 76, 151

## U

U.S. National Longitudinal Mortality Study, 106, 108, 109
UK, 2, 50, 51, 52, 57, 69, 102, 103, 112, 113, 132, 139, 140, 151, 160, 161, 162, 172, 176, 178, 182, 198, 218, 247, 259
Ukraine, 123, 128, 193, 198, 249, 251, 258
UN, 160, 239
unemployed individuals, 226
unemployment rate, 99, 102
unhappiness, 31
unification, 153
uniform, 193
United, 57, 73, 90, 95, 96, 97, 103, 106, 110, 112, 117, 125, 136, 138, 148, 239
United Kingdom, 125
United Nations, 136, 239
United States, 57, 73, 90, 95, 96, 97, 103, 106, 110, 112, 117, 136, 138, 148
universality, 131, 213
urban, 111, 112, 113, 114, 115, 116, 117, 118, 119, 139, 148, 153, 221, 222, 223, 228, 247, 251, 255, 258, 260
urban areas, 111, 112, 114, 115, 228, 251, 255
urban life, 148
urban population, 260
urbanicity, 111, 113, 114, 118

urbanization, 49, 113, 116, 123, 124, 128, 197, 210, 217, 219
Uruguay, 177, 181
USA, 55, 73, 95, 96, 99, 100, 102, 111, 113, 114, 115, 125, 131, 132, 133, 134, 135, 137, 139, 141, 142, 148, 166, 171, 178, 183
**USSR**, viii, 181, 193, 194, 195, 196, 197, 198, 199, 215, 216
Uzbekistan, 194, 245

## V

valence, 38, 41
variables, 9, 30, 32, 38, 40, 45, 47, 50, 60, 61, 62, 78, 86, 94, 95, 107, 114, 122, 124, 142, 146, 158, 165, 167, 171, 173
variations, 21, 58, 93, 98, 113, 119, 126, 166, 201, 211, 221, 225, 226, 229, 233, 258
vasectomy, 31
vehicles, 226
vein, 142
veneration, 202, 203
Venezuela, 178, 180
victimization, 67
victims, 59, 151, 155, 156, 158, 160, 161, 205
Vietnam, 243
violence, 49, 53, 56, 58, 97, 122, 129, 149, 153, 154, 156, 157, 159, 186, 188, 229, 230, 231, 238, 260
voters, 126
vulnerability, 10, 13, 14, 15, 17, 22, 26, 40, 46, 47, 52, 57, 61, 71, 85, 151, 169, 177, 182, 204, 231
vulnerability to depression, 15, 17, 26, 169

## W

wages, 109
Wales, 106, 114, 117, 118, 119, 131, 137, 183, 204

war, 106, 153, 157, 160, 161, 191, 214, 236, 238
war years, 157
Washington, 16, 17, 25, 79, 110, 143, 150, 161, 162, 257
wealth, 105, 106
weapons, 157
welfare, 24, 31, 229
welfare reform, 24
well-being, 17, 77, 80, 161
West Africa, 259
Western countries, 111, 123, 167, 168, 182, 183, 203, 205, 246
Western Developed Countries (WDC), 175
white-collar workers, 210
WHO, 54, 56, 119, 121, 123, 127, 129, 133, 138, 159, 175, 181, 183, 185, 188, 191, 193, 201, 202, 204, 205, 215, 218, 235, 239, 242, 243, 244, 245, 247, 249, 260
workers, 35, 50, 56, 100, 102, 128, 146, 158, 159, 169, 170, 205, 206, 207, 210, 237, 252
working population, 207
workplace, 207, 208, 209
World Bank, 236, 239
World Health Organisation, 183, 190
World Health Organization, 28, 35, 53, 58, 111, 119, 121, 129, 138, 162, 166, 190, 204, 209, 210, 211, 215, 218, 231, 232, 235, 238, 239, 247, 260
World Health Organization (WHO), 53, 58, 215
World War I, 194
worldwide, 5, 23, 87, 121, 131, 159, 235, 242
wrongdoing, 186

## Y

Yale University, 25
yield, 94
young adults, 16, 38, 63, 118, 183, 186
young people, 21, 42, 78, 88, 139, 148, 157, 186, 231, 243, 250, 256
young women, 148, 185, 186, 246, 250
Yugoslavia, 160, 161

## Z

Zimbabwe, 235
Zulu, 52